Toward Emotional Competences

Toward Emotional Competences

Edited by:
Francisco Pons
Marie-France Daniel
Louise Lafortune
Pierre-André Doudin
Ottavia Albanese

AALBORG UNIVERSITY PRESS 2006

Toward Emotional Competences
Francisco Pons, Marie-France Daniel, Louise Lafortune, Pierre-André Doudin, and Ottavia Albanese (eds.)

© The Authors and Aalborg University Press

Cover: Sisse Harrington
Layout: Lars Pedersen / Anblik
Printed by Publizon A/S
ISBN-13: 978-87-7307-785-6
ISBN-10: 87-7307-785-2

Distribution:
Aalborg University Press
Niels Jernes Vej 6B
9220 Aalborg
Denmark
Phone: (+45) 96 35 71 40, Fax: (+45) 96 35 00 76
E-mail: aauf@forlag.aau.dk
www.forlag.aau.dk

All rights reserved. No part of this book may be reprinted or reproduced or utilized in any form or by any electronic, mechanical, or other means, now known or hereafter invented, including photocopying and recording, or in any information storage or retrieval system, without permission in writing from the publishers, except for reviews and short excerpts in scholarly publications.

CONTENT

List of contributors   9

INTRODUCTION

Toward emotional competences: An introduction   13
Francisco Pons, Marie-France Daniel, Louise Lafortune, Pierre-André Doudin, and Ottavia Albanese

CHAPTER 1

Emotion understanding as a reflective emotional competence: Between experiences and symbols   19
Francisco Pons, Marc de Rosnay, Pierre-André Doudin, Paul Harris, and Frédérique Cuisinier

    1. Introduction   19
    2. The power of symbols and the power of experiences   21
    3. Empirical illustration   25
    4. Discussion   29
    5. Conclusion   31
    References   32

CHAPTER 2

Children's emotion understanding: Preliminary data from the Italian validation project of *Test of Emotion Comprehension* (TEC)   39
Ottavia Albanese, Ilaria Grazzani Gavazzi, Paola Molina, Carla Antoniotti, Laura Arati, Eleonora Farina, and Francisco Pons

    1. Introduction   39
    2. Test of Emotion Comprehension (TEC)   40
    3. The Italian standardization   44
    4. Results   45
    5. Discussion and conclusion   50
    References   51

CHAPTER 3

Adolescence and awareness of positive emotions: A diary study — 55
Ilaria Grazzani Gavazzi, Ottavia Albanese, and Elaine Duncan

- 1. Introduction — 55
- 2. Adolescence and emotions — 56
- 3. The research — 58
- 4. Results — 61
- 5. Discussion and conclusion — 64
- References — 67

CHAPTER 4

Guilt as information mechanism in adolescents — 73
Francesco Mancini and Amelia Gangemi

- 1. Introduction — 73
- 2. Method — 76
- 3. Results — 78
- 4. Discussion and conclusion — 81
- References — 84

CHAPTER 5

Emotions and individual differences: the cognitive constructive model applied to eating disorders in childhood — 87
Maria Grazia Strepparava

- 1. Introduction — 87
- 2. Emotion awareness: from lived experience to subjective narrative — 87
- 3. The clinical background: the cognitive-constructive approach — 92
- 4. Eating disorders and emotions — 100
- 5. Overeating or weight and shape concerned children — 101
- 6. Children, emotional narrative, eating and weight problems — 104
- 7. Conclusion — 118
- References — 123

CHAPTER 6

A reflection on the relationship between emotions and critical thinking   131

Louise Lafortune and Andrée Robertson

  1. Introduction   131
  2. The role of emotions in the expression of critical thinking   132
  3. The role of critical thinking in the expression of emotions   133
  4. Actions which favor intervention   137
  5. Conclusion: Discussion and perspectives   149
  References   150

CHAPTER 7

The development of emotional competency: Using interactive-reflexive activities as a family assistance program in mathematics   155

Louise Lafortune

  1. Introduction   155
  2. Validation of interactive-reflexive activities in mathematics   157
  3. Theoretical concepts: Emotion, meta-emotion, and emotional competency   158
  4. Implementation and evaluation of the implementation of interactive-reflexive activities: description and results   164
  5. Links with emotional competency   166
  6. Pupil perceptions regarding parent beliefs toward mathematics   167
  7. Interpretation, discussion and conclusion   168
  References   171

CHAPTER 8

Emotional competency in accompaniment: Analysis of the manifestations of emotions in a context of change   177

Louise Lafortune, Lise St-Pierre, and Daniel Martin

  1. Introduction   177
  2. Reflection resulting in theoretical choices   178
  3. Emotional competency   179

  4. Self-analysis of taking into account the affective dimension in a context of an accompaniment project   183
  5. Analysis of data from accompaniers: Quebec and Switzerland   191
  6. Discussion and conclusion   198
  References   201

CHAPTER 9

A study of children's representations of four basic emotions   205

Marie-France Daniel, Emmanuelle Auriac, Catherine Garnier, Martine Quesnel, and Michael Schleifer

  1. Introduction   205
  2. Primary prevention of violence   206
  3. Social representations of emotions   207
  4. Method of analysis   212
  5. Results   215
  6. Discussion and conclusion   222
  References   224

CHAPTER 10

Training social workers in intercultural realities: A teaching model to counter unreasoned affectivity and contribute to the development of reflective judgment   229

Jo Ann Lévesque

  1. Introduction   229
  2. Social workers and intercultural realities   230
  3. The course on interethnic realities and social intervention   231
  4. An analytical tool and a methodology   232
  5. The teaching model based on the development of reflective judgment   235
  6. Conditions derived from the data on each axis of the model   237
  7. The reflective judgment development model and pedagogy   246
  References   247

LIST OF CONTRIBUTORS

Ottavia Albanese
University of Milano Bicocca (Italy)
ottavia.albanese@unimib.it

Carla Antoniotti
University of Milano Bicocca (Italy)
carla.antoniotti@unimib.it

Laura Arati
University of Torino (Italy)
arati@psych.unito.it

Emmanuelle Auriac
IUFM of Auvergne (France)
emma.auriac@wanadoo.fr

Frédérique Cuisinier
University of Paris X (France)
fcuisinier@free.fr

Marie-France Daniel
University of Montréal (Canada)
marie-france.daniel@umontreal.ca

Pierre-André Doudin
University of Lausanne and High School of Pedagogy (Lausanne, Switzerland)
pierre-andre.doudin@hepl.ch

Elaine Duncan
Glasgow Caledonian University (United Kingdom)
e.duncan@gcal.ac.uk

Eleonora Farina
University of Milano Bicocca (Italy)
eleonora.farina@unimib.it

Amelia Gangemi
University of Cagliari (Italy)
gangemi@unica.it

Catherine Garnier
University of Québec at Montréal (Canada)
catherine.garnier@uqam.ca

Ilaria Grazzani Gavazzi,
University of Milano-Bicocca (Italy)
ilaria.grazzani@unimib.it

Paul L. Harris
Harvard University (USA)
paul_harris@gse.harvard.edu

Louise Lafortune
University of Québec at Trois-Rivières (Canada)
louise.lafortune@uqtr.ca

Jo Ann Lévesque
McGill University (Canada)
joann.levesque@mcgill.ca

Francesco Mancini
School of Cognitive Psychotherapy (Italy)
mancini@apc.it

Daniel Martin
High School of Pedagogy (Lausanne, Switzerland)
daniel.martin@hepl.ch

Paola Molina
University of Torino (Italy)
molina@psych.unito.it

Francisco Pons
University of Aalborg (Denmark)
pons@hum.aau.dk

Martine Quesnel,
University of Québec at Montréal (Canada)
martine.quesnel@uqam.ca

Andrée Robertson
University of Québec in Outaouais (Canada)
anrobertson@videotron.ca

Marc de Rosnay
University of Sydney (Australia)
marcd@usyd.edu.au

Maria Grazia Strepparava
University of Milano-Bicocca (Italy)
mariagrazia.strepparava@unimib.it

Michael Schleifer
University of Québec at Montréal (Canada)
schleifer.michael@uqam.ca

Lise St-Pierre
University of Sherbrooke (Canada)
lise.st-pierre@usherb.ca

INTRODUCTION

Toward emotional competences: An introduction

Francisco Pons, Marie-France Daniel, Louise Lafortune, Pierre-André Doudin, and Ottavia Albanese

This book is the result of a collaboration by twenty-four scholars in developmental psychology, clinical psychology and educational sciences from Europe (Denmark, France, Italy, Switzerland, and United Kingdom), North America (Canada and United States), and Oceania (Australia). It provides an overview of novel and significant research on emotional competences from psychological, clinical and pedagogical points of view. Indeed, emotional competences have emerged as one of the main factors of psychological functioning and development and of individual differences in this functioning and development.

At a general level, emotional competences can be defined as the abilities to (1) experience, (2) recognize, (3) express, (4) control the expression of, (5) regulate the experience of and (6) understand emotions. In line with the work of Saarni (2000), the term "emotional competence" will be used in this text to describe these six competences. However, other terms such as "emotional intelligence" (Goleman, 1995; Salovey & Grewal, 2005) or "metaemotion" (Pons, Doudin, Harris & de Rosnay, 2002) could have been also used.

The book is divided into 10 chapters, and each one explores at least one of these six emotional competences. Some of the chapters are theoretical (theory-driven) while others are empirical (data-driven). Some report basic research (epistemologically orientated) whereas others report "applied" research (pragmatically orientated). Depending on the chapter, the participants involved in the research (case or group studies) are typically-developing children, adolescents and adults and non-typical people from Western and non-Western societies and cultures. Depending on the chapter, the methodologies of the research are: naturalistic observations, interviews, diary methods, self-reports, questionnaires or psychometric tests, and the analyses are either qualitative or quantitative. Depending on the chapter, one or several basic or complex emotions are investigated (e.g. from happiness, anger, fear, sadness to guilt, shame or pride). With this book, the reader will achieve an up-to-date and extensive understanding of emotional competences, their natures, developments, causes, consequences and possibilities for improvement.

In the first chapter, "Emotion understanding as a reflective emotional competence: Between experiences and symbols" Pons, de Rosnay, Doudin, Harris, and Cuisinier investigate the impact of affective experiences and symbolic cognitions on emotion understanding. Recent studies have suggested that children's symbolic cognitive abilities and affective experiences may have an impact on their understanding of emotion. However, the specific contributions of these characteristics have rarely been examined. The aim of the research introduced in this chapter is to evaluate the specific effect(s) of learning difficulties (as symbolic cognitive characteristics) as well as previous abuse (as experiential and affective characteristics) on adolescents' understanding of several simple and complex components of emotion understanding. Both theoretical and applied implications of this research are analyzed.

In the second chapter, "Children's emotion understanding: Preliminary data of the Italian validation project of Test of Emotion Comprehension (TEC)" Albanese, Grazzani Gavazzi, Molina, Antoniotti, Arati, Farina, and Pons present the first results of the Italian standardization of the TEC. The validity and the reliability of the TEC have been evaluated in previous studies. However, no proper standardization of this instrument was available until now. This chapter is the first step toward the resolution of this gap within the context of a Western Latin society and culture: Italy. When completed, this standardization should permit researchers and clinicians to locate a child (3 to 11 years of age) in terms of emotional understanding with respect to his or her reference population. This localization can either be general (with respect to the child's overall level of emotion understanding) or more specific (with respect to the child's understanding of a specific component of emotion understanding).

In the third chapter, "Adolescence and awareness of positive emotions: A diary study", Grazzani, Albanese, and Duncan investigate awareness of positive emotions as a dimension of subjective well-being and as a protective factor in adolescents. Most of the studies on emotions in adolescents focus on negative emotions such as anger, fear, sadness, depression or anxiety. However, an increasing number of studies in line with the wave of interest for positive psychology are starting to address the question of positive emotions. The main goal of the research presented in this chapter is to study both well-being and related positive emotions in adolescents using a diary method. More specifically, the three main goals of the research are to investigate in adolescent girls and boys: (1) positive emotions and emotions in everyday life; (2) gender differences and similarities in relation to positive emotions and life satisfaction and (3) the relationships between positive emotions and subjective well-being. Both theoretical and applied implications of this research are analyzed.

In the fourth chapter, "Guilt as an information mechanism in adolescents" Mancini and Gangemi examine the impact of guilt on adolescents' reasoning according to the "affect-as-information mechanism" hypothesis in which emotions are used as salient information in the formulation of judgments and evaluations. To this aim a study is presented in which the impact of adolescents' experience of guilt on their judgments of danger and the effectiveness of preventive performance are investigated. Both clinical and psycho-educational implications of this research are analyzed.

In the fifth chapter, "Emotions and individual differences: the cognitive constructive model applied to eating disorders in childhood" Strepparava starts by presenting a general overview of the cognitive-constructive approach and continues by discussing eating disorders personality with the main focus on related emotional experiences. The chapter ends with the preliminary results of a study on emotional narrative concerning happiness, sadness, anger and fear in school-aged children with and without eating disorders and/or body image disturbances. The relevance of this research for the field of eating disorders studies is discussed.

In the sixth chapter, "A reflection on the relationship between emotions and critical thinking" Lafortune and Robertson look at the relation between emotions and critical thinking. Underlying their chapter are questions such as: Can the manifestation of emotions influence (positively or negatively) the expression of critical thought? Can the development of critical thinking influence the expression or comprehension of emotions? Are there actions or interventions that would make it possible to improve the regulation of emotions and thereby promote the expression of critical thought? Can the development of skills linked to critical thinking promote better regulation of emotions? The authors also explore possible actions directed at both emotions and critical thinking in order to reach pupils in different ways.

In the seventh chapter, "The development of emotional competency: Using interactive-reflective activities as a family assistance program in mathematics" Lafortune analyses emotions according to a cognitive perspective with regard to parental interventions with children learning mathematics. To pursue this issue three research results are presented in relation to: (1) the validation of

Interactive-Reflexive Activities in mathematics to ensure a home follow-up, (2) the implementation and evaluation of the implementation of Interactive-Reflexive Activities at home and (3) an exploratory study of pupils' beliefs about their parents' beliefs about mathematics. These results provide possible avenues of solutions and future research.

In the eighth chapter, "Emotional competency in accompaniment: Analysis of the manifestations of emotions in a context of change" Lafortune, St-Pierre, and Martin reflect on the influence of emotions during the accompaniment process and contribute to the deployment of new ways of approaching continuing education. They suggest a theoretical reflection on the influence of emotions during accompaniment and on the development of emotional competency in accompaniers. This work, based on the description of a self-analysis approach, considers emotions in preparation for an accompaniment task, and it includes a training-intervention study from which an analysis grid is drawn. Subsequently, results of this exploratory research, focused on the knowledge and the analysis of situations of accompaniment influenced by emotions are presented.

In the ninth chapter, "A study of children's representation of four basic emotions" Daniel, Auriac, Garnier, Quesnel, and Schleifer study the process by which pre-school-aged children modify their representations of certain basic emotions. The specific questions treated in this chapter are: (1) What are 5- and 6-year-old children's social representations of four basic emotions (happiness, anger, fear and sadness)? (2) Without specific stimulation, are the social representations of children in this age group stable? (3) With cognitive stimulation, how is the process of modifying representations manifested by these children? The study was exploratory; the principal instrument employed an individual interview based on word association.

Finally, in the tenth chapter, "Training social workers in intercultural realities: A teaching model to counter unreasoned affectivity and contribute to the development of reflective judgment" Lévesque describes the research approaches which led to the discovery of a systemic teaching model based on the development of reflective judgment and the conditions for this model's privileged strategies: the transmission of information, educational conversation and writing. The results of the pretest and post-tests on cognitive reflection are also presented, and they confirm that the reflective judgment development model contributes to the development of reflective capacity or the maintenance of high-level reflective skills.

References

Goleman, D. (1995). *Emotional intelligence.* New York: Batman.

Salovey, P., & Grewal, D. (2005). The science of emotional intelligence. *Current Directions in Psychological Sciences, 14*(6), 281-285.

Pons, F., Doudin, P.-A., Harris, P., & de Rosnay, M. (2002). Métaémotion et intégration scolaire. In L. Lafortune & P. Mongeau (Eds.), *L'affectivité dans l'apprentissage* (pp. 7-28). Sainte-Foy: Presses de l'Université du Québec.

Saarni, C. (2000). Emotional competence: A developmental perspective. In R. Bar-On & J.D. Parker (Eds.), *The handbook of emotional intelligence* (pp. 68-91). San Francisco: Jossey-Bass.

CHAPTER 1

Emotion understanding as a reflective emotional competence: Between experiences and symbols

Francisco Pons, Marc de Rosnay, Pierre-André Doudin, Paul Harris, and Frédérique Cuisinier

1. Introduction

Emotional competences have emerged as one of the main factors of psychological functioning and development and of individual differences in this functioning and development (e.g. Goleman, 1995; Mayer & Salovey, 1997; Pons, Hancock, Lafortune & Doudin, 2005; Saarni, 2000 for discussion). However, the definitions of the terms "emotions" and "emotional competences" are still quite controversial (e.g. alternatives include: "sentiments", "feelings", "affects" and "moods" as well as "emotional intelligence" and "metaemotion"). In this chapter we propose two working definitions.

Emotions are states not only of the mind and but also of the body (and perhaps also of the group) that are caused by and that cause biological (physiological), psychological and social (cultural) changes. These states of the body and the mind, these emotions, can be within an individual but can also stem from another person. They can be positive (pleasant) or negative (unpleasant). They can be more or less basic (happiness, anger, fear, sadness, anxiety, etc.) or complex (guilt, shame, pride, etc.). They can be real but also fictional (experienced by a puppet, an imaginary companion, etc.). They can be present but also past (memories, ruminations, etc.) or future (potential, anticipation, etc.) They can last less than a second or an entire lifetime.

At least six emotional competences have been identified — the competence: (1) to experience emotions; (2) to recognize emotions (in faces, voices, postures, gestures, words, etc.); (3) to express emotions (verbally and non-verbally); (4) to control the expression of emotions (hiding, simulation, etc.); (5) to regulate the experience of emotions; and last but not least (6) to understand the natures, causes (and maybe also the development), consequences and possibilities of control and regulation of emotions (i.e. emotion understanding, emotion comprehension). In other words, emotional competences can be defined as the abilities to experience, recognize, express, control the expression of, regulate the experience of and understand emotions.

In the last three decades, a substantial body of research has demonstrated that normal children progress through a series of landmarks in developing their emotion understanding (i.e. the sixth emotional competence). For example, at 2-3 years of age, most children are capable of identifying basic emotions such as happiness, anger, fear and sadness just by looking at the faces of other people. They also understand the typical emotional responses to external events such as getting a gift, being annoyed by a little brother, being chased by a monster or losing a loved object. At 6-7 years of age the majority of children understand the impact of mental states such as beliefs on emotions. They are also able to discern/appreciate the difference between what people feel and what they express. Around the age of 10-11 years, most children understand more complex reflective emotions such as guilt, shame, pride and ambivalence. They also understand how to control their feelings efficiently via psychological strategies (e.g. Pons, Harris & de Rosnay, 2004 for a review). The order of these landmarks appears to be universal across cultures (e.g. Tenenbaum, Visscher, Pons & Harris, 2003). Several studies have also showed that there are clear typical individual differences in the development of children's emotion understanding. For example, some typical children at the age of 2-3 years generate spontaneously more than 25 emotional statements, whereas others generate none. Some typical children between 4 and 5 years of age have a level of emotion understanding that is superior to other typical children aged between 10 and 11 years (see Pons & Harris, 2005 for a review).

Today there are at least two explanatory approaches to the development of emotion comprehension in children and of the individual differences in this development. Both approaches recognize the influence of children's idiosyncratic characteristics and of their family environment. However, these two approaches differ in their conception of the nature of these influences. In the first approach these influences are considered as primarily symbolic and cognitive. Children do not necessarily have to experience an emotion to understand it. In the second approach these influences are viewed under a more experiential and affective angle. Children do not necessarily need to symbolically and cognitively represent an emotion to be able understand it.

2. The power of symbols and the power of experiences

The power of symbols

In the first approach, which might be qualified as "developmental and cognitive" because of its theoretical background, the quality of the symbolic and cognitive capacities of children and their family (primarily the mother) is considered to have a primary effect upon children's emotion understanding. Here, the basic hypothesis is that the greater these symbolic and cognitive capacities are the greater children's emotion understanding.

Several studies provide evidence in support of this hypothesis (e.g., Harris, 2005; Harris, de Rosnay & Pons, 2005; Pons, Harris & de Rosnay, in press for reviews and discussions). For instance, Cutting and Dunn (1999), de Rosnay and Harris (2002), Pons, Lawson, Harris and de Rosnay (2003) and de Rosnay, Pons, Harris and Morrell (2004) have shown a robust, positive correlation between language abilities (e.g., grammar, lexical and narrative reception) and emotion understanding (e.g. recognition of basic emotions such as happiness, sadness, fear or anger and understanding of mixed and moral emotions such as ambivalence, pride and guilt) in children between 3 and 11 years of age. Other studies have shown that deaf children, particularly those with restricted access to sign language, have difficulties in understanding mental states (Deleau, 1996; Figueras-Costa & Harris, 2001; Peterson & Siegal, 1995, 1999). Research with mentally retarded adults has also revealed significant, positive correlations between IQ (average IQ = 50) and the understanding of mixed and moral emotions, the influence of belief on emotions and strategies for regulating emotions (Hernández-Blasi, Pons, Escalera & Suco, 2003). Similar results have been found with children with autism (Buitelarr, et al., 1999).

Finally, several studies have shown that when the family, and in particular the mother, talks frequently and coherently to her child about mental states, including the causes and the consequences of emotions, this has a positive influence on the child's emotion understanding (e.g. de Rosnay, Pons, Harris & Morrell, 2004; Meins et al., 2002). The lapse of time between the assessment of family discourse and the assessment of the child's level emotion understanding can be brief: some days or weeks (Dunn, Brown, Slomkowski, Tesla & Youngblade, 1991; Garner, Jones, Gaddy & Rennie, 1997), extended over several months (Ruffman, Slade & Crowe, 2002), over one year (Meins & Fernyhough, 1999) and even over 3 years (Dunn, Brown & Beardsall, 1991; Brown & Dunn, 1996).

These different studies suggest the symbolic and cognitive influences on children's emotion understanding are bi-directional: the familial communicative environment impacts on the child's emotion understanding, but the child also brings her/his own linguistic competencies to this communicative environment. We can therefore imagine how a positive cycle can become established within the child's social world: children with good language skills have more opportunities to communicate with others more easily and make appealing conversational partners. Thus, they have more opportunity to communicate about their emotions or those of others (e.g. Pons, Lawson, Harris & de Rosnay, 2003 for a discussion).

In sum, in this first approach, the child's and caregiver's abilities to symbolically and cognitively represent emotions are considered more important determinants of children's emotion comprehension than the child's or caregiver's experience of affective well-being.

The power of experiences

According to the second approach, that might be qualified as "psychodynamic and ethological" because of its theoretical background, the quality of children's affective experience, especially in relation to their caretakers (generally their mother) is assumed to have a primary influence on children's understanding of emotions. The underlying hypothesis is that children's experience of affective well-being, particularly within their family environment, facilitates their exploration of, acceptance of and, ultimately, their understanding of emotions.

Various studies support this hypothesis (e.g. Fonagy & Target, 1997, 1999; Thompson, 1999 for reviews and discussions). They show, for example, that there is a link between children's understanding of emotions and their attachment relationship to their caretaker, as measured via standardized instruments such as "The Strange Situation" or "The Separation Anxiety Test". Securely attached children (versus children who are ambivalently or insecurely attached) have a better understanding of the emotional implications contained in fictional stories (Bretherton, Ridgeway & Cassidy, 1990; Main, Kaplan & Cassidy, 1985), the influence of desires on emotions (Fonagy, Redfern & Charman, 1997), of beliefs on emotions (de Rosnay & Harris, 2002) and of the mixed nature of certain emotions (Steele, Steeel, Croft & Fonagy, 1999). Fonagy, Target and Gergely (2000) also showed that there was a clear relation between attachment behaviors and the capacity for representing the mental states of self and others among patients with borderline personality disorders (see also Fonagy, Target, Steele, Steele, Leigh, Levison & Kennedy, 1997). Steele, Steele, Croft and Fonagy (1999) showed that the representation that expectant mothers have of their attachment relationship (as assessed with the Adult Attachment Interview) predicts the understanding that their children have of certain mixed emotions some six or seven years later when the child is 6 years old (see also

Fonagy, Steele, Moran & Steele, 1993; Fonagy, Steele & Steele, 1991; Main, Kaplan et Cassidy, 1985). Laible and Thompson (1998) showed that mothers who represent their attachment with their child as secure (as assessed with the Attachment Q-set) have children (ranging from 2 ½ to 6 years) with a good understanding of negative emotions (see also de Wollf & van IJzendoorn, 1997; van IJzendoorn, Jufffer & Duyvesteyn, 1995).

A small number of studies has shown that the distortion or absence of attachment relationships, as in the case of abuse, is associated with a strong negative impact on the emotion understanding of children and their families (e.g. Aber & Allen, 1987). Camras, Ribordy, Hill & Martino (1990) showed that abused children (between 3 and 7 years old) were less accurate in recognizing certain basic emotions (e.g. happiness, sadness, anger, fear, disgust and surprise) than non-abused children (see also Camras, Grow & Ribordy, 1983; Camras, Ribordy, Hill, Martino, Spaccarelli & Stefani, 1988). Shipman, Zeman, Penza and Champion (2000) found that girls (between 6 and 12 years old) who had been sexually abused by their fathers or paternal figures had a lower level of emotion understanding (e.g., of the causes and consequences of emotions) than girls who had not been sexually abused. Shipman and Zeman (2001) also found that physically abused children (between 6 and 12 years old) had more difficulties in understanding how to control feelings such as anger than non-abused children. In addition, the mothers of these abused children were less able to recognize their children's emotional displays and to understand how to help their children to cope with negative emotions than the mothers of non-abused children (see also Shipman & Zeman, 1999 for similar results).

In sum, the second approach proposes that the greater the affective well-being of the child and caregiver, the better the child understands or will understand emotions. In this approach, emphasis is placed on children's and caregivers' affective experience, the basic premise being that these experiences are one of the necessary conditions, albeit insufficient, for children's developing understanding of emotions.

Four open questions

These various studies represent a considerable advance in the exploration of individual differences in emotion understanding. They demonstrate strong relations between children's emotion understanding and some of their own characteristics or some of the characteristics of their family, be they either mostly experiential and affective (e.g. affective experiences, attachment relationships, abuse) or mostly symbolic and cognitive (e.g. language skills, IQ). However, at least four open questions have emerged from these studies.

First, it is difficult to evaluate the specific contribution of these two groups of characteristics and their interaction (see Harris, 1999; de Rosnay & Harris, 2002 for discussion). For example, several studies have indicated a co-variation between the quality of the mother-child attachment and the quality of mother-child discourse about emotions. Secure mothers speak more easily about their attachment relationship with their own mothers (e.g., van IJzendoorn, 1995). Meins, Fernyhough, Fradley and Tuckey (2001) found that mothers' appropriate mind-related comments about mental states, including emotions, when their infants were 6 months old proved to be good predictors of their children's attachment security at 12 months. Laible and Thompson (2000) found that the attachment relationship was a good predictor of mothers' and children's discourse about emotions (both being good predictors of children's early conscience development at the age of four years). Fonagy, Redfern and Charman (1997) showed that the mother-child attachment relationship was a good predictor of the child's emotion understanding, even when the child's level of language skill was controlled for (see also Steele, Steele, Croft & Fonagy, 1999). On the other hand, de Rosnay (2003) showed that the frequency of mental state comments by mothers of children aged 4½ to 6 years was a good predictor of children's emotion understanding even when the mother-child attachment relationship was controlled for. However, some studies have reported contradictory results. For instance, Humfress, O'Connor, Slaughter, Target and Fonagy (2002), showed that young adolescents' representation of their attachment relationships was correlated with their understanding of mental states but not with their language skills. On the other hand, Meins, Fernyhough, Wainwright, Gupta, Fradley and Tuckey (2002) found that mothers' use of mental state language and children's verbal ability predicted children's mental state understanding but their earlier attachment relationship did not. Finally, Ciarrochi, Chan and Caputi (2000) observed no relation between IQ and emotion understanding but, as reported before, Hernández-Blasi et al. (2003) and Buitelarr, et al. (1999) did find such a relation.

Second, most research on individual differences in emotion understanding has focused on pre-school or young school children. Studies of emotion understanding by early adolescence are rare.

Third, in the majority of these studies emotion understanding was assessed with respect to a small number of components or relatively simple components of emotion understanding (e.g., the recognition of basic emotions or the understanding of external causes of emotions). For this reason, it is difficult to evaluate the level of generality of the results obtained in these studies.

Finally, few empirical studies have investigated the impact of abuse and learning difficulties at school on the understanding of emotions. Therefore, it would be interesting to push forward the investigation of the role of these two issues on emotion understanding.

3. Empirical illustration

Goal of the research

The aim of the present research was to try to answer to these four questions. The primary goal was to evaluate the effects of abuse (an experiential-affective factor), learning difficulties (a symbolic-cognitive factor) and their interaction on adolescents' understanding of various simple and complex components of emotion.

Participants

Four groups of adolescents were tested (N = 28 adolescents):
- Group 1: Abused adolescents with learning difficulties (A+ LD+)
- Group 2: Abused adolescents without learning difficulties (A+ LD−)
- Group 3: Non-abused adolescents with learning difficulties (A− LD+)
- Group 4: Non-abused adolescents without learning difficulties (A− LD−)

Four types of abuse were identified in accordance with the literature: (1) Psychological abuse (e.g. verbal abuse, depreciation, terrifying symbolic acts, psychological cruelty); (2) Neglect (e.g., deficient care, rejection, absence of physical and psychological attention); (3) Sexual abuse (e.g. incest, rape and attempted rape, sexual contact, exposure to pornography or indecent acts) and (4) Physical abuse (e.g., physical violence and aggression, brutality, sadism) (e.g. Aber & Zigler, 1981; Barnett, Manly & Cicchetti, 1993; Calverley, Fischer & Ayoub, 1994; Christoffel, Schiedt, Agran, Kraus, McLoughlin & Paulson, 1992; Doudin & Erkohen-Marküs, 2000).

Two non-exclusive types of learning difficulties at school were identified in accordance with the literature: (1) Placement in classes for pupils with special needs ("structural differentiation") and (2) Repetition of at least one school year. These placements and repetitions resulted from adolescents' unsatisfactory marks in primary subjects (Native literacy, foreign language, mathematics, physics, biology, history and geography) (e.g. Bottani & Walberg, 1992; Doudin, 1996; OCDE, 1996; Nuttall, 1992).

The adolescents in Groups 1 and 2 had been psychologically abused (100%), neglected (71%), sexually abused (14%) and/or physically abused (14%) by at least one of their parents. All were separated from their parent by social services and were living in a specialized boarding institution in one of the main cities of the French-speaking part of Switzerland. Both parents of all these adolescents had been abused by their own parents when they were children (they had suffered either from psychological abuse or neglect). More generally, the family background of these adolescents included a variety of risk factors (e.g., parental separation, divorce, or mental illness) and in a minority of cases included dramatic life-events (e.g. murder, suicide or death of a close family member, prison, drug abuse). Among the adolescents with learning difficulties (Groups 1 and 3), a majority were placed in classes for pupils with special needs (57%) and almost all of them had repeated at least one school year (86%). The average age and age range were similar in all four groups (13 years and 3 months). The proportion of girls and boys was also similar in all four groups (between 43 and 57%). All participants spoke French as their first language. All were tested at the same local school.

Procedure, instrument, and score

Adolescents were seen individually in a quiet room at their school. Testing was carried out over one session. To assess adolescents' understanding of emotions, the Test of Emotion Comprehension (TEC) was used (Pons & Harris, 2000). This instrument is based on an extensive review of the experimental literature on the development of emotion understanding. A substantial body of research has shown that at least nine more or less complex components of emotion understanding develop during childhood and adolescence: Recognition of emotion on the basis of expressive cues; understanding the role of external causes, desires, beliefs and reminders; understanding the control of either expressed or experienced emotions; understanding the mixed nature of emotions and understanding of moral or social emotions (see Harris, 1989; Lewis & Haviland-Jones, 2000; Pons, Doudin, Harris & de Rosnay, 2005; Saarni & Harris, 1989; Saarni, Mumme & Campos, 1998, for reviews). The TEC permits the measurement of the understanding of these nine components from the age of 3 years until adolescence. The TEC has been translated into English, French, Spanish, Italian, Dutch, Quechua, Danish, Arabic, German, Greek, Fongbé and will soon be available in Norwegian and Portuguese. It has been validated and its reliability has been evaluated positively. The TEC will soon be standardized in Italian (e.g. Albanese et al., 2006). A computerized colored version is also under progress. The TEC is currently used by dozens of research, pedagogical and clinical institutions in Europe, America, Africa, Asia and Oceania as a diagnostic instrument, and as either an independent or a dependent measure.

The TEC consists of a picture book with a simple cartoon scenario on the upper part of each page. Beneath each scenario, on the lower part of the page, are four emotional outcomes, typically represented as facial expressions. The four possible outcomes are two negative emotions (sad/scared, sad/angry, or scared/angry) and two non-negative emotions (happy/just alright). Testing was conducted on an individual basis. The general procedure was divided into two steps: (1) While showing a given cartoon scenario, the experimenter read the accompanying story about the depicted character(s); (the face(s) of the characters in the cartoon were left blank). (2) After hearing the story, the adolescent was asked to make an emotion attribution to the main character by pointing to the most appropriate of the four possible emotional outcomes (the adolescents' responses were non-verbal). The test was divided into 9 blocks presented in a fixed order. Each block assessed a particular component of the understanding of emotion:

- Recognition of emotions on the basis of facial expression (e.g. recognition of the face of a happy person);
- Understanding of external causes of emotions (e.g. attribution of an emotion to a character being chased by a monster);
- Understanding of desire-based emotions (e.g. attribution of an emotion to two characters in the same situation but having opposite desires);
- Understanding of belief-based emotions (e.g. attribution of an emotion to a rabbit who is enjoying a carrot without knowing that a fox is hiding behind the bushes);
- Understanding the influence of a reminder on a present emotional state (e.g. attribution of an emotion to a character who is reminded of the loss of a pet);
- Understanding of the regulation of an experienced emotion (e.g. attribution of a psychological strategy such as "think about something else" to a character who wants to stop feeling sad);
- Understanding of the possibility of hiding an underlying or true emotional state (e.g. attribution of an emotion to a character who is smiling in order to hide his or her distress from another character engaged in teasing);
- Understanding of mixed emotions (e.g. attribution of an emotion to a character who has just received a bicycle for his or her birthday but who is wondering, as a novice, if he or she might fall off and get hurt); and
- Understanding of moral emotions (e.g. attribution of an emotion to a character who has done something naughty and who fails to confess to his or her mother).

An overall level of emotion understanding was calculated by summing the components correctly answered with a minimum of 0 points (none of the nine components passed) and a maximum of 9 points (all nine components passed).

Preliminary results

Table 1 shows the percentage of adolescents by overall level of emotion understanding by group. The majority (57%) of the abused adolescents with learning difficulties (Group 1) understood no more than 7 components of emotion understanding. None was able to understand all 9 components. The majority (57%) of the abused adolescents without learning difficulties (Group 2) understood at least 8 components of emotion understanding. A substantial minority (43%) understood all 9 components. The majority (71%) of the non-abused adolescents with learning difficulties (Group 3) understood no more than 7 components of emotion understanding. Only a tiny minority (14%) understood all 9 components. Finally, the majority (57%) of non-abused adolescents without learning difficulties (Group 4) understood at least 8 components of emotion understanding. Almost half of them (43%) were able to understand all 9 components.

Table 1
Percentage of adolescents by overall level of emotion understanding and by group

Group	Overall level of emotion understanding					
	4	5	6	7	8	9
Group 1 (A+ LD+)	14		14	29	43	
Group 2 (A+ LD-)			14	29	14	43
Group 3 (A- LD+)		14	14	43	14	14
Group 4 (A- LD-)					57	43

Note: None of the adolescents got an overall level of emotion understanding lower than 4 points.

Statistical analyses (analyses of variance and regression analyses) revealed no significant main effect for abuse but a significant main effect of learning difficulties. A similar proportion (respectively, 78% and 71%) of abused (Groups 1 and 2) and non-abused (Groups 3 and 4) adolescents understood at least 8 components of emotion understanding. The majority (64%) of the adolescents with learning difficulties (Groups 1 and 3) understood no more than 7 components whereas a clear majority (79%) of the adolescents without learning difficulties (Groups 2 and 4) understood either 8 or 9 components of emotions understanding. Finally, there was no significant interaction between abuse and learning difficulties. The abused adolescent without learning difficulties (Group 2) understood more components of emotion understanding than the abused adolescents with learning difficulties (Group 1). The situation was similar with the non-abused adolescents; those without learning difficulties (Group 4) understood more components of emotion understanding than those with learning difficulties (Group 3).

In summary, learning difficulty but not abuse had an impact on adolescents' emotion understanding. Abused and non-abused adolescents with learning difficulties displayed less overall understanding of emotion than did abused and non-abused adolescents without learning difficulties.

4. Discussion

The aim of this research was to evaluate the effects of abuse (experiential-affective factor), learning difficulties (symbolic-cognitive factor) and the potential interaction of these variables on adolescents' understanding of several components of emotion understanding that vary in difficulty, emotion understanding being considered as one of the most important emotional competences, the reflective one.

A surprising and important result of this study is that there was no difference between abused and non-abused adolescents' overall level of emotion understanding. Only learning difficulties had a significant impact on their emotion understanding. Adolescents with learning difficulties had a significantly lower overall level of emotion understanding than those without learning difficulties. Only one third of the adolescents with learning difficulties (36%) were able to understand eight or nine components of emotion understanding whereas more than three quarters of those without learning difficulties (79%) were able to do so. Finally, no significant interaction was found between abuse and learning difficulties. Adolescents without learning difficulties always had a higher overall level of emotion understanding than those with learning difficulties, irrespective of any history of abuse.

The overall level of emotion understanding of the adolescents with learning difficulties was comparable to that found for typically developing children of 9 years of age whereas the overall level of the adolescents without learning difficulties was comparable to that found with typically developing children of 11-12 years and adults in previous research using the same methodology (e.g.

Hernández-Blasi, Pons, Escalera & Suco, 2003; Pons, Harris & Doudin, 2002; Pons, Lawson, Harris & de Rosnay, 2003; Pons & Harris, 2005; Pons, Harris & de Rosnay, 2004). The overall level of the later group was also consistent with what may be inferred from the literature on the development of emotion understanding (e.g., Harris, 1989; Lewis & Haviland-Jones, 2000; Pons, Doudin, Harris & de Rosnay, 2005; Saarni & Harris, 1989; Saarni, Mumme & Campos, 1998).

In other words, the results of this research are consistent with previous studies showing an impact of language and IQ on emotion understanding but not with those showing an impact of attachment relationships and abuse on emotion understanding. These concordances and discrepancies can be interpreted in different ways.

Symbols are more powerful than experiences!

One possible interpretation is that symbolic and cognitive characteristics are actually better predictors of emotion understanding than affective experience. However, as mentioned in the introduction, several studies have shown an impact of affective experience on emotion understanding, especially in very young children.

Do symbols and experiences have the same impact whatever the age of the individual?

A second possible interpretation is that affective experience has an influence on young children's emotion understanding because of their greater affective sensitivity and dependency. Furthermore, this relation could be reversed for symbolic and cognitive characteristics. The older children get, the more their symbolic and cognitive characteristics influence their emotion understanding because of the impact of intellectual capacities that naturally improve with age. Consequently, an alternative interpretation of the results of this research is that the abused adolescents with good intellectual capacities had had the time to compensate for the impact of their dramatic affective experience. Further longitudinal research with toddlers and school children with and without abuse and learning difficulties could determine whether this hypothesis is correct or not.

Do all types of abuse have the same impact?

Third, it is an open question whether the absence of a relationship between abuse and emotion understanding holds for all types of abuse. For example, we can hypothesize that physical, sexual and psychological abuses differ from neglect in their impact on emotion understanding. Physical, sexual and psychological abuse may be considered as serious distortions of the attachment relationship whereas neglect amounts to a dramatic absence of an attachment relationship. Clinical observations have shown that the absence of a relationship often yields many more grave consequences than do distorted relationships (e.g., Doudin & Erkohen-Marküs, 2000). A qualitative inspection of abused adolescents' overall level of emotion understanding supports this hypothesis. It shows that the abused adolescents who were not neglected (i.e. they were sexually, physically and psychologically abused) had the tendency to have a higher overall level (around 8 points) than the ten neglected adolescents (around 7 points). In the future, it would be interesting to study the interaction between the types of abuse (sexual, physical and psychological versus negligence) and emotion understanding in adolescents and also in children (in a larger scale) to investigate the impact of the types of abuse on emotion understanding.

5. Conclusion

In summary, the present empirical research showed that (1) symbolic and cognitive (i.e. learning difficulties at school) but not experiential and affective (i.e. abuse) characteristics have an impact on adolescents' reflective emotional competence; emotion understanding and (2) there is no interaction between these symbolic-cognitive and experiential-affective characteristics in adolescents. These findings suggest that adolescents' emotion understanding extends beyond their first-hand affective experience. The results of this research contribute to our comprehension of some of the origins of emotion understanding and of individual differences in this understanding in adolescents. In the future, it would be interesting to examine toddlers and school children using the same methodology and design to evaluate the generality of these results. It would also be interesting to examine the differential impact of negligence versus sexual, physical and psychological abuse to refine these results.

Two additional complementary questions may be asked in conclusion. First, why do some abused adolescents have learning difficulties and others not? Various answers can be proposed to this question. Briefly, this difference among abused adolescents could be due to some characteristics of the individual such as his/her resilience (Rutter, 1989; Werner & Smith, 1992) or capacity to develop along distinctive pathways (Fischer, Ayoub, Singh, Noam, Maraganore & Raya, 1997). It could also be due to some characteristics of his/her family, school environment and/or social services (Cicchetti & Toth, 1993; Doudin & Erkohen-Marküs, 2000). Second, why do some non-abused adolescents have learning difficulties and others not? Learning difficulties are not always correlated with IQ deficits or cognitive dysfunctions. Emotional (and motivational) issues, in other words experiential-affective characteristics, may also have a reciprocal impact on learning processes, in other words on symbolic-cognitive characteristics. The question of the impact of emotions (and motivation) on learning processes at school is still quite open (e.g. Pons, Hancock, Lafortune & Doudin, 2005). Therefore in the future, it would also be interesting to investigate these different individual and environmental characteristics to better understand the results of this research.

Finally, it should be noted that a better understanding of the impact of symbolic-cognitive and experiential-affective factors on emotion understanding could be useful both in psychotherapy or educational psychology. Indeed, a limited understanding of emotions, reflective competence on emotions, has long been identified in the clinical world as an important source of patients' affective difficulties. An increasing number of studies have also converged on the idea that the higher a pupil's emotion understanding is, the better his or her relationships with schoolmates and teachers are (e.g. Pons, Harris & Doudin, 2002; Thompson, Laible & Robbennolt, 1997; Villanueva, Clemente & Garcia, 2000 for reviews and discussions). A better understanding of the impact of symbolic-cognitive and experiential-affective factors on emotion understanding could contribute to the construction of new and more targeted clinical and educational programs of intervention and prevention. For example, depending on the age group and on the characteristics of the individual and his or her family or school, such programs would focus either on symbolic and cognitive dimensions (e.g., discussion about emotions) or on experiential and affective dimensions (e.g., re-enactment of emotions) to help the individual and his or her family, schoolmates or teachers to improve their emotion understanding.

References

Aber, J., & Allen, P. (1987). The effects of maltreatment on young children's socio-emotional development: An attachment theory perspective: *Developmental Psychology, 23*, 406-414.

Aber, J., & Zigler, E. (1981). Developmental considerations in the definition of child maltreatment. *New Directions for Child Development, 11*, 1-29.

Albanese, O., Grazzani, I., Molina, P., Antoniotti, C., Arati, I, Farina, E., & Pons, F. (2006). La comprensione delle emozioni nei bambini: Dati preliminari del progetto Italiano dei validazione del Test of Emotion Comprehension (TEC). In O. Albanese, M.-F. Daniel, P.-A. Doudin, L. Lafortune & F. Pons (Eds.),

Competenza emotive tra psicologia ed educazione (pp. 35-47). Milano: Franco Angeli.

Barnett, D., Manly, J., & Cicchetti, D. (1993). Defining child maltreatment: The interface between policy and research. In. D. Cicchetti & S. Toth (Eds.), *Child abuse, child development and social policy advances in applied developmental psychology* (pp. 7-73). Norwood, NJ: Ablex Publishing Company.

Bottani, N., & Walberg, H. (1992). A quoi servent les indicateurs internationaux de l'enseignement? In *L'OCDE et les indicateur internationaux de l'enseignement* (pp. 7-13). Paris: CERI.

Bretherton, I., Ridgeway, D., & Cassidy, J. (1990). Assessing internal working models of attachment relationship. In T. Greenberg, D. Ciccehetti & E. Cummings (Eds.), *Attachment in the preschool years* (pp. 273-308). Chicago: University of Chicago Press.

Brown, J., & Dunn, J. (1996). Continuities in emotion understanding from three to six years. *Child Development, 67*, 789-802.

Buitelaar, J., van der Wees, M., Swaab-Barneveld, H., & Jan van der Gaag, R. (1999). Verbal memory and performance IQ predict theory of mind and emotion recognition ability in children with autistic spectrum disorders and psychiatric control children. *Journal of Child Psychology and Psychiatry, 40*, 869-881.

Calverley, R., Fischer, K., & Ayoub, C. (1994). Complex splitting of self-representations in sexually abused adolescent girls. *Development and Psychopathology, 6*, 195-213.

Camras, L., Grow, J., & Ribordy, S. (1983). Recognition of emotional expression by abused children. *Journal of Clinical Child Psychology, 12*, 325-328.

Camras, L., Ribordy, S., Hill, J., & Martino, S. (1990). Maternal facial behavior and the recognition and production of emotional expression by maltreated and nonmaltreated children. *Developmental Psychology, 26*, 304-312.

Camras, L., Ribordy, S., Hill, J., Martino, S., Spaccarelli, S., & Stefani, R. (1988). Recognition and posing of emotional expressions by abused children and their mothers. *Developmental Psychology, 24*, 776-781.

Christoffel, K., Schiedt, P., Agran, J., Kraus, J., McLoughlin E., & Paulson, J. (1992). Standard definitions for childhood injury research. *Pediatrics, 89*, 6, 1027-1034.

Cicchetti, D., & Toth, S.L. (Eds.) (1993). *Child Abuse, Child Development and Social Policy. Advances in Applied Developmental Psychology*. Norwood, NJ: Ablex Publishing Company.

Ciarrochi, J., Chan, A., & Caputi, P. (2000). A critical evaluation of the emotional intelligence construct. *Personality and Individual Differences, 28*, 539-561.

Cutting, A., & Dunn, J. (1999). Theory of mind, emotion understanding, language, and family background: Individual differences and interrelations. *Child Development, 70*, 853-865.

Deleau, M. (1996). L'attribution d'états mentaux chez des enfants sourds et entendants: une approche du rôle de l'expérience langagière sur une théorie de l'esprit. *Bulletin de Psychologie, 427*, 48-56.

Doudin, P.-A. (1996). Elèves en difficultés: la pédagogie compensatoire est-elle efficace? *Psychoscope, 17*, 4-7.

Doudin, P.-A., & Erkohen-Marküs, M. (Eds.) (2000), *Violence à l'école: fatalité ou défi?* (pp. 17-46). Bruxelles: De Boeck.

Dunn, J., Brown, J., & Beardsall, L. (1991). Family talk about feeling states and children's later understanding of other's emotions. *Developmental Psychology, 27*, 448-455.

Dunn, J., Brown, J., Slomkowski, C., Tesla, C., & Youngblade, L. (1991). Young children's understanding of other people's feelings and beliefs: Individual differences and their antecedents. *Child Development, 62*, 1352-1366.

Fischer, K., Ayoub, C., Singh, I., Noam, G., Maraganore, A., & Raya, P. (1997). Psychopathology as adaptive development along distinctive pathways. *Development and Psychopathology, 9*, 749-779.

Figueras-Costa, B., Harris, P.L. (2001). Theory of mind development in deaf children: A nonverbal test of false-belief understanding. *Journal of Deaf Studies and Deaf Education, 6*, 92-102.

Fonagy, P., Redfern, S., & Charman, T. (1997). The relationship between belief-desire reasoning and a projective measure of attachment security (SAT), *British Journal of Developmental Psychology, 15*, 51-61.

Fonagy, P., Steele, M., Moran, G., & Steele, H. (1993). Measuring the ghost in the nursery: An empirical study of the relation between parent's mental representations of childhood experiences and their infants' security of attachment. *Journal of the American Psychoanalytic Association, 41*, 957-989.

Fonagy, P., Steele, H., & Steele, M. (1991). Maternal representations of attachment during pregnancy predict the organization of infant-mother attachment at one year of age. *Child Development, 62*, 891-905.

Fonagy, P., & Target, M. (1997). Attachment and reflective function: Their role in self-organisation. *Development and Psychopathology, 9*, 679-700.

Fonagy, P., & Target, M. (1999). An interpersonal view of the infant. In A. Hurry (Ed.), *Psychoanalysis and developmental therapy* (pp. 3-31). Madison, CT: International University Press.

Fonagy, P., Target, M., & Gergely, G. (2000). Attachment and borderline personality disorder: A theory and some evidence. *Psychiatric Clinics of North*

America, 23, 103-122.

Fonagy, P., Target, M., Steele, M., Steele, H., Leigh, T., Levison, A., & Kennedy, R. (1997). Morality, disruptive behavior, borderline personality disorder, crime and their relationship to security of attachment. In L. Atkinson & K. Zucker (Eds.), *Attachment and psychopathology* (pp. 223-274). New York: Guilford Press.

Garner, P., Jones, D., Gaddy, G. & Rennie, K. (1997). Low-income mothers' conversations about emotions and their children's emotional competence. *Social Development, 6*, 37-52.

Harris, P. L. (1989). *Children and emotion*. Oxford: Blackwell.

Harris, P. L. (1994). The child's understanding of emotion: Developmental changes and the family environment. *Journal of Child Psychology and Psychiatry, 35*, 3-28.

Harris, P. L. (1999). Individual differences in understanding emotion: The role of attachment status and psychological discourse. *Attachment and Human Development, 1*, 307-324.

Harris, P. L. (2005). Conversation, pretense, and theory of mind. In J. W. Astington & J. A. Baird (Eds.), *Why language matters for theory of mind* (pp. 70-83). Oxford: Oxford University Press.

Harris, P.L., de Rosnay, M., & Pons, F. (2005). Language and children's understanding of mental states. *Current Directions in Psychological Sciences, 14*(2), 69-73.

Hernández Blasi, C., Pons, F., Escalera, C., & Suco, A. (2003, June). *On the role of intelligence on emotional comprehension*. Poster, 33rd Annual Meeting of the Jean Piaget Society, Chicago, USA.

Humfress, H., O'Connor, T., Slaughter, J., Target, M., & Fonagy, P. (2002). General and relationship-specific models of social cognition: Explaining the overlap and discrepancies. *Journal of Child Psychology and Psychiatry, 43*, 873-883.

van IJzendoorn, M.H. (1995). Adult attachment representations, parental responsiveness, and infant attachment: A meta-analysis on the predictive validity of the adult attachment interview. *Psychological Bulletin, 117*, 387-403.

van IJzendoorn, M.H., Juffer, F. & Duyvesteyn, M.G.C. (1995). Breaking the intergenerational cycle of insecure attachment: A review of the effects of attachment-based interventions on maternal sensitivity and infant security. *Journal of Child Psychology and Child Psychiatry, 36*, 225-248.

Laible, D., & Thompson, R. (1998). Attachment and emotional understanding in preschool children. *Developmental Psychology, 34*, 1038-1045.

Laible, D., & Thompson, R. (2000). Mother-child discourse, attachment security, shared positive affect, and early conscience development. *Child Development, 71*, 1424-1440.

Lewis, M., & Haviland-Jones, J. (Eds.) (2000), *Handbook of emotions*. New York: The Guilford Press.

Main, M., Kaplan, N., & Cassidy, J. (1985). Security in infancy, childhood and adulthood: A move to the level of representation. *Monographs of the Society for Research in Child Development, 50*, 66-104.

Meins, E., & Fernyhough, C. (1999). Linguistic acquisitional style and mentalising development: The role of maternal mind-mindedness. *Cognitive Development, 14*, 363-380.

Meins, E., Fernyhough, C., Fradley, E., & Tuckey, M. (2001). Rethinking maternal sensitivity: Mother's comments on infants' mental processes predict security of attachment at 12 months. *Journal of Child Psychology and Psychiatry, 42*, 637-648.

Meins, E., Fernyhough, C., Wainwright, R., Gupta, M., Fradley, E., & Tuckey, M. (2002). Maternal mind-mindedness and attachment security as predictors of theory of mind understanding. *Child Development, 73*, 1715-1726.

Nuttall, D. (1992). Les indicateurs internationaux de l'enseignement: leurs fonctions et leurs limites. In *L'OCDE et les indicateur internationaux de l'enseignement* (pp. 15-25). Paris: CERI.

OCDE. (1996). *Regards sur l'éducation. Les indicateurs de l'OCDE*. Paris: CERI.

Peterson, C. & Siegal, M. (1995). Deafness, conversation and theory of mind. *Journal of Child Psychology and Psychiatry, 36*, 459-474.

Peterson, C. & Siegal, M. (1999). Representing inner worlds: Theory of mind in autistic, deaf and normal hearing children. *Psychological Science, 10*, 126-129.

Pons, F., Doudin, P.-A., Harris, P., & de Rosnay (2005). Helping children to improve their emotion comprehension. In F. Pons, D. Hancock, L. Lafortune & P.-A. Doudin (Eds.), *Emotions in learning* (pp. 15-39). Aalborg: Aalborg University Press.

Pons, F., Hancock, D., Lafortune, L., & Doudin, P.-A. (Eds.) (2005). *Emotions in learning*. Aalborg: Aalborg University Press.

Pons, F., & Harris, P. (2000). *Test of emotion comprehension (TEC)*. Oxford: University of Oxford.

Pons, F., & Harris, P. (2005). Longitudinal change and longitudinal stability of individual differences in children's emotion understanding. *Cognition and Emotion, 19*(8), 1158-1174.

Pons, F., Harris, P. L., & Doudin, P.-A. (2002). Teaching emotion understanding. *European Journal of Psychology of Education, 17*(3), 293-304.

Pons, F., Harris, P., & de Rosnay, M. (2004). Emotion comprehension between 3 and 11 years: Developmental periods and hierarchical organizations. *European Journal of Developmental Psychology, 1*(2), 127-152.

Pons, F., Harris, P., & de Rosnay, M. (in press). Betydningen af barnets sprog og familiens samtaleaktiviteter for barnets Theory of Mind. In C. Jantzen & T. Thellesen (Eds.), *Videnskabelig begrebsdannelse*. Aalborg: Aalborg Universitrtsforlag.

Pons, F., Lawson, J., Harris, P. L., & de Rosnay, M. (2003). Individual differences in children's emotion understanding: Effects of age and language. *Scandinavian Journal of Psychology44*(4), 347-353.

de Rosnay, M. (2003). *Childen's understanding of emotion: The roles of attachment and maternal discourse*. Unpublished Doctoral Thesis, Department of Experimental Psychology, University of Oxford.

de Rosnay, M., & Harris, P. L. (2002). Individual differences in children's understanding of emotion: The role of attachment and language. *Attachment and Human Development, 4*, 39-45.

de Rosnay, M., Pons, F., Harris, P., & Morrell, J. (2004). A lag between understanding false belief and emotion attribution in young children: Relationships with context, language ability, and mother's mental state language. *British Journal of Developmental Psychology, 22*, 197-218.

Ruffman, T., Slade, L., & Crowe, E. (2002). The relationship between children's and mother's mental state language and theory-of-mind understanding. *Child Development, 73*, 734-751.

Rutter, M. (1989). Psychosocial resilience and protective mechanisms. In D. Cicchetti & V. Carlson (Eds.), *Child maltreatment: Theory and research on the causes and consequences of child abuse and neglect* (pp. 181-214). New York: Cambridge University Press.

Saarni, C., & Harris, P. L. (Eds.) (1989). *Children's understanding of emotion*. Cambridge: Cambridge University Press.

Saarni, C., Mumme, D., & Campos, J. (1998). Emotional development: Action, communication, and understanding. In W. Damon (Series Ed.), & N. Eisenberg (Ed.), *Handbook of child psychology: Vol. 3. Social, emotional and personality development* (5th edition, pp. 237-309). New York: John Wiley.

Shipman, K., & Zeman, J. (1999). Emotional understanding: A comparaison of physically maltreating and nonmaltreating mother-child dyads. *Journal of Clinical Child Psychology, 28*, 407-417.

Shipman, K., & Zeman, J. (2001). Socialization of children's emotion regulation in mother-child dyads: A developmental psychopathology perspective. *Development and Psychopathology, 13*, 317-336.

Shipman, K., Zeman, J., Penza, S., & Champion, K. (2000). Emotion management skills in sexually maltreated and nonmaltreated girls: A developmental psychopathology perspective. *Development and Psychopathology, 12*, 47-62.

Steele, H., Steele, M., Croft, C., & Fonagy, P. (1999). Infant-mother attachment at one year predicts children's understanding of mixed emotions at six years. *Social Development, 8*, 161-178.

Tenenbaum, H., Visscher, P., Pons, F., & Harris, P. (2003). *Emotion understanding in Quechua children from an agro-pastoralist village.* Manuscript submitted for publication.

Thompson, R. A. (1999). Early attachment and later development. In J. Cassidy & P. R. Shaver (Eds.), *Handbook of attachment: Theory, research, and clinical applications* (pp. 265-286). London: The Guilford Press.

Thompson, R., Laible, D., & Robbennolt, J. (1997). Child care and preventing child maltreatment. In C. Dunst & M. Wolery (Eds.) *Advances in early education and child care. Vol. 9: Family policy and practice in early child care. Advances in early education and day care* (pp. 173-202). Stamford, CT: JAI Press.

Villanueva, L., Clemente, R., & Garcia F. (2000). Theory of mind and peer rejection at school. *Social Development, 9*, 271-283.

Werner, E. & Smith, R. (1992). *Vulnerable but invincible: A longitudinal study of resilient children and youth.* New York: Adams, Bannister and Cox.

de Wolff, M. & van IJzendoorn, M. H. (1997). Sensitivity and attachment: A meta-analysis on parental antecedents of infant attachment. *Child Development, 68*, 571-591.

CHAPTER 2

Children's emotion understanding: Preliminary data from the Italian validation project of *Test of Emotion Comprehension* (TEC)

Ottavia Albanese, Ilaria Grazzani Gavazzi, Paola Molina, Carla Antoniotti, Laura Arati, Eleonora Farina, and Francisco Pons

1. Introduction

Children's understanding of emotions is an aspect or ability which has met with special attention within the body of research devoted to the development of emotional competence. Emotional competence is the set of skills that help one to recognize, understand, and respond consistently to other people's emotions as well as regulate the expression of one's own (Saarni, 1999). With respect to emotional competence, the literature produced in the field of developmental psychology falls within the theoretical framework of studies on children's theory of mind and meta-representational skills (Astington, Harris & Olson, 1988; Harris, 1989).

Based on extensive investigations conducted in the last two decades (e.g. Harris, 1983;1991; Harris, Olthof & Meerum Terwogt, 1981; Harris, Donnelly, Guz & Pitt-Watson, 1986; Bretherton, Fritz, Zahn-Waxler & Ridgeway, 1986; Kestenbaum & Gelman, 1995; Lagattuta, Wellman & Flavell, 1997; Lagattuta & Wellman, 2001; Pons, Lawson, Harris & de Rosnay, 2003; for a review: Grazzani & Antoniotti 2006), authors have described well-identified developmental stages and outlined their hierarchical relations in the development of emotion understanding (Pons, Harris & de Rosnay, 2004).

The chapter by Pons, de Rosnay, Doudin and Harris in this book illustrates the hierarchical model, emphasizing nine distinct components concerning the nature, the causes and the regulation of emotions. Children develop an understanding of the different components between three and eleven years of age. Three different stages may be identified (external, mental, reflective), and the experimental tasks performed by children are connected, at each stage, to the understanding of a few specific interrelated components (Pons, Harris & de Rosnay, 2004).

2. Test of Emotion Comprehension (TEC)

Based on a systematic analysis of the empirical literature on children's emotion understanding development Pons and Harris (2000) developed a tool named TEC (*Test of Emotion Comprehension*). TEC is meant to assess the understanding of emotions in children aged three to eleven. Such an understanding includes nine components concerning the nature of emotions (for a detailed description of these, see the contribution of Pons et al. in this book). These nine components include: recognition of basic emotions and understanding of mixed emotions (two components); the causes of emotions (five components: understanding of the impact of external causes, reminders, desires, beliefs and moral values on emotions); and the possibility of controlling the expression and the experience of emotions (two components: distinguishing apparent and felt emotions, regulation of current experience).

TEC consists of an A4 book (male and female versions) presenting a series of cartoon scenarios placed on the top of each page. The bottom part of each page shows four possible emotional outcomes depicted by facial expressions. In using TEC, the researcher reads a short story while the child looks at the cartoon scenario, and then the child is asked to point to the facial expression that fits best with the story (the child's answer is typically non-verbal).

For instance, in order to assess children's understanding of the external causes of emotions (one component belonging to the "understanding of the causes" category) on the top of the page there is a face without expressive cues and a present; the bottom part of the page shows four faces expressing different emotions (Fig. 1). The researcher, pointing at the expressionless image says: "This child has just received a present for his birthday" and then asks, still pointing at the different expressions: "How does the child feel? Happy, sad, just alright or scared?"

Figure 1.
Understanding of external causes of emotions (Component II) (Pons & Harris, 2000)

With the aim of assessing children's understanding of mixed emotions (a component included in the category "understanding the nature of emotions"), the top of another page shows a face without expressive cues and a bicycle. The bottom part of the page includes four frames, only two of which show a single face expressing an emotion, while the remaining two include two faces expressing different emotions. The researcher, pointing at the child's image says: "This child is looking at the beautiful bike he has just received as a present for his birthday. At the same time he is wondering whether he will fall and get hurt, as he cannot ride the bike yet"; then he asks, still pointing at the different expressions, "How does this child feel? Does he feel: happy, sad and scared, happy and scared, or scared?" (Figure 2).

Figure 2.
Understanding of mixed emotions (Component VIII) (Pons & Harris, 2000)

The test was initially administered on a sample of 100 British children aged 3, 5, 7, 9 and 11, uniformly distributed by age and gender (Pons, Harris & de Rosnay, 2004); the findings of this early research were largely confirmed by other investigations with Western children (e.g. Pons & Harris, 2005; Pons, Harris & Doudin, 2002; Pons, Lawson, Harris & de Rosnay, 2003) and Quechua children from Peru (Tennenbaum, Visscher, Pons & Harris, 2004). The overall score and the answers to individual components grow fairly regularly with age, even though high individual variability is recorded in children's responses. The range within which correct answers fall, for each type of component is very broad, even though a clear developmental pattern can be identified, as shown by hierarchical analyses (e.g. Pons & Harris, 2005; Pons, Harris & de Rosnay, 2004). These hierarchical analyses reveal that the nine components are arranged in groups of three: within each group, an equivalent level of difficulty can be observed. Moreover, while the three groups are hierarchically arranged the correct answer in a higher level group implies the ability to correctly answer questions in the lower level group(s). The components relevant to emotion recognition (I), to the influence of external causes of emotions (II) and to the role of memory (V) are to be found in the lower level of difficulty. The understanding of the role of desires (III), beliefs (IV) and the possible difference between felt emotion and facial expression (VII) is acquired at a subsequent stage. Finally, the understanding of emotional ambivalence (VIII), of the moral dimension of emotions (IX) and of possibility of regulation (VI) reflect a higher level of mental elaboration attained only in late childhood or even later. Empirical findings, therefore, outline a developmental pattern that differs slightly from the theoretically postulated developmental order (reflected by the roman number identifying each component). In particular, the understanding of the role played by desires is acquired later than is predicted by the theoretical model, based on the research conducted on the individual features of emotion understanding. Table 1, below, shows the differences vis-à-vis the theoretical developmental model; these are marked with an arrow.

Table 1
The development of emotion comprehension (e.g. Pons, Harris & de Rosnay, 2004)

Age	Understanding of emotion's *nature*	Understanding of emotion's *causes*	Understanding of emotion's *control*
3-5 years *External*)	Categorization of basic emotions on the basis of facial expression (I)	External causes of emotions (II)	
		Role of memory on present emotional states (V)	
		Role of desires on emotions (III) ▼	
6-7 years (*Mental*)	Mixed emotions (VIII) ▼	Role of beliefs on emotions (IV)	Hiding an emotional state (VII)
9-11 years (*Reflective*)		Role of morals on emotions (IX)	Controlling an experienced emotion (VI)

TEC has shown good test-retest reliability correlation when administered to children aged 9 years after three months ($r(18) = .84$) (Pons, Harris & Doudin, 2002); TEC has also shown good stability in its administration to children of 7,

9 and 11 years after thirteen months ($r(40) = .68$) checking by age and gender, $r(38) = .54$) (Pons & Harris, 2005). TEC also correlates strongly with language ability ($r = 81$ and $.52$ when the effects of age and gender were controlled) (Pons, Lawson, Harris & de Rosnay, 2003) and with IQ (r = between .62 and .78) (Hernández-Blasi, Pons, Escalera & Suco, 2003).

3. The Italian standardization

In Italy, a TEC Standardization Project has been started by a group of researchers from different universities, coordinated by Ottavia Albanese. The project currently involves Università degli Studi di Milano Bicocca, Università degli Studi di Torino and Università degli Studi di Roma "La Sapienza"; groups of researchers from other universities will soon join in. The Italian version of the test has been translated by the Project group and edited by Francisco Pons, one of the authors of the TEC, with whom administering procedures as well as inclusion criteria for children in the sample have been discussed.

In this chapter we shall present preliminary findings collected in Turin and Milan. The main objective of this first phase was to find out whether the results obtained in the original English sample (Pons, Harris & de Rosnay, 2004) could be repeated in the Italian context. Our questions, therefore, concerned (i) the possibility of comparing the data collected in the two cities (Milan and Turin), with the results obtained after collecting data from the English sample, and, above all, (ii) the possibility of identifying a hierarchical pattern in children's answers. This phase of the research involved the participation of 367 children attending kindergarten and primary schools in Milan and Turin, aged 4-10, evenly distributed by gender and age, as shown in Table 2.

Table 2
Number of children by age group and by gender

Age	Boys	Girls	Total
4 years	10	9	19
5 years	12	9	21
6 years	33	44	77
7 years	32	26	58
8 years	33	34	67
9 years	35	33	68
10 years	33	24	57
Total	188	179	367

4. Results

Data were collected in kindergartens in Turin and in primary schools in Milan. Data relevant to children aged 6 were collected in both cities (77 children, 22 in Turin and 55 in Milan): a comparison between the two groups showed no significant differences (t-test on independent samples conducted on overall score: t (75) = .377, P = .707). On this basis, we concluded that the two samples could be considered as a single group.

As regards possibility of comparison with the English sample, a first descriptive analysis highlighted that only component IV – understanding the role of beliefs - showed a pattern substantially different from that which we expected based on English findings. As a matter of fact, as shown in Table 3, the correct answer "happy" seems to become fairly stable starting with children 6-8 years of age, while the answer "just alright", which is wrong, seems to grow.

Table 3
Responses on the Component IV (Comprehension of the impact of beliefs)

Age	Happy	Just alright	Angry	Scared	Missing
4 years	4	3	3	9	
5 years	7	2	1	11	
6 years	37	13	1	26	
7 years	30	13		15	
8 years	41	19		7	
9 years	39	24		5	
10 years	36	16		4	1
Total	194	90	5	77	1

This particular pattern led us to think that children gave a different interpretation to the story than that hypothesized by the authors, and one possibility is that this interpretive difference was linked to a translation problem: in other words, children would answer "just alright" giving priority to the fact that the little rabbit did not worry (since it did not know that the fox was hiding behind the nearby bush), rather than "happy" because it was eating a carrot. We thus recoded the score relevant to Component IV, considering correct both answers ("happy" and "just alright")[1]. Having done so, our data widely overlap with those

---

[1] We have discussed such a choice with one of the authors (Francisco Pons): it clearly needs further checking, through a change in the vocabulary used, which we intend to do in the subsequent phases of the research.

obtained in the original study by Pons and Harris. In subsequent stages of the research we will therefore use this new coding for component IV (Figure 3).

Figure 3
Component IV and recoded Component IV by age

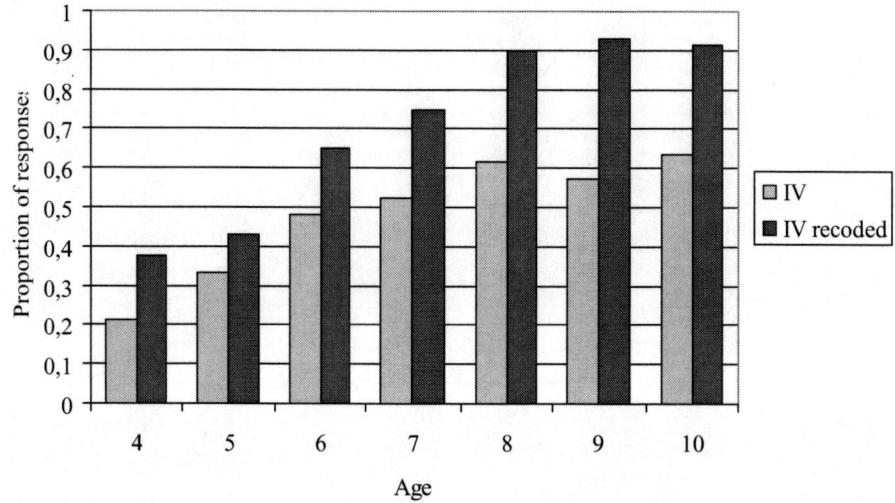

Figure 4 shows the developmental pattern of the answers for all components: correct answers for all components regularly increase with age, and the difference in scores related to age is significant for all components (chi square (6), Kruskall Wallis Exact Test, Montecarlo Method: P = .000).

Figure 4
Profiles of responses for the nine components by age

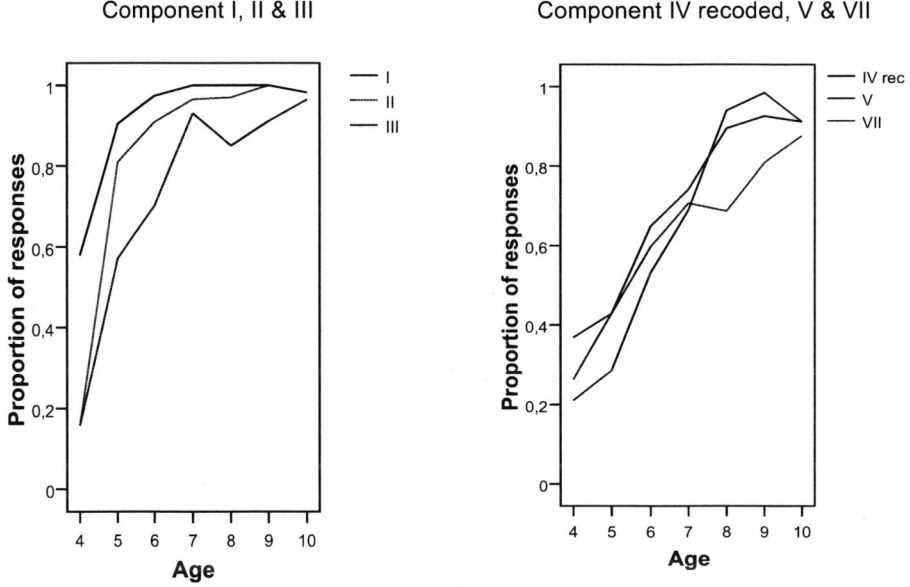
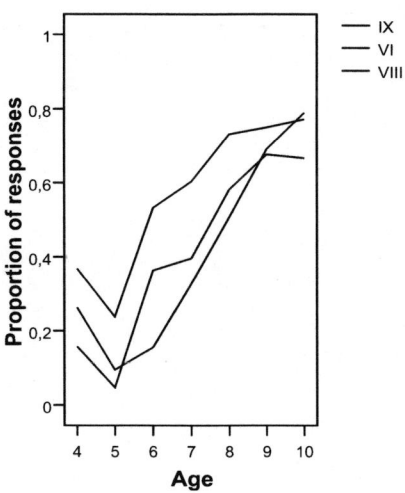

Children's emotion understanding 47

Overall score as well regularly increases with age. However, as observed also by Pons et al. (2004), individual differences are remarkable at any age (see Figure 5).

Figure 5
Overall score by age

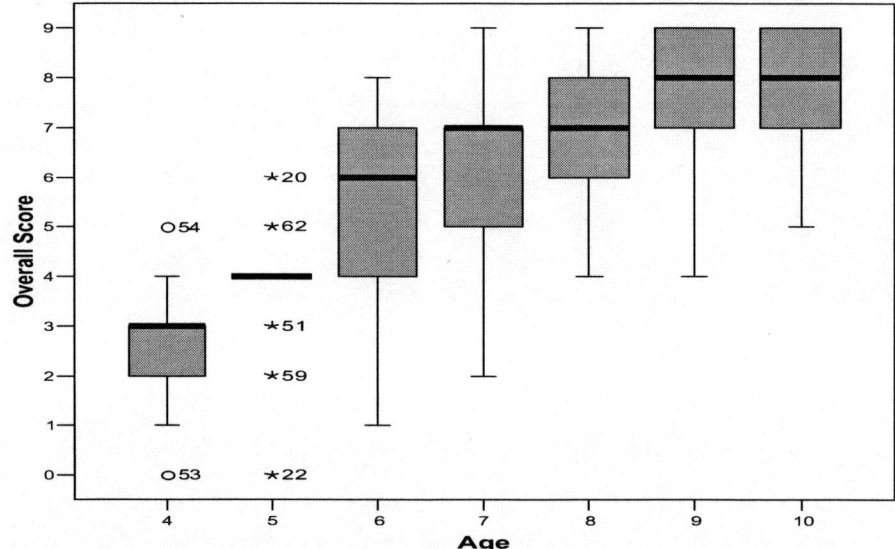

Note: These graphs are Box-Plot Graphs: the lower boundary of the box is the 25th percentile, and the upper is the 75th; the horizontal bold line inside the box represents the median value; vertical lines (whiskers) indicate the range of responses. Extreme cases, i.e. cases with values that are more then 3 box-lengths from the upper or lower edge of the box, are reported with an asterisk (*); outliers, i.e. cases with values that are between 1.5 and 3 box-lengths from the upper or lower edge of the box, are reported with a circle (°).

No differences in overall score are recorded in relation to gender; we have checked through ANOVA [one-way ANOVA: F (366) = .529; P = .468]. The same is true for children having/not having siblings; in this case too we carried out an ANOVA on the overall score: F (366) = .291; P = .590. Individual differences appear therefore to be linked neither to gender nor to presence of siblings and call for further investigation.

Unlike Pons et al. (2004), in order to analyze the hierarchical pattern of answers, we used Mokken Scales (Mokken, 1971, van Schuur, 2003). Such a scale performs a hierarchical analysis to obtain items rank-ordered by difficulty. It calculates a homogeneity index (H-Item) for the various items and a cumulative index (H-Scale) for the whole scale. "Homogeneity [...] is defined by relating the number of model violations observed (denoted as the number of *errors observed* or *E(obs)*) to the number of violations that can be expected under the model of stochastic independence (denoted as *E(exp)*)" (van Schuur, 2003, p. 17-18). This index helps determine whether the lower number of correct answers for a given item which is considered more difficult than another varies significantly with respect to the number of expected answers in case of stochastic independence, and therefore of equivalent difficulty for the two items considered. Empirically, Scales with H >.30 and Rho >=.70 are considered acceptable (van Schuur, 2003).

The hierarchical pattern recorded among the various scales, even though not thoroughly satisfactory, is encouraging: seven out of nine items provide an acceptable Mokken scale (H = 0.40, Rho = 0.68). The pattern, shown in Table 4, is in line with what is theoretically expected.

Table 4
Mokken Scale (N=367)

Items	Mean	H Item
Included		
Component I	0.96	0.68
Component II	0.91	0.53
Component III	0.81	0.39
Component IV	0.77	0.32
Component V	0.74	0.37
Component VII	0.69	0.32
Component VIII	0.45	0.49
Excluded:		
Component IX		
Component VI		

Note: H Scale (7 items) = 0.40, Rho = 0.68

5. Discussion and conclusion

The TEC offers promising features vis-à-vis the objective of performing an overall assessment of children's competence in understanding the nine components of emotional experience over a wide range of ages (4-10, in our case). In particular, results show a clear developmental pattern which is not linked to gender or to experience with siblings. While meaningful efforts are still required in order to achieve a true standardization of the tool, our first analyses are promising. Our work highlights a developmental pattern which is partially different from that identified by Pons et al. (2004). However, the developmental profile obtained by our group largely matches the expected one, based on theoretical as well as experimental evidence, as shown by the comparison between our profile and that outlined in the English study presented in Table 5.

Table 5
Hierarchical pattern in English and Italian samples

England N=100 (3-11 years)		Italy N=367 (4-10 years)	
I	Recognition	I	Recognition
V	*Reminder*	II	Cause
II	Cause	III	*Desire*
IV	Belief	IV	Belief
III	*Desire*	V	*Reminder*
VII	Hiding	VII	Hiding
IX	Morality	IX	Morality
VI	Regulation	VI	Regulation
VIII	Mixed	VIII	Mixed

We have not discussed in depth here the hypothesis put forward by Pons et al. (e.g. 2004) concerning the possibility of arranging the development of emotional understanding into three periods, each grouping several competences considered to be equivalent. This is in part because the hierarchical development observed in the present sample is different and therefore calls for further reflection on the developmental pattern of this kind of competences with respect to what has been theoretically put forward and empirically investigated. Additionally, the use of a hierarchical analysis tool (such as Mokken Scales) supports the hierarchical pattern, thereby leading to a legitimate use of the overall score. Nevertheless, as charts in Figure 4 show, the pattern of answers could be referred to different profiles for the different components, profiles which can in turn be grouped into three different modalities. Should such differences be stable in the overall sample on which the Italian standardization will be performed, we would certainly be faced with an interesting situation calling for further and deeper investigation.

In our view, the primary assets of the TEC lie in the facts that it is simple in conception and that it leads to a clear identification of a developmental pattern, including different components and varying levels of difficulty. While this involves some degree of simplification for a few aspects of the more complex components, such simplification is compensated for by the usefulness of a tool that can assess the development of children's understanding of emotions in a wide range of ages. Furthermore, the role cognitive competence plays with respect to specific aspects of emotional comprehension is still an open issue. In order to address this issue, the development of emotional understanding in non-normative samples of children with specific relational problems or cognitive delays must be investigated.

Scholars in the field of metacognition and learning (Albanese, Doudin & Martin, 2003; Lafortune & Mongeau, 2002; Pons, Hancock, Lafortune & Doudin, 2005 Pellerey, 2003; Grazzani Gavazzi, 2004) emphasize how several difficulties in the school context would be relate to disorders in emotion understanding that TEC could help detect. The use of TEC would, on the one hand, help identify these disorders, and on the other provide a basis for conceiving of emotional education projects from a metacognitive perspective (Pons, Harris & Doudin, 2002) which may jointly address cognitive and emotional-affective developmental issues.

References

Albanese, O., Doudin, P.A., & Martin, M. (Eds.) (2003). *Metacognizione ed educazione*. Milano: Franco Angeli.

Astington, J., Harris, P.L., & Olson, D.R. (Eds.) (1988). *Developing theories of mind*. Cambridge, MA: Cambridge University Press.

Bretherton, I., Fritz, J., Zahn-Waxler, C., & Ridgeway, D. (1986). Learning to talk about emotions: A functionalist perspective, *Child Development*, 57, 529-548.

Grazzani Gavazzi, I. (Ed.) (2004). *La competenza emotiva*. Milano: Unicopli.

Grazzani Gavazzi, I., & Antoniotti, C. (2006). La comprensione delle emozioni nei bambini. Bibliografia ragionata. *Età Evolutiva, 83,* 117-128.

Harris, P.L. (1983). Children's Understanding of the Link Between Situation and Emotion. *Journal of Experimental Child Psychology, 9,* 215-234.

Harris, P.L. (1989). *Children and emotion: The development of psychological understanding.* Oxford: Blackwell.

Harris P.L. (1991). The work of the imagination. In A. Whiten (Ed.), *Natural theories of mind: Evolution, development and simulation of everyday mind-reading* (pp. 283-304). Oxford: Oxford University Press.

Harris, P.L., Donnelly, K., Guz, G., & Pitt-Watson, R. (1986). Children's understanding of the distinction between real and apparent emotion. *Child Development, 57,* 895-909.

Harris, P.L., Olthof, T., & Meerum Terwogt, M. (1981). Children's Knowledge of Emotion. *Journal of Child Psychology and Psychiatry, 22,* 247-261.

Hernández Blasi, C., Pons, F., Escalera, C., & Suco, A. (2003, June). *On the role of intelligence on emotional comprehension.* Poster, 33rd Annual Meeting of the Jean Piaget Society, Chicago, USA.

Kestenbaum, R., & Gelman, S. (1995). Preschool children's identification and understanding of mixed emotions. *Cognitive Development, 10,* 443-458.

Lafortune, L., & Mongeau, P. (2002). *L'affectivité dans l'apprentissage.* Sainte-Foy: Presses de l'Université du Québec.

Lagattuta, K., & Wellman, H. (2001). Thinking about the past: Early knowledge about links between prior experience, thinking and emotion. *Child Development, 72,* 82-100.

Lagattuta, K., Wellman, H., & Flavell, J. (1997). Preschoolers' understanding of the link between thinking and feeling: Cognitive cueing and emotional change. *Child Development, 68,* 1081-1104.

Mokken, R.J. (1971), *A theory and procedure of scale analysis,* The Hague-Paris: Mouton.

Pellerey, M. (2003). Metacognizione e processi affettivi, motivazionali e volitivi. In O. Albanese (Eds.), *Percorsi metacognitivi. Esperienze e riflessioni.* (pp. 57-73). Milano: Franco Angeli.

Pons, F., Doudin, P.A., Harris, P., & de Rosnay, M. (2002). Métaemotion et integration scolaire. In L. Lafortune, & P. Mongeau (Eds.), *L'affectivité dans l'apprentissage* (pp. 7-28). Sainte-Foy: Presses de l'Université du Québec.

Pons, F., Hancock, D., Lafortune, L., & Doudin, P.-A. (Eds.) (2005). *Emotions in learning.* Aalborg: Aalborg University Press.

Pons, F., & Harris, P.L. (2000). *TEC (Test of Emotion Comprehension).* Oxford: Oxford University Press.

Pons, F., & Harris, P. (2005). Longitudinal change and longitudinal stability of individual differences in children's emotion understanding. *Cognition and Emotion, 19*(8), 1158-1174.

Pons, F., Harris, P., & de Rosnay, M. (2004). Emotion comprehension between 3 and 11 years: developmental period and hierarchical organization. *European Journal of Developmental Psychology, 1*(2), 127-152.

Pons, F., Harris, P., & Doudin, P.-A. (2002). Teaching emotion understanding. *European Journal of Psychology of Education, 17*(3), 293-304.

Pons, F., Lawson, J., Harris, P., & de Rosnay, M. (2003). Individual differences in children's emotion understanding: Effects of age and language. *Scandinavian Journal of Psychology, 44*(4), 347-353.

Saarni, C. (1999). *The development of emotional competence.* New York: The Guilford Press.

Tenenbaum, H.R., Visscher, P., Pons, F., & Harris, P.L. (2004). Emotional understanding in Quechua children from an agro-pastoralist village. *International Journal of Behavioral Development, 28* (5), 471-478.

van Schuur, W.H. (2003). Mokken Scale Analysis: Between the Guttman scale and parametric Item Response Theory, *Political Analysis, 11* (1), 139-163.

CHAPTER 3

Adolescence and awareness of positive emotions: A diary study

Ilaria Grazzani Gavazzi, Ottavia Albanese, and Elaine Duncan

1. Introduction

Research in the study of emotions, in part due to clinical implications, has focused on negative or unpleasant emotions such as anger, fear, sadness, depression or anxiety. A survey of recent Italian literature reveals plenty of monographic studies on specific unpleasant feelings (e.g., Anolli, 2000; Ciceri, 2002; D'Urso, 2001a; Di Blasio & Vitali, 2001). However, due to a recent wave of interest in positive psychology, pleasant emotions are now the object of a systematic and original investigation as well. Three major reasons could explain this interest.

First, within theories of emotions, positive ones have been problematic for a long time. In fact, whereas the function of negative emotions, from an evolutionary point of view, has been well known for several years (e.g., Ekman, Levenson & Friesen, 1983; Oatley & Johnson Laird, 1987) the role of positive feelings has only lately been clarified. Feeling anger allows one to react to a frustration. Fear is connected to avoiding dangers, and experiencing sadness facilitates coping with losses. Negative emotions when elicited by such events change goal priorities and affect a person's plans. On the other hand, it's not so easy to explain why people feel happy or experience intense joy or an aesthetical emotion. In this regard, Fredrickson's theory (2001; 2004) is particularly interesting. She offers the broaden-and-build model of positive emotions, a new view of their functional meaning. In her perspective, not only do positive emotions regulate negative ones, including their cardiovascular aftereffects, but they also broaden individuals' momentary thought-action repertoires and build individuals' personal resources. These resources are more durable than the transient emotional states, and can be drawn on later, in other contexts and in other emotional states. In other words, happiness, joy, contentment – recall Aristotelian *eudaimonia* – have beneficial effects.

Moreover, health psychology has recently contributed to focusing attention not only on risk but also on protective factors in physical and emotional subjective well-being. In this regard, the experience of happiness, joy, interest, contentment and the like is an important dimension in individuals' evaluation of quality of life. Following Schwarz and Strack (1999), what is known about subjective well-being is largely based both on reports of happiness episodes and upon answers to questions on life-satisfaction. Diener, Suh, Lucas and Smith (1999) think that well-being includes different dimensions such as emotions, negative and positive affects, and judgments on life satisfaction. Psychological well-being, in substance, takes in both affective and cognitive aspects. Affective aspects regard the balance between positive feelings (e.g., joy, contentment, pride, and so on) and negative emotions (guilt, shame, sadness…). Cognitive aspects concern personal evaluation of life-satisfaction, for instance the wish to change one's life style, the appreciation of actual life or the weight of others' point of view on specific issues. Different aspects are partially independent of each other, and consequently subjective well-being is not a global, compact phenomenon (Lucas, Diener & Suh, 1996) but something complex and changeable.

Finally, the approach of positive psychology (Seligman & Csikszentmihalyi, 2000; Delle Fave, 2004) represents a welcome move away from a dominant disease-model approach, and it focuses on factors that allow individuals and communities to flourish. It is a perspective that underlines the deep, internal, subjective experience of well-being in considering people's evaluation of their own life in different cultures (Diener, 1996). Positive psychology studies the weight of those factors that foster individual development, examining among other things the link between positive emotions and quality of life (Gill & Fenstein, 1994), or being aware of the modest importance of financial prosperity. The same social indicators by themselves couldn't explain and define people's life satisfaction: age, gender, culture, moral values, expectations and a variety of experiences can explain individual differences in the evaluation of specific events.

2. Adolescence and emotions

In the present work, positive emotions are investigated in relation to adolescence. Whereas a large body of studies shows adolescence as a life period characterized by confusion, doubt and crisis (e.g., Blos, 1979; Erikson, 1982; Laufer & Laufer, 1984) little is known about adolescent emotional experiences in everyday life.

Matarazzo (2001) underlines that extensive work must be carried out in order to understand adolescents' knowledge, experience, mental representations, and coping strategies in relation to emotional events.

Research on emotions in adolescence predominantly deals with negative feelings. Csikszentmihalyi and Larson (1984), for instance, found that in this time of life the frequency of negative emotions increases significantly (see also Larson & Amussen, 1991; Stapley & Haviland, 1989). Abe and Izard (1999) noted that a deeper self awareness leads adolescents to frequent and intense evaluations of themselves and, consequently, to the experience of negative emotions, such as fear (e.g., because of feeling inadequate), sadness (loss), and disgust (e.g., towards one's body). Tangney, Wagner, Fletcher and Gramzow (1992) state that feeling shame can provoke anger with the aim to protect one's personal image. D'Urso (2001b) found that the experience of anger is more frequent and less regulated in adolescents than in young adults, above all in those who engage in sport activities and consider the expression of anger as a tool to acquire authority and leadership within a group. Grazzani Gavazzi et al. (1998), with a sample from Milan, found that the experience of fear and anxiety is frequent in typical adolescents, and it is often associated with the context of interpersonal relationships. Pietropolli Charmet (2000) underlined the link between sadness, shame and fear on one hand, and the developmental tasks of identity construction and autonomy on the other. Barone and Zaccagnino (2004) found that fear is related to physical and psychological safety and health, whereas sadness frequently arises when affective relationships finish or personal objectives fail. They also found that experiencing shame in adolescence is related to others' evaluation and judgment and is connected to the difficulty in projecting one's self into the future. Jealousy is connected to the fear of being less satisfactory than others in the fields of friendship and romantic relationships.

Recently, in relation to economic, social and cultural changes and new parental styles, adolescence has been considered in continuity with previous and following phases of life cycle (Rutter & Rutter, 1995; Pietropolli Charmet, 2000). Adolescents deal with several developmental tasks, primarily with identity construction (Erikson, 1982; Marcia, 1980). This means that they confront physical, cognitive and relational concerns (Palmonari, 1997; Confalonieri & Grazzani Gavazzi, 2002). The physical task deals with the positive integration between body and mind, in the light of important physical and mental changes during puberty. The cognitive concern deals with the acquisition of formal and abstract modes of thought as well as metacognitive and emotional competences (Confalonieri & Grazzani Gavazzi, 2005). In terms of social tasks, adolescents are involved in the construction of new kinds of relationships with parents, teachers and friends. To summarize, adolescence is a process of identity construction that implies dealing with different tasks in the context of family, school and peer interactions. In this regard, positive emotions – such as happiness, joy, satisfaction, contentment (for classification: Johnson-Laird & Oatley, 1989; Storm, Jones & Storm, 1996) – can play an important function: alleviating the developmental difficulties; they can, therefore, be a component of subjective well-being (Schimmack, Oishi & Diener, 2002).

Regarding positive emotions, studies have examined neuropsychological aspects (Ekman, Levenson & Friesen, 1983; Fredrikson & Levenson, 1998), expressive correlates (Argyle, 1987), personality and positive emotions (Myers & Diener, 1995; Peterson, 2000), cultural facets (Suh, Diener, Oishi & Triandis, 1998), antecedents and social variables (Scherer, Wallbott & Summerfield, 1986; Myers, 2000; Grazzani Gavazzi & Ornaghi, 2001), job (Argyle, 1987), leisure (Csikszentmihalyi & Wong, 1991) and religious practices (Gartner, Larson, & Allen, 1991). By contrast, few studies focus on these aspects in relation to adolescence, and investigating the link between subjective well-being and the experience of positive emotions (Armezzani, 1998); it's still a challenge to explore the personal meaning of well-being without using a psychometric approach.

3. The research

The present research is part of an ongoing project, influenced by narrative cultural psychology (Bruner, 1990), on "emotions in everyday life"[1]. In this perspective, narrative is a tool of reality construction.[2].

We carried out research on adolescents since few studies have, so far, investigated positive emotions in this time of life span development. We realized that there was a gap in the literature regarding antecedents, contexts, activities and relationships accompanying the experience of positive emotions. Most studies, in fact, adopted a psychometric approach (Argyle, 1987; Legrenzi, 2001; Strack, Argyle & Schwarz, 1991). Therefore, we used a semi-structured diary in order to investigate well-being and related emotions through narrative data that would be possible to analyze both with quantitative and qualitative procedures. We aimed at:

---

[1] For a survey of research on this issue, see Grazzani & Ornaghi (2001).

[2] In Bruner's perspective (1990), narrative is an instrument used to know and interpret the reality and the Self. Selves are constructed through narratives in the context of interpersonal relationships. By means of autobiographical and diary narratives (Bruner, 1993) people can better know themselves and share with others (readers or listeners) the constructed knowledge (Groppo, Ornaghi, Grazzani & Carrubba, 1999).

- Describing positive moments and emotions in daily life (antecedents, typology, intensity, social correlates);
- Exploring gender similarities and differences in relation to positive emotions and life-satisfaction;
- Discussing the relationship between positive emotions and subjective well-being.

Method

In this section we present the sample, the research instrument, its procedure, and the coding system used to analyze data.

Participants

The sample consisted of 250 adolescents equally divided by gender. They were recruited in high schools situated in Lecco, Milan and hinterland (Lombardia). Diaries were written by 222 middle class participants (mean age: 17; range: 16-19).[3] They recorded 665 positive incidents and related emotions (333 from females and 332 from males).

Instrument

We utilized an emotion diary designed for ease of carriage and use (the Italian version of: Duncan & Grazzani Gavazzi, 2000). It was A5 in size, consisting of five pages in total. The first-page was a cover-page containing researchers' names and affiliations. The second contained instructions to each participant and asked for demographic details. This was followed by five identical pages on which participants recorded positive experiences (each page for one episode). Precisely, the diary asked for a description of the situation, accompanying emotions, their intensity, whether they were alone or with others and whether they talked to others about their positive experience and accompanying emotions. Participants were also asked about whether memories for past events had been brought to mind during the present emotional state. We hoped that the participants would be able to feel committed to this study for around one week. The final-page contained a question on life-satisfaction. For this we adopted the faces scale previously used by Andrews and Withey (see Diener, 1996) in a survey of Americans' perception of life quality. The scale consisted of 7 schematic faces, from A to G, with varying degrees of smile expressions. The participant was invited to circle the face that

---

[3] Similarly to other diary studies, the number of participants who kept correctly the emotion diary was less than the number who initially agreed to take part in the research.

most matched their level of life satisfaction. The researcher collected the anonymous diaries a week after the presentation and going personally to the school.

Coding procedure

We collected 665 diary pages. Two researchers independently coded the data. When necessary, agreement was reached by discussion. For each participant (N = 222) age, gender and life-satisfaction score were scored. Responses were subject to content-analysis in accordance with existing coding schema (Duncan & Grazzani, 2000, 2004; Grazzani Gavazzi & Duncan, 2002).

From Question 1 we could determine where the incident took place, whether the participants were alone or accompanied, and the antecedent. Accordingly, the location in which the incident occurred was coded for five distinct environments, namely "public place/building", "university", "home", "work", or "sport/exercise context". In relation to whom the participants were with, we adopted the following categories: "alone", "with family", "with partner", "friends and acquaintances" and finally "colleagues". The antecedent categories were as follows: "work at university issue", "other tasks not related to university work", "hobby/leisure pursuit", "social event with friends", "relaxing alone", or "being intimate with partner". The presence/absence of emotions was coded. As a result of many participants employing more than one label for their feeling states (Question 2), it was decided that the first label written would be adopted. Thus classification under 8 terms was possible namely "Happiness", "Joy", "Love", "Satisfaction", "Cheerfulness", "Relief", "Contentment", "Excitement". In addition, we had to create an "Other" category for miscellaneous terms. In response to Question 3 regarding intensity of emotion we simply noted the number circled on a 1-10 scale where 1 stood for "not noticeable" and 10 for "the most intense I have felt in my life". Question 4 concerning behavioral reactions or urges contained the following pre-determined categories – "moving closer or touching someone or something", "talking or laughing", "withdrawing", "no emotional actions or urges to act", and an "other" category where participants could enter their own phrase. Question 5 and 6 asked about 'sharing feelings with others' and the 'triggering of memories similar events'. Each participant simply answered "Yes" or "No" to these questions. Coding of the recalled memory was not carried out in this study. On the final-page the life satisfaction rating was coded numerically with "A" representing 7 and 'very satisfied with my life' through to "G" which represented a score of 1 and 'very unsatisfied with my life'.

4. Results

The results will be split into two sections, in accordance with the aims of the research: at first we focus on overall results, and then on gender differences.

Overall results

Two hundred and twenty-two participants recorded 665 positive incidents and related emotions. Eighty-three percent of incidents were accompanied by one or more than one positive emotion. Emotional intensity was high since the average score (scale 1-10) was 7.0.

Participants chose a variety of *labels for the emotional states* that accompanied each positive episode. The most frequent emotions were happiness (25.1%), joy (15.7%) and satisfaction (9.9%). Moreover they reported contentment (4.7%), cheerfulness (4.4%), love (2.9%), and excitement (1.8%). The category "other" (34.4%) referred to many labels that could not be coded using our existing schema; nevertheless, participants used them to give a name to their own emotional states (Figure 1). Some of these labels belong to the semantic field of happiness and joy (e.g., excitement, peace), others are phrases related to feeling felt in relation to the specific positive moment (e.g., "I felt free", "I felt unconscious", and so on).

Figure 1
Percentage of answers by type of positive emotion

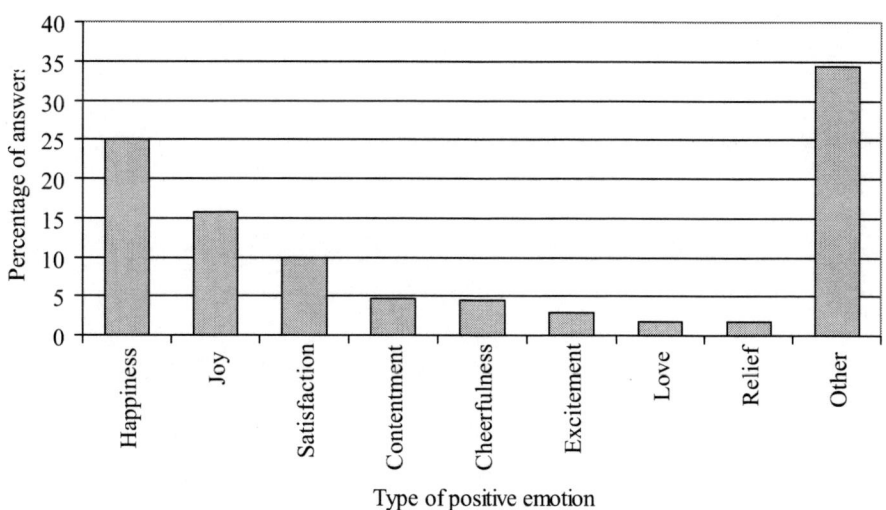

There was a great deal of variation regarding the type of event which served as the *antecedents* or triggers of the positive incident. The most frequent events were *hobby/leisure pursuit* (34.6%), *task* (28.2%), *affects* (16.6%), *relaxing* (11%) and *social events* (8.8%). *Job* was categorized only in 0,5% of episodes.

We found that happiness was more frequently related to leisure and affects; joy was more commonly associated to affect, and satisfaction to task events.

Regarding the *context* of positive moments, the most frequent locations were *public place* (41.8%), *home* (30.9%), *and school* (22.3%). Table 1 illustrates type of emotion, antecedents and context distribution according to the coding schema.

Table 1
Percentage of answers by type of emotion, type of antecedent, and context

Type of emotion		Type of antecedent		Context	
Happiness	25.1	Hobby/leisure	34.6	Public place	41.8
Joy	15.7	Task	28.2	Home	30.9
Satisfaction	9.9	Affects	16.6	School	22.3
Contentment	4.6	Relaxing	11.0	Job	1.0
Cheerfulness	4.5	Social	8.2	Sporting	1.0
Excitement	1.8	Job	0.5	context	3.0
Love	1.3			Not classified	
Relief	1.1				
Other	36				

Regarding *with whom* the participant was when a positive incident occurred, the majority of episodes happened when adolescents were engaged in activities with friends and acquaintances (62.8%), but, interestingly, several positive emotions reported occurred when the participant was in fact alone (16.7%). Then we have the following distribution: with partner (10.3%), with family members (9.7%), and with colleagues (0.5%). Public places (pub, cinema and the like) and school were the contexts that were most frequently associated with experiencing positive emotions with friends. The home context was most frequently related to the experience of positive moments and emotions being with parents, other family members or partner.

The distribution of behavioral reactions (*actions*) as a consequence of the positive incidents is the following: "talk and laugh" (35%), "getting closer/talk" (16.9%) and "getting closer" (14.1%). Participants recorded "withdrawing" only 2.0% of incidents. It can be seen that positive incidents facilitate moving closer to, talking and laughing with others.

The experience of *sharing* positive moments and emotions occurred in 59.2% of incidents. Participants most often shared their emotions with friends and people affectively close to them.

Finally, the average score for life-satisfaction (for which the scale consisted of 7 schematic faces with varying degrees of smile expressions) was 5.4.

Gender comparison

A gender comparison was carried out to investigate similarities and differences within our sample. Firstly, regarding *type of emotion*, no difference was found between males and females.

Regarding *type of event (antecedents)*, we found differences as a function of gender (*Chi square* = 14.4, df = 5, p = .013). Male adolescents reported more leisure episodes than females (126 males *versus* 90 females); on the contrary, girls recorded affects more frequently than boys (64 females *versus* 40 males). See Figure 2.

Figure 2
Percentage of answers by type of event antecedent to positive emotion

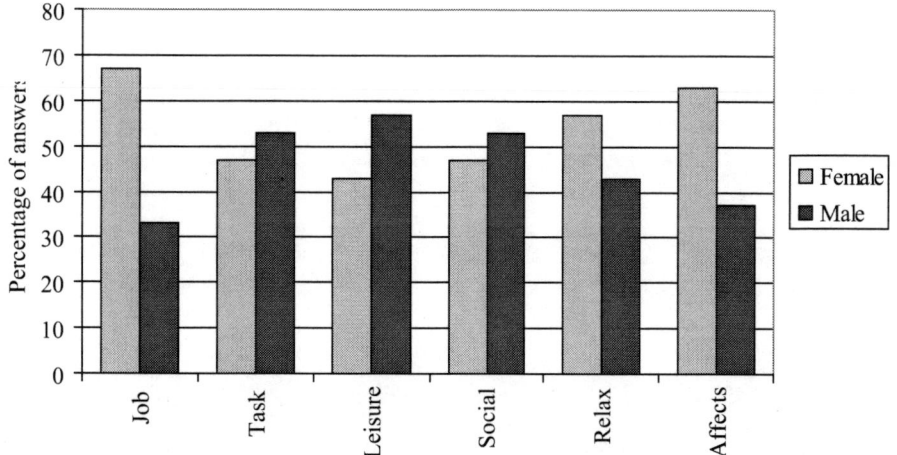

Regarding *context*, we found significant statistical differences (*chi square* = 21.9, df = 5, p = .0005). In fact, it can be seen that although "public place" is the most frequent context across genders, males reported more public place incidents than females (142 males versus 119 females); by contrast, "home" is more frequently related to female episodes (114 females) than to male incidents (79 males). The overall distribution is illustrated in Table 2.

Table 2
Percentage of answers by type of emotion, type of event and context and by gender

Type of emotion[a]			Type of event			Context		
	Female	Male		Female	Male		Female	Male
Happiness	39.6	40.8	Leisure	26.1	37.3	Public place	36.3	41.6
Joy	28.6	19.7	Task	24.1	28.2	Home	34.0	24.3
Satisfaction	12.6	17.1	Affects	20.5	12.5	School	17.8	23.9
Cheerfulness	6.0	8.6	Relaxing	12.4	9.5	Workplace	1.0	0.7
Contentment	7.1	6.6	Social	7.3	8.9	Sport	1.0	0.3
Excitement	2.2	3.9	Job	0.7	0.3	Not classified	9.9	9.2
Relief	2.2	1.3	Not classified	8.9	3.3			
Love	1.7	2.0						

Note: a = "Other" has not been included here.

Finally, males and females differ in self-reported *life-satisfaction*, with males recording a significantly higher score (df = 1, F = 9.4, p=.002).

No significant differences were found about type of emotions, nor regarding: their mean intensity, the type of actions accompanying them, the type of person with whom participants were when the positive moments occurred or the frequency of social sharing of emotion.

The gender comparison yielded the same results even when allowing for a split into two age groups (16 to 18 years old).

5. Discussion and conclusion

Overall results

This diary focused on positive moments, positive emotions and affects in adolescent daily life. The sample consisted of boys and girls with typical development, recruited both in a small and in a big town located in a northern Italian region (Lombardia). We had two aims: describing positive moments and emotions in daily life, and exploring gender similarities and differences. Results allow us to reflect on and think about adolescent emotions and well-being.

First of all, it would appear that positive incidents are frequent in the course of daily life even if we can't say anything about the precise frequency (we did not investigate this aspect since previous research indicates that there are many difficulties in obtaining a correct information). Eighty-nine percent of initial participants reported episodes and related emotions; these participants kept the diary with satisfying precision.

Positive incidents are triggered by a variety of personal, social and environmental antecedents. Moreover, it seems that participants were satisfied about their life, supporting the idea of adolescence as an 'almost-normal' phase in the cycle of life since socio-cultural conditions and parents' educational styles have helped to facilitate navigation through challenging tasks (Confalonieri & Grazzani Gavazzi, 2005).

The psychological vocabulary associated with positive emotions is varied. Participants not only used common terms such as *happiness, joy* and *satisfaction* but also a large proportion of more refined labels associated with the semantic area of happiness and well-being: *tenderness, serenity, peace, relax, ecstasy, elation* are some of the terms absorbed by category 'other' in our classification.

Positive emotions are experienced more commonly in pubs, cinemas and social contexts or in parks, mountains and holiday places; nevertheless, they were also felt at home and at school, a place where adolescents spend much part of their daily life. Positive moments at school are associated with academic achievement, sporting performances (above all for males), friendship and romantic relationships. We wish to present some examples: [*]

Participant 208, M – *We were in the school gym talking about the last year school outing in Barcelona; we were remembering the beautiful moments spent together.*
Participant 246, M – *I was at school; I was content because I finished a project planned with my class-mates in January.*

Regarding the antecedents, emotions are frequently associated with leisure (games, sport activities, outings, concerts), the accomplishment of school tasks, and to relationships with friends, relatives and partners.

Participant 247, M – *During gym class at school many class-mates positively appraised my athletic performances. Mates who I did not believe could appreciate me, paid me many compliments on my sporting performance.*

Participant 276, F – *I have just returned after a beautiful week-end spent in Mantova with my boy friend and some of his friends. Everything was exciting.*

Participant 100, F – *Since it was 'father feast', we went to Mass and then I did a lot of things to alleviate him from any efforts and labor: I did not want him to work.*

Participant 311, F – *I was with my friends at the Arcimboldi Theatre for a Vivaldi concert.*

---

[*] Subject numbers correspond to those appeared in a general data base containing several other participants to research conducted with the diary of positive emotions.

Positive moments are experienced when participants are by themselves as well. In these circumstances adolescents reported important emotional states in terms of psychological well-being such as relaxed, peaceful, quiet and personal satisfaction. Some of these states are related to aesthetic emotions (Zammuner, 2001) and their typical antecedents.

Participant 291, F – *I was alone at my home watching outside: there were no clouds, everything was nice. I stayed at the balcony looking at the garden, the birds and the sky.* The experience of positive emotions is associated with actions linked to the relationship with others such as getting close and talking, or talking and laughing. Moreover, sharing emotions is frequent, and it is reported in connection with the intensity of emotions (Rimé, 1995).

Gender comparison

Regarding the average score related to the life-satisfaction scale, a quantitative difference emerged. Males rated themselves higher than female adolescents did, namely they seem to be more satisfied and happy. Although in the narrative perspective of our work this result has to be considered cautiously (it's a result associated with the simple choice of a smiling face instead of a narrative report of an emotional episode), it is an interesting finding. In fact, it is in accordance with Italian and international literature on females' cognitive and emotional features in adolescence, namely their greater aptitude to introspection, reflection, and critical thought (Palmonari, 1997; Grazzani et al., 1998; Vianello, 1999; Confalonieri & Scaratti, 2000; Petter, 1990; Vegetti Finzi & Battistin, 2000; Grazzani Gavazzi & Antoniotti, 2005; Rosenblum & Lewis, 2003). A consequence of critical thought is greater uncertainty and less satisfaction in daily life. Nevertheless, it would be useful to verify whether this gender difference appears in other phases of life. Warr and Payne (1982) did not find any difference in adult British participants regarding life-satisfaction and well-being. Therefore, this issue has to be further investigated.

Regarding the typology of positive emotions reported, we did not find important differences since both males and females frequently recorded happiness, joy and satisfaction episodes. Emotional intensity was not significantly different on the basis of gender either, corroborating what we found in other diary research: intensity varies more across cultures than across gender (Grazzani Gavazzi & Duncan, 2002; Duncan & Grazzani Gavazzi, 2004).

Nevertheless, we found interesting differences regarding the context of positive moments and emotions: males recorded more school-related incidents than females who reported more home episodes; male episodes were more frequently associated to friendship and interactions with class-mates, whereas females' episodes were more commonly associated to affects (romantic relationships and family interactions). These findings corroborate a common point of view regarding gender differences in adolescence: males seem to be more interested in actions (challenges, risk) and their own visibility, whereas females seem to be committed to affective matters and introspection and reflection on themselves (Pietropolli Charmet, 2000).

In general, both girls and boys are engaged in physical, cognitive and relational tasks associated with identity construction. In this phase, when the desire to explore urges adolescents toward the world situated outside the secure family home, positive experiences and associated emotions are a protective factor. They positively influence general mood and help adolescents to be creative and, particularly, to set up a 'stock of resources' to be used in the critical moments, such as when they have to cope with negative situations.

Spangler and Zimmermann's thesis (1999), that stresses the importance of positive relational experience in improving the resources to explore cognitively and emotionally possible growing paths, deserves to be examined carefully. In the present study we used the diary and the narrative approach that encourages participants to look at their own internal world, producing knowledge and awareness, and therefore developing cognitive and emotional competence – an important protective factor.

We expect both future studies with larger samples and educational projects aimed at using emotion diaries in a meta-cognitive perspective (Doudin, Martin & Albanese, 2001) to improve emotional awareness by helping participants to acquire an improved ability to regulate negative emotions and learn to look for positive moments and emotions.

References

Abe, J.A., & Izard, C.E. (1999). The developmental functions of emotions: An analysis in terms of differential emotions theory. *Cognition and Emotion*, *13*(5), 523-549.

Anolli, L. (2000). *La vergogna*. Bologna: Il Mulino..

Argyle, M. (1987). *The psychology of happiness*. London: Methuen.

Armezzani, M. (1998). La ricerca sui significati soggettivi di salute e benessere. Una riflessione epistemologica e una proposta di metodo. In G. Tibaldi (Ed.), *I significati soggettivi della salute e del ben-essere*, (pp. 11-24). Padova: UNIPRESS.

Barone, L., & Zaccagnino, M.. (2004). Eventi di vita e costruzione della semantica emozionale in adolescenza. In I. Grazzani Gavazzi (ed.), *La competenza emotive* (pp. 207-241). Milan: Unicopli.

Blos, P. (1979). *The adolescence passage.* New York: International Universities Press.

Bruner, J.S. (1990). *Acts of meaning.* Cambridge, MA: Harvard University Press.

Bruner, J.S. (1993). The autobiographical process. In R. Folkenflick (Ed.), *The culture of autobiography* (pp. 38-56). Stanford: Stanford University Press.

Ciceri, R. (2002). *La paura.* Bologna: Il Mulino.

Confalonieri, E., & Grazzani Gavazzi, I. (2002). *Adolescenza e compiti di sviluppo.* Milan: Unicopli.

Confalonieri, E., & Grazzani Gavazzi, I. (2005). *Adolescenza e compiti di sviluppo. Edizione riveduta ed ampliata.* Milan: Unicopli.

Confalonieri, E., & Scaratti, G. (Eds.) (2000). *Storie di crescita.* Milan: Unicopli.

Csikszentmihalyi, M., & Larson, R. (1984). *Being adolescent.* New York: Basic Books.

Csikszentmihalyi, M., & Wong, M. (1991). The situational and personal correlates of happiness: a cross-national comparison. In F. Strack, M. Argyle, & N. Schwarz (Eds.), *Subjective well-being. An interdisciplinary perspective* (pp. 193-212). Oxford: Pergamon Press.

Delle Fave, A. (2004). Positive psychology and the pursuit of complexity. *Ricerche di Psicologia, 1,* 7-12.

D'Urso, V. (2001a). *La rabbia.* Bologna: Il Mulino.

D'Urso, V. (2001b). "La rabbia giovane". In O. Matarazzo (Ed.), *Emozioni e adolescenza* (pp. 269-300). Naples: Liguori.

Di Blasio, P., & Vitali, R. (2001). *Sentirsi in colpa.* Bologna: Il Mulino.

Diener, E. (1996). Subjective well-being in a cross-cultural perspective. In H. Grad, A. Blanco, & J. Georgas (Eds.), *Key issues in cross-cultural psychology* (pp.). Liese: Swets & Zeitlinger.

Diener, E., Suh, E.M., Lucas, E., & Smith, H.L. (1999). Subjective well-being: three decades of progress. *Psychological Bulletin, 125* (2), 276-302.

Doudin, P.A., Martin, D., & Albanese, O., (Eds.) (2001). *Métacognition et éducation. Aspects transversaux et disciplinaires.* Berne: Peter Lang.

Duncan, E., & Grazzani Gavazzi, I. (2002) What makes people happy? A prospective diary study on positive emotions in Scottish and Italian young adults. On-line *Proceedings of the First European Conference on Positive Psychology*, Winchester.

Duncan, E., & Grazzani Gavazzi, I. (2004). Positive emotional experiences in Scottish and Italian young adults: a diary study. *Journal of Happiness Studies, 5,* 359-384.

Ekman, P., Levenson, R.W., & Friesen, W.V. (1983). Autonomic nervous system activity distinguishes among emotions. *Science, 221*, 1208-1210.

Erikson, E. (1982). *The life cycle completed. A review.* New York: Norton.

Evans, P., & Edgerton, N. (1991). Life events and moods as predictors of the common cold. *British Journal of Medical Psychology, 64*, 35-44.

Fredrickson, B.L. (2001). The role of positive emotions in positive psychology. *American Psychologist, 56* (3), 218-226.

Fredrickson, B.L. (2004). The role of positive emotions in positive psychology. Paper presented at the 2nd European Conference on Positive Psychology, Pallanza, 5-8 July.

Fredrikson, B.L., & Levenson, R.W. (1998). Positive emotions speed recovery from the cardiovascular sequelae of negative emotions. *Cognition and Emotion, 12*, 191-220.

Frijda, N. (1986). *Emotions.* Cambridge: Cambridge University Press.

Frijda, N. (1999). Emotions and hedonic experience. In D. Kahneman, E. Diener, & N. Schwarz (Eds.), *Well-being. The foundations of hedonic psychology* (pp. 190-210). New York: Russell Sage Foundation.

Gartner, J., Larson, D.B., & Allen, G.D. (1991). Religious commitment and mental health: a review of the empirical literature. *Journal of Psychology and Religion, 19*, 6-25.

Gill, T.M., & Feinstein, A.R. (1994). A critical appraisal of the quality of Quality-of-Life-Measurements. *Journal of Personality and Social Psychology, 272*, 8.

Grazzani Gavazzi, I. (2002). Positive emotions in everyday life: A study with Italian adolescents. Paper, *XVII ISSBD Meeting, Ottawa.*

Grazzani Gavazzi, I. (2005). Lo sviluppo emotivo in adolescenza, in E. Confalonieri, & I. Grazzani Gavazzi (eds.), *Adolescenza e compiti di sviluppo. Edizione riveduta ed ampliata* (pp. 93-104). Milan: Unicopli.

Grazzani Gavazzi, I., & Antoniotti, C. (2005). Mentalising emotions in adolescence: effects of age, gender, and type of emotion. Paper, XIIth European Conference on Developmental Psychology, Tenerife, August 24-28.

Grazzani Gavazzi, I., & Duncan, E. (2002). A diary study on positive emotions and well-being in Scottish and Italian young adults. In G. Bellelli, & A. Curci (Eds.) *Emozioni: cultura, comunicazione, benessere* (pp. 157-162). Bari: Progedi.

Grazzani Gavazzi, I., Groppo, M., Marchetti, A., Confalonieri, E., Pirovano, N., & Righi, L. (1998). Adolescenti, emozioni e narrazione di Sé. Uno studio attraverso il diario. *Età evolutiva, 61*, 41-55.

Grazzani Gavazzi, I., & Ornaghi, V. (2001). Esperienza e racconto delle emozioni in adolescenza: uno studio attraverso il diario. In O. Matarazzo (Ed.), *Emozioni e adolescenza* (pp. 87-109). Naples: Liguori.

Groppo, M., Ornaghi, V., Grazzani, I., & Carrubba, L. (1999). *La psicologia culturale di Bruner*. Milan: Raffaello Cortina.

Isen, A.M. (1993). Positive affect and decision making. In M. Lewis, & J.M. Haviland (Eds.), *Handbook of emotions* (pp. 261-277). New York: Guilford Press.

Johnson-Laird, P.N., & Oatley, K. (1989). The language of emotions: an analysis of a semantic field. *Cognition and Emotion*, 3(2), 447-465.

Larson, R., & Amussen, L. (1991). Anger, worry, and hurt in early adolescence: An enlarging world of negative emotion. In M. Colton, & S. Gore (Eds.), *Adolescent stress: causes and consequences* (pp. 21-42). New York: Aldine de Gruytet.

Laufer, M., & Laufer, M.E. (1984). *Adolescence and developmental breakdown: A psychoanalytic view*. New Haven: Yale University Press.

Legrenzi, P. (1998), *La felicità*. Bologna: Il Mulino.

Lucas, R.E., Diener, E., & Suh, E. (1996). Discriminant validity of well-being measures. *Journal of Personality and Social Psychology*, 71, 616-628.

Marcia, J.E. (1980). Identity in adolescence. In J. Adelson (Ed.), *Handbook of adolescent psychology* (pp. 159-187) .New York: Wiley.

Matarazzo, O. (Ed.) (2001). *Emozioni e adolescenza*. Naples: Liguori.

Myers, D.G. (2000). The funds, friends, and faith of happy people. *American Psychologist*, 55(1), 56-57.

Myers, D.G., & Diener, E. (1995). Who is happy? *Psychological Science*, 6, 10-19.

Oatley, K., & Johnson-Laird, P.N. (1987). Towards a cognitive theory of emotion. *Cognition and Emotion*, 1(1), 29-50.

Peterson, C. (2000). The future of optimism. *American Psychologist*, 55(1), 44-55.

Palmonari, A. (Ed.) (1997). *Psicologia dell'adolescenza*. Bologna: Il Mulino.

Petter, G. (1990). *Problemi psicologici della preadolescenza e dell'adolescenza*, Florence: Giunti.

Pietropolli Charmet, G. (2000), *I nuovi adolescenti*. Milan: Raffaello Cortina.

Rimé, B. (1995). Mental rumination, social sharing and the recovery from emotional exposure. In J.W. Pennebaker (Ed.), *Emotion, disclosure and health* (pp. 195-233). Washington: APA.

Rosenblum, G.D., & Lewis, M. (2003). Emotional development in adolescence. In G.R. Adams, & M.D. Berzonsky (Eds.), *Blackwell Handbook of Adolescence* (pp. 269-289). Oxford: Blackwell Publishing.

Rutter, M., & Rutter, M. (1995). *L'arco della vita*. Florence: Giunti.

Salovey, P., Rothman, A.J., Detweiler, J.B., & Steward, T. (2000). Emotional states and physical health. *American Psychologist, 55*(1), 110-121.

Sartorius N. (1993). A WHO method for assessment of health related quality of life (WHOQOL). In S. Walker, & R.M. Rosser (Eds.), *Quality of life assessment: key issue in the 1990s*. Dordrecht: Kluwer Academic Publishing.

Scherer, K.R. (1982). Emotion as a process: function, origin and regulation. *Social Science Information, 21*, 555-570.

Scherer, K.R., Walbott, H.S., & Summerfield, A.B. (1986). *Experiencing Emotion*. Cambridge: Cambridge University Press.

Schimmack, U., Oishi, S., & Diener, E. (2002). Cultural influences on the relation between pleasant emotions and unpleasant emotions: Asian dialectic philosophies or individualism-collectivism? *Cognition and Emotion, 16*(6), 705-719.

Schwarz, N., & Strack, F. (1999). Reports of subjective well-being: judgmental processes and their methodological implications. In D. Kahneman et al. (Eds.), *Well-being. The foundations of hedonic psychology* (pp. pp. 61-84). New York: Russell Sage Foundation.

Seligman, M., & Csikszentmihalyi, M. (2000). Positive psychology: an introduction. *American Psychologist, 55*, 5-14.

Spangler, G., & Zimmermann, P. (1999). Attachment representation and emotion regulation in adolescents: A psychobiological perspective on internal working model. *Attachment and human development, 1*, 270-290.

Stapley, J., & Haviland, J.M. (1989). Beyond depression: Gender differences in normal adolescents. *Sex Roles, 20*, 295-308.

Strack, F., Argyle, M., & Schwarz, N. (Eds.) (1991). *Subjective well-being*. Oxford: Pergamon Press.

Suh, E., Diener, E., Oishi, S., & Triandis, H.C. (1998). The shifting basis of life satisfaction judgements across cultures: emotions versus norms. *Journal of Personality and Social Psychology, 74*, 482-493.

Tangney, J.P., Wagner, P.E., Fletcher, C., & Gramzow, R. (1992). Shamed into anger? The relation of shame and guilt to anger and self-reported aggression. *Journal of Personality and Social Psychology, 62*, 669-675.

Vegetti Finzi, S., & Battistin, A.M. (2000). *L'età incerta*. Milan: Mondadori.

Vianello, R. (1999). *Psicologia dello sviluppo*. Bergamo: Edizioni Junior.

Warr, P., & Paine, R. (1982). Experience of strain and pleasure among British adults. *Social Science and Medicine, 16*, 1691-1697.

Zammuner, V. (2001). L'emozione estetica negli adolescenti. In O. Matarazzo (Ed.), *Emozioni e adolescenza* (pp. 301-334). Naples: Liguori.

CHAPTER 4

Guilt as information mechanism in adolescents

Francesco Mancini and Amelia Gangemi

1. Introduction

A key issue in developmental psychology in the study of self-regulation is the relationship between cognitive processes and emotional experiences, with most research focusing on the impact of affective states on cognition.

One of the several ways in which affect may influence cognition is by using affect as a source of information (*affect-as-information*). According to this mechanism, which may lead people to take account of their emotions as information concerning the real world, emotional states influence judgments when they are experienced as providing judgment-relevant information (emotional reasoning; Arntz, Rauner, & van den Hout, 1995; Butler & Mathews, 1987; Forgas & Bower, 1988; Johnson & Tversky, 1983; Salovey & Birnbaum, 1989; Schwarz & Clore, 1983). In this chapter, we will focus on this mechanism because of its relevance to understanding the relationship among conscious experience, emotion and cognition.

The question addressed here is whether the activation of a guilt emotion influences cognition, and thus reasoning, in adolescents by using affect as source of input to the inferential reasoning process (*affect-as-information*). To this aim, an experiment will be presented in which we examined the influence of an emotional state that was induced by asking our participants to remember a previous guilt event on judgments of danger (likelihood and severity of a negative event) and on the effectiveness of one's own preventive performances in a group of adolescents. We will investigate the role played by *trait*-guilt, defined as "the chronic disposition to experience guilt", in their evaluation of danger and on their preventive performance.

Let us now explain what we mean by *affect as a source of information*. According to this mechanism, also called "*ex consequentia* reasoning", "emotional reasoning" and "affect-as-information", emotional states influence judgments when they are experienced as a source of judgment-relevant information (Clore, 1992; Schwartz & Clore, 1988; 1996). In other words, affects function as information, influencing judgments in a direction congruent with the *state*-affect, defined as "a temporary experience of emotion" (Butler & Mathews, 1987; Forgas & Bower, 1998; Johnson & Tversky, 1983; Salovey & Birnbaum, 1989; Schwarz & Clore, 1983).

The apparent informational value of affective cues may be influenced by chronic affective differences. The more people experience a particular kind of affect, the more fully they may rely on it as a source of valid information. Indeed, a number of cited studies have found that adult anxious patients tend to use their feelings to confirm their thoughts, in this case their thoughts or judgments of danger (Arntz et al., 1995; Engelhard, Macklin, McNally, van den Hout & Arntz, 2003; Engelhard, van den Hout & Arntz, 2001; Engelhard, van den Hout, Arntz & McNally, 2002). For this reason, anxious patients often engage in emotional reasoning: they draw invalid conclusions about a situation on the basis of their subjective emotional response. Anxious subjects strongly believe in the proposition: "If I feel anxious, there must be danger" (Arntz *et al.*, 1985). The authors argue that this tendency to infer danger on the basis of subjective anxiety may play a role in the development and maintenance of anxiety disorders, by starting a vicious circle like the following one: "If I feel anxious, then there must be danger. This perception of danger increases my anxiety, and as a consequence I more strongly believe that there is danger, and so on."

Research on normal adults, in whom affect is induced in the laboratory by giving instructions, is also extremely interesting. In their numerous and widely cited studies, Gasper and Clore (1998) and Scott and Cervone (2002) investigated the *affect-as-information* mechanism in normal subjects using the same induction procedure. Scott and Cervone (2002) found that negative affect can lead to the construction of higher performance standards even if the nature of the performance is unrelated to the source of the negative affect. Scott and Cervone argue that their results have implications for the understanding and treatment of depression. They suggest that depressed individuals tend to use their negative feelings to validate their thoughts and start a vicious circle that contributes to the maintenance of their depression. We can imagine this vicious circle as follows: "if I feel depressed, then my performance standards get higher. If I fail to respect these standards (and this is very likely), then my negative affect will be further increased and, as a consequence, there will be a further raising of my performance standards," and so on.

Moreover, Gasper and Clore (1998) showed that negative affect influences risk estimates and specifically the likelihood and the severity of a negative outcome in normal subjects. These findings are consistent with those of Arntz and colleagues (1995) as regards the role of emotional reasoning in the maintenance of anxiety disorders. In this case, anxious individuals use their emotional state as information to confirm their beliefs of danger, that is, that the aversive event will occur and that it will be very serious. The authors also found a relationship between *trait*-affect and *emotional reasoning*, thus demonstrating the predominant role of *trait* affect in people's use of *state* affect when making judgments of risk. From this perspective, greater chronic anxiety may lead to greater perceived risk.

The emotional reasoning phenomenon also characterizes children's thinking. In recent work Murris, Merckelbach and Spauwen (2003) showed that children, like adult individuals, tend to infer danger on the basis of their emotional state. In this study, children aged from 8 to 12 years were asked to rate danger levels of scripts in which objective danger *versus* objective safety and anxiety response *versus* no anxiety response were systematically varied. Evidence of a general emotional reasoning effect was found. That is, children's danger ratings were not only a function of objective danger information, but also, in the case of objective safety scripts, of the presence of anxiety response information. Indeed, children's high danger ratings occurred in safety situations in which the protagonist of the script reacted with an anxiety response. According to Gasper and Clore (1998), Murris and colleagues (2003) found that emotional reasoning was more frequent in the children who scored high in a questionnaire assessing *trait* anxiety, where the questionnaire was completed two weeks before the experiment. This result confirms that, in children, and specifically in anxious children, emotional reasoning plays a fundamental role in danger estimates.

On this basis, the question addressed in this chapter is *what about guilt-affect*, and more specifically, *what about guilt for having acted irresponsibly in normal adolescents?* In three different experiments with normal adults (Mancini, Gangemi & van den Hout, 2005), we found that the induction of guilt for having acted irresponsibly led our participants to:
(1) Overestimate the likelihood and severity of a negative outcome.
(2) Elevate the level of performance they adopt as a personal standard for evaluating their achievement.
(3) Prefer risk-averse choices.

According to Gasper and Clore (1998) and Muris and colleagues (2003), we observed that trait-guilt assessed by an ad hoc questionnaire, plainly influenced individuals' emotional reasoning.

On the basis of the above studies, the main purpose of the present study is to examine whether the induction of guilt affect also influences cognitive processes and specifically reasoning in adolescents. To this aim we investigated how low- and high-*trait*-guilt normal adolescents use negative (guilt-affect) and positive affect (in this case pride-affect, i.e. pride at having acted in such a way as to feel satisfied with oneself) induced in the laboratory. More specifically, we examined how *trait* guilt, i.e. guilt experienced chronically, may influence how *state* guilt, i.e. guilt experienced momentarily, is used as information on the judgment of risk (likelihood and severity of a negative outcome), and on the evaluation of preventive performance in adolescents. State affect was manipulated by getting participants to write about a life event in which they had felt either guilty or proud (Gasper & Clore, 1998). *Trait-* and *state-*guilt were assessed by the Guilt Inventory (Jones & Kugler, 1990; Jones, Schratter & Kugler, 2000). We predicted that increasing the perception of guilt-affect in normal adolescent participants would: (a) increase their estimate of risk and (b) generate higher dissatisfaction with preventive performance. We also predicted that adolescents high in trait-guilt would: (a) estimate more risk than participants low in trait-guilt and (b) make lower evaluative judgments of their preventive performance than individuals low in *trait*-guilt.

2. Method

Participants and design

Participants consisted of 248 randomly selected students (127 boys and 121 girls) recruited from a high school in Palermo. Their mean age was 14 years (SD = 1.6; range 13 to 16 years). Students were randomly assigned to one of the two groups of induced emotional state (*affect-induction condition*): 123 in the group of guilt affect and 125 in the group of pride affect (see Table 1). A 2 × 2 factorial design was used. The between subjects factors were Affect-induction (negative/guilt *versus* positive/pride) and Trait-guilt (high *versus* low).

There are two reasons for the decision not to use a control group (i.e. a group in which no emotion was induced). The first reason requires a premise: it is unrealistic to imagine a group of subjects lacking any active emotional state. Indeed, inside the non-induced group there could be individuals with heterogeneous emotional states. For instance, it would be reasonable to imagine that several individuals are sad, others happy, others worried and others fearful, and so on. The control group could therefore produce responses attributable to a mean of emotional states. This makes it advisable to render the active emotional state uniform for all subjects. The second reason is to bring our procedure into line with the accredited international literature (e.g. Gasper & Clore, 1998). The experiments carried out by authoritative researchers in this field always oppose a negative emotional state (such as that of guilt at having acted irresponsibly for us) to a positive one (that of pride for us).

Materials and procedure

Participants were tested in eight groups. They received a booklet with written manipulation instructions, a story and a number of 100 mm visual analogue scales (VASs). After the affect induction, a questionnaire was administered in order to check the effectiveness of instruction manipulation (induction of guilt or pride).

The experiment was conducted in a large room. An experimenter told participants that the study was about how personality differences might affect students' perceptions. The informed consent of both parents and adolescents was obtained. Participants had to solve the problem individually.

Affect induction

Affect was manipulated by having participants describe a life event in which they had felt either guilty or proud (Schwarz & Clore, 1998). Students were instructed to describe in fifteen minutes a recent life event as vividly as possible and to include details of what they were feeling and thinking.

The scenarios

After having described the guilt/pride event, all participants read a scenario like this:

> You are at your grandparents' place together with your cousins. Your grandparents are away and you and your cousins decide to go and reach them. You and your cousins are fooling around and thus you forget to close the bathroom window before leaving the house. Later, while watching TV, you worry that burglars may have got into your grandparents' home through the window.

The questionnaire

After having read the story, all participants completed the survey questionnaire regarding the scenario. It includes the dependent measures for this experiment.

This questionnaire contains two sections: the first includes visual analogue scales to assess the evaluative judgments of the likelihood of the negative event occurring, and the estimation of the severity of the negative event. Ratings of likelihood were made over the range from 0 to 100, with anchors at 0 ("not at all likely") and 100 ("extremely likely"). Ratings of severity were made within the range from 0 to 100, with anchors at 0 ("not at all severe") and 100 ("extremely severe"). The second section includes visual analogue scales to assess satisfaction with preventive performance. Ratings of satisfaction were made over the range from 0 to 100, with anchors at 0 ("totally satisfied") and 100 ("not at all satisfied").

Guilt inventory

All participants then filled out the Guilt Inventory (Jones & Kugler, 1990; Jones, Schratter & Kugler, 2000). The Guilt Inventory consists of 45 items which assess three content domains as follows: *trait guilt*, defined as "an ongoing sense of guilt beyond immediate circumstances"; *state guilt*, defined as "present guilty feelings based on current or recent transgressions"; and *moral standards*, defined as "subscription to a code of moral principles without reference either to specific behaviors or overly specific beliefs". Responses are rendered using a 5-points scale: 1 = strongly agree, 2 = agree, 3 = undecided, 4 = disagree, and 5 = strongly disagree. A total score (10-215), a total trait guilt score (18-90) and a total state guilt score (10-50) were calculated by adding the ratings across items.

3. Results

Trait guilt

The high- and low-*trait*-guilt groups were established using a media split.

Affect manipulation check

To assess the effectiveness of the affect manipulation, we performed a 2 × 2 (affect × *trait*-guilt) analysis of variance (ANOVA) on the state guilt scores. The affect manipulation was effective, as indicated by reports of greater guilt after writing a guilty story (M=34.76; SD=10.21) than a proud story (M = 30.36; SD = 8) (F (1, 244) = 15.51, p < .001). In addition, high-*trait*-guilt participants (M = 34.37; DS=10) reported more state guilt than did low-*trait*-guilt participants (M = 30; DS= 7), as indicated by a *trait*-guilt main effect (F (1, 244) = 16.05, p < .001). Finally, high-*trait*-guilt individuals were no more responsive to the affect induction than low-*trait*-guilt individuals, as indicated by the lack of any significant Affect × *Trait*-Guilt interaction (F (1, 244) = 2.95, n.s.). Consequently, it is unlikely that any differences in risk estimates and in performance standards were due to high-*trait*-guilt individuals experiencing a greater change in state guilt than low-*trait*-guilt individuals.

Risk estimates (likelihood and severity)

A 2 × 2 (affect: guilt *versus* pride × *trait*-guilt: high *versus* low) analysis of variance (ANOVA) was performed on risk ratings. As predicted, "guilty" subjects rated the likelihood and the severity of the negative outcome higher than "proud" participants (likelihood: F (1, 244) = 89.92, p < .001; severity: F (1, 244) = 25.62, p < .001) (see Table 1). Moreover, low-*trait*-guilt individuals estimated less risk than high-*trait*-guilt individuals (likelihood: F (1, 244) = 23.55, p < .001; severity: F (1, 244) = 39.14, p < .001) (see Table 1). Finally, affect manipulation affected risk estimates through an interaction with *trait*-guilt, (likelihood: F (1, 244) = 26.16, p < .001; severity: $F(1, 244) = 39.37$, p < .001).

Table 1
Mean and (standard deviation) risk (likelihood and severity) and preventive performance standard ratings for all the experimental conditions

Experimental condition	N= 248	Likelihood	Severity	Preventive performance
Affect induction				
Guilt	123	67.3 (24)	68.3 (23)	68 (20)
Pride	125	38.2 (21.5)	39.8 (23.6)	39.4 (19.7)
Trait-guilt				
High	144	68.2 (28)	68.4 (24)	68.7 (20.3)
Low	104	39.7 (21.3)	41.1 (22)	41 (18.8)

The data indicate that high *trait*-guilt individuals used the information provided by their negative affective state as a basis for judgment, whereas low trait-guilt individuals did not. The mean likelihood and severity ratings are shown in Figures 1 and 2 as a function of Affect Condition (guilt *versus* pride) and *Trait*-guilt (high *versus* low).

Figure 1
Mean likelihood performance ratings as a function of guilt *versus* pride affect and high *versus* low *trait*-guilt for the total sample (N= 248)

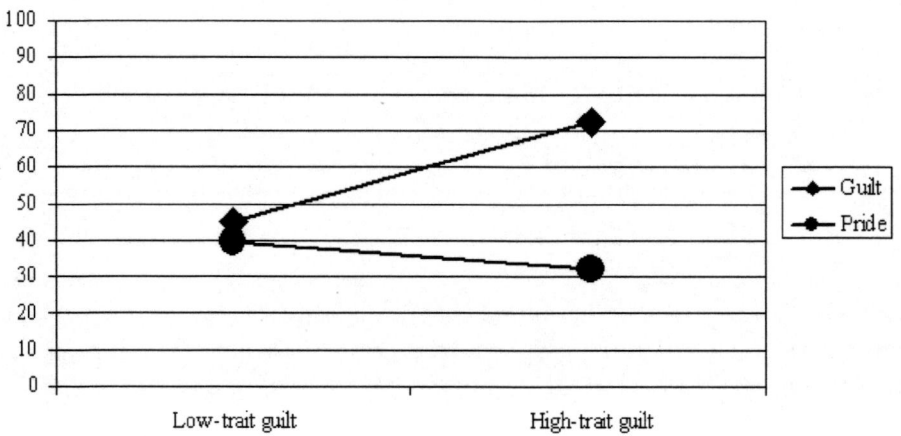

Figure 2
Mean severity ratings as a function of guilt *versus* pride affect and high *versus* low *trait*-guilt for the total sample (N= 248)

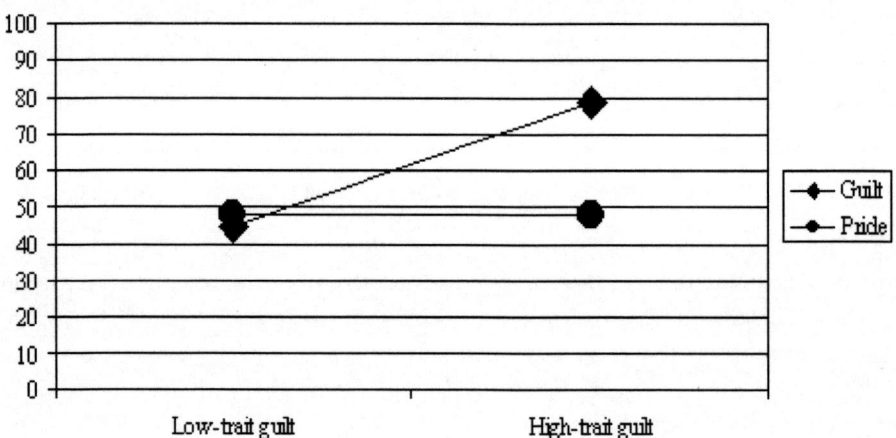

Performance evaluations

A 2 × 2 (affect: guilt *versus* pride × *trait*-guilt: high *versus* low) analysis of variance (ANOVA) was performed on preventive performance standards ratings. Consistent with our hypothesis, "guilty" subjects expressed higher dissatisfaction with their preventive performance than "proud" participants ($F (1, 244) = 11.86, p < .002$). As predicted, low-*trait*-guilt individuals expressed lower dissatisfaction with their preventive performance than high-*trait*-guilt individuals ($F (1, 244) = 26.43, p < .001$). The affect manipulation affected evaluative judgment of preventive performance through an interaction with *trait*-guilt ($F (1, 244) = 9.73, p < .005$). This result indicates that high *trait*-guilt individuals used the information provided by their negative affective state as a basis for the evaluation of their performance, whereas low *trait*-guilt individuals did not. The mean preventive performance ratings as a function of Affect Condition (guilt *versus* pride) and *Trait*-guilt (high *versus* low) are shown in Figure 3.

Figure 3
Mean preventive performance ratings as a function of guilt *versus* pride affect and high *versus* low *trait*-guilt for the total sample (N= 248)

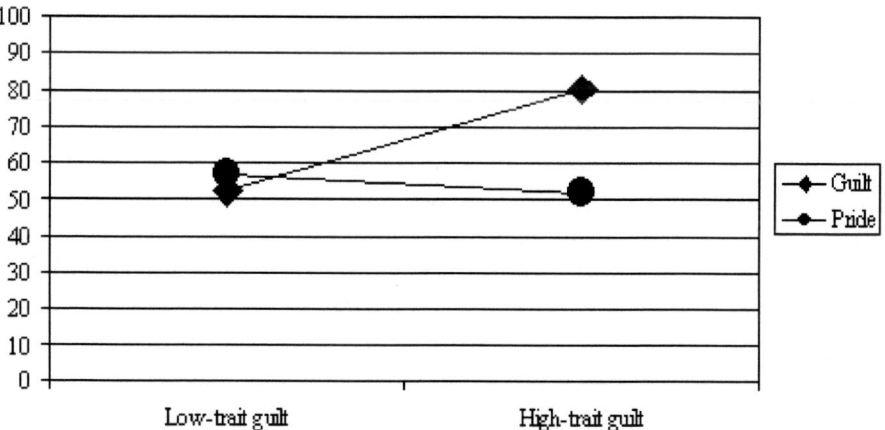

4. Discussion and conclusion

The current study examined the *guilt-as-information* mechanism in a group of normal high-school adolescents. We investigated how *trait*-guilt influences how *state*-guilt is used as information on the judgment of the likelihood and severity of a negative outcome, and on evaluation of preventive performance. We observed how adolescents with low- and high-*trait*-guilt used laboratory-induced negative (guilt-affect) and positive (pride-affect) affects. Affect was manipulated by making participants write about either a negative or a positive life event.

The results can be summarized as follows. To begin with, evidence was found of a general *guilt-as-information* effect. That is, compared to proud adolescents, guilty ones tended to rate negative outcomes as being more likely and more severe. Moreover, "guilty" adolescents showed higher dissatisfaction with their preventive performances.

Second, this *guilt-as-information* mechanism was associated with levels of *trait*-guilt. High levels of *trait*-guilt were accompanied by a greater tendency to overestimate risk and to elevate preventive performance standards. This result suggests that an important difference between individuals scoring high and low in *trait*-guilt may be their trust in their own guilty feelings. In this perspective, trait affect influences the apparent in formativeness of state affective information.

Taken with the earlier findings of Arntz et al. (1995), Scott and Cervone (2002), and Gasper and Clore (1998), the current data suggest that adolescents in general use guilt affect information when evaluating the potential risk of an outcome and their ability to avoid a negative outcome.

The conclusion that guilt-negative affect influences judgment on risk and standards is consistent with theories emphasizing the constructive nature of judgments and standards. The criteria people adopt to evaluate events and themselves are not necessarily always pre-stored and directly accessible cognitive contents. Instead, standards can be constructed through implicit psychological processes. Moreover, as per Scott and Cervone (2002) and Gasper and Clore (1998), our findings also suggest that risk expectancies and performance standards can be substantially emotion-based.

We assume that this type of emotional reasoning (Arntz et al., 1995) plays an important role in the onset of vicious circles: individuals use negative affect to validate thoughts and beliefs that are consistent with the initial negative affect. This mechanism has important clinical implications: It can allow the development, maintenance and aggravation of psychopathological disorders (Salkovskis & Forrester, 2002; Mancini & Gangemi, 2002a; 2002b; Clark, 1986). For example, it is applicable to psychopathologies such as Obsessive Compulsive Disorder (OCD). Obsessive patients chronically experience guilt for having acted irresponsibly (Mancini, 2001; Mancini & Gangemi, 2004; Niler & Beck, 1989; Rachman, 1993). They could thus use this feeling as information to confirm that an aversive event will occur, that it will be very serious and that their preventive performance will not meet their moral standards. As a consequence, they will be almost certainly guilty of having caused harm to themselves or to other people. The *guilt as information* mechanism thus would start a vicious circle in which negative emotion would be used as criterion for evaluating performance as unsatisfactory, and this evaluation would reinforce the initial negative emotion. Consequently, we believe that the role of emotional reasoning in adolescents should also be considered from a preventive point of view.

Finally, we claim that our work can make an useful contribution to an important but still unresolved question: Why in only a small number of adolescents (and not in all of them) does an emotional state become an important source of information about reality, setting up vicious circles which reinforce beliefs on the basis of the emotional state and thus of psychopathology?

We believe that the answer is provided by studies specifically investigating the role of *trait*-affect (*trait*-anxiety or *trait*-guilt) in the use of a state emotion when making judgments and evaluations (Arntz et al., 1995; Gasper & Core, 1998; Scott & Cervone, 2002). These experiments clearly demonstrate that:
(a) *State*-affect and *trait*-affect are two different sources of information.
(b) *State*-affect and *trait*-affect interact.
(c) The apparent informational value of chronic affect is higher than *state*-affect.

Consistent with the above mentioned studies (Arntz et al., 1995; Gasper & Core, 1998; Scott & Cervone, 2002), information from *state*-affect is more reliable when it is consistent with backup information provided by dispositional or *trait*-affect. By contrast, *state*-affect may be relied on less when it is inconsistent with the information provided by *trait*-affect. Thus, the apparent informational value of *trait*-affect may be considered on the basis of individual differences in using *state*-affect as information. The more often people experience a particular kind of affect, the more fully they may rely on it as a source of valid information. For example, high-*trait*-anxious individuals have an attentional bias toward threatening information (e.g. Broadbent & Broadbent, 1988; MacLeod & Cohen, 1993). They are more likely than low-*trait*-anxious individuals to notice and to rely on cues that signal danger, interpret ambiguous stimuli in a more threat-relevant manner (MacLeod & Cohen, 1993), and believe that negative events are more likely to happen to them (Butler & Mathews, 1987).

Although further studies are needed to fully answer this question, we believe that some psycho-education about the knowledge of emotions and their tendency to promote emotional reasoning could be useful. This psycho-education ought to include the way in which such emotional reasoning might contaminate judgments about aspects of the self (including performance evaluations), the future and the world. Of course, future studies are necessary to replicate and extend the present findings.

References

Arntz, A., Rauner, M., & van den Hout, M. (1995). "If I feel anxious, there must be danger": *ex-consequentia* reasoning in inferring danger in anxiety disorder. *Behaviour Research and Therapy, 33,* 917-925.

Broadbent, D., & Broadbent, M. (1988). Anxiety and attentional bias: State and trait. *Cognition and Emotion, 2,* 165-183.

Butler, G., & Mathews, A. (1987). Anticipatory anxiety and risk perception. *Cognitive Therapy and Research, 11,* 551-565.

Clark, D.M. (1986). A cognitive approach to panic. *Behaviour Research and Therapy, 24,* 461-470.

Clore, G. L. (1992). Cognitive phenomenology: Feelings and the construction of judgement. In L.L. Martin, & A. Tesser (Eds.), *The construction of social judgement* (pp.133-163). Hillsdale, NJ: Erlbaum.

Engelhard, I. M., Macklin, M., McNally, R. J., van den Hout, M.A., & Arntz, A. (2003). Emotion- and intrusion-based reasoning in Vietnam veterans with and without chronic posttraumatic stress disorder. Behaviour Research and Therapy, 39, 11, 1339-1348.

Engelhard, I. M., van den Hout, M. A., & Arntz, A. (2001). Posttraumatic stress disorder after pregnancy loss. General Hospital Psychiatry, 23, 2, 62-66.

Engelhard, I. M., van den Hout, M.A., Arntz, A., & McNally, R. J. (2002). A longitudinal study of "intrusion-based reasoning" and posttraumatic stress disorder after exposure to a train disaster. Behaviour Research and Therapy, 40, 12, 1415-1424.

Forgas, J. P., & Bower, G. H. (1988). Affect in social and personal judgments. In K. Fiedler & J. Forgas (Eds.), *Affect, cognition and social behavior: New evidence and integrative attempts* (pp. 183-208). Toronto: Hogrefe.

Gasper, K., & Clore, G. L. (1998). The persistent use of negative affect by anxious individuals to estimate risk. *Journal of Personality and Social Psychology, 5,* 1350-1363.

Johnson, E. J., & Tversky, A. (1983). Affect, generalization, and the perception of risk. *Journal of Personality and Social Psychology, 45,* 21-31.

Jones, W.H., & Kugler, K. (1990). *Preliminary manual for the Guilt Inventory (GI).* Unpublished manuscript, University of Tennessee, Knoxville, TN.

Jones, W.H., Schratter, A.K., & Kugler, K. (2000). The Guilt Inventory. *Psychological Reports, 87,* 1039-42.

MacLeod, C., & Cohen, I.L. (1993). Anxiety and the interpretation of ambiguity: A text comprehension study. *Journal of Abnormal Psychology, 102*, 238-247.

Mancini, F. (2001). El trastorno obsessivo-compulsivo. *Revista de Psicoterapia. 42*, 7-25.

Mancini, F., & Gangemi, A. (2002a). Ragionamento e irrazionalità. In C. Castelfranchi, F. Mancini, & M. Miceli (Eds.), *Fondamenti di cognitivismo clinico* (pp. 156-199). Torino: Bollati Boringhieri.

Mancini, F., & Gangemi, A. (2002b). Il paradosso nevrotico, ovvero della resistenza al cambiamento. In C. Castelfranchi, F. Mancini, & M. Miceli (Eds.), *Fondamenti di cognitivismo clinico* (pp. 200-226). Torino: Bollati Boringhieri.

Mancini, F., & Gangemi, A. (2004). Fear of guilt of behaving irresponsibly in obsessive-compulsive disorder. *Journal of Behavior Therapy and Experimental Psychiatry, 35*, 109-120.

Mancini, F., Gangemi, A., & van den Hout, M. (2005). Guilt-as-information mechanism. *Submitted for publication*.

Muris, P., Merckelbach, H., & Van Spauwen, I. (2003). The emotional reasoning heuristic in children. *Behaviour Research and Therapy, 41*, 261-272.

Niler, E. R., & Beck, S. J. (1989). The relationship among guilt, dysphoria, anxiety and obsessions in a normal population. *Behaviour Research and Therapy, 27*, 213-220.

Rachman, S. (1993). Obsessions, responsibility and guilt. *Behaviour Research and Therapy, 31*, 149-154.

Salkovskis, P.M., & Forrester, E. (2002), Responsibility. In R.O. Frost, & G. Steketee (Eds.), *Cognitive Approaches to Obsessions and Compulsions* (pp. 45-63). Oxford: Pergamon.

Salovey, P., & Birnbaum, D. (1989). Influence of mood on health relevant cognitions. *Journal of Personality and Social Psychology, 57*, 539-551.

Schwarz, N., & Clore, G. L. (1983). Mood, misattribution, and judgments of well-being: Informative and directive functions of affective states. *Journal of Personality and Social Psychology, 45*, 513-523.

Schwarz, N., & Clore, G. L. (1988). How do I feel about it? Informative functions of affective states. In K. Fiedler, & J. Forgas (Eds.), *Affect, cognition and social behaviour* (pp. 44-62). Toronto: Hogrefe.

Schwarz, N., & Clore, G. L. (1996). Feelings and phenomenal experiences. In E.T. Higgins, & A. Kruglanski (Eds.), *Social psychology: A handbook of basic principles* (pp. 433-465). New York: Guilford Press.

Scott, W. D., & Cervone, D. (2002). The impact of negative affect on performance standards: Evidence for an affect-as-information mechanism. *Cognitive Therapy and Research, 26*, 1, 19-37.

CHAPTER 5

Emotions and individual differences: the cognitive constructive model applied to eating disorders in childhood

Maria Grazia Strepparava

1. Introduction

The first section presents a general overview of the cognitive-constructive approach to individual development, and in the next section the "eating disorders personality" is discussed with primary focus on its emotional experience. The chapter ends with the preliminary results of an enquiry on emotional narratives concerning happiness, sadness, anger and fear in school-aged children with eating disorders and/or body image disturbances[1].

2. Emotion awareness: from lived experience to subjective narrative

Research on emotional experience is a complex matter, with many possible levels of analysis: emotion awareness, appraisal, physiological patterns, regulation processes, cognitive labeling, and social and cultural components of the subjective emotional experience. From my point of view, one level deserving great attention is the narrative construction of emotions during an individual history.

We use our language abilities to construct personal experience as narratives: narrative communicates mental representations of experience as well as the roles of the self and of the others in the described event; narratives are central to our capacity to symbolize experience. That is the reason why we can be es

---

[1] This research was supported by the partial financial contribution given to the author by the Italian Ministry for University and Research (MIUR) in the year 2003.

sentially defined as *narrative beings* and our minds as based on *narrative brains* (Goncalves et al., 2004), not because we tell stories, but because our conscious experience is narrative.

Children acquire the capacity for narrative at around three years of age and since this very beginning they become narrative beings who can: translate their subjective sensory experience into a linguistic description of inner states and feelings, build a net of representations and explanations of themselves and of the world around, and frame each experience in their timeline.

Narratives exemplify a vital process of meaning making in everyday life, a process we can tap into by using the spontaneous production of children in play and story telling (Emde, 2003) or by clinical interview.

Narratives can be studied from many different perspectives; in this chapter the focus will be on individual differences in meaning making, on the emotional tone and the emotional quality of narratives and on the interpersonal scheme depicted in the stories that were collected. When completing, generating or remembering a story, children are involved in an activity of *emotional meaning making*. Emotions, regarded as active, ongoing and adaptive processes, have four central functions in defining the *meaning* of an experience: motivation, communication, continuity of the self, and understanding of others. Personal narrative provides young children and adults with the means to regulate, understand and communicate their affective experience. Narratives must be considered as shared forms of making sense of experiences. Building narratives implies also an evaluation act: in telling a story, in telling *our* story, we select and highlight some information as the most relevant to communicate someone the *true* meaning (true *from our point of view*) and to allow the listener to understand how our personal world was affected by the mentioned event (Wolf, 2003). More generally stated: we depend on narrative for our own sense of evolving personal identity. This view on narrative has great relevance to the cognitive constructive clinical approach that will be presented more in detail in section 3. We can approach individual differences observing how many possible descriptions can be evoked from the very same event. In agreement with Neymeyer (2000), I consider *self* as a narrative construction, an ordering of experience into a durable sense of identity. This ordering process is the result of the interaction between some core emotional immediate and tacit feelings and their cognitive, linguistic, explicit descriptions (Guidano, 1987; 1991). The linguistic description of our emotional experience is the basis of our "narrative identity". Its function is to build meaning and ordered structure form the chaotic multiplicity of the experience (Goncalves, Korman & Angus, 2000), a tendency we can find at all of the levels of mind functioning (Gopnik & Melzoff, 1997;

Spelke, 1994; Welman & Gellman, 1992). The narrative function has the goal of establishing the continuity of meaning processes by integrating different life experiences in meaningful unities and building regularities (Mancuso & Sarbin, 1983; Neimeyer, 1995). In this framework, psychopathology is seen as a product of the patient's narrative construction (Capps & Ochs, 1995; Goncalves et al., 1999).

Core emotions are the nuclear basis of the narrative process, as they operate as tacit grids that filter each new experience. Our *conscious* emotion experience is the result of this process of translation and organization from the tacit to the explicit level; the narrative we share with others is the translation into our language of this experience.

Subjective emotional experience changes deeply in lifetime; activation and deactivation of emotional states becomes more self regulated and complex emotions can emerge due to changes in social skills. An example are the two forms of embarrassment/shame mentioned by Lewis (1993), the first emerging early due to the feeling of being exposed to view, and the second emerging at around three years of age when the child can cognitively recognize a discrepancy between his behavior and the social or familiar norms and/or expectations. The awareness of causes, consequences and possible coping strategies in emotional experience increases with age (Lewis, Sullivan, Stanger & Weiss, 1989; Saarni 1999; Sroufe 1996), as well as the reflective mechanism and the meta-cognitive processes applied to emotional experience (Albanese, Doudin & Martin, 2003; Mayer & Salovey 1997; Pellerey, 2003; Pons, Doudin, Harris & de Rosnay, 2002). Emotions are essential for self-awareness and self-knowledge; they are a guide in interacting with the physical and social environment, play a central role in consciousness development (Cacioppo & Gardner, 1999; Damasio, 1999; Rolls, 1999).

There are no standards in emotional experience and a deep comprehension of individual differences is possible only if we can study the *process* by which the *meaning* of each emotion was built by each person along time and life events. The subjective meaning that underlies an *emotion's name* relies upon many elements: upon the episodes in which each specific internal state was experienced, upon the values it received by the very same person and by its attachment figure, upon the shared social value in a given culture, upon the way in which any single episode was integrated in the individual's history (Villegas, 1994; Emde, Wolf & Oppenheim, 2003; Rezzonico & Strepparava, 2002).

Damasio (1999) offers a very interesting account that puts emotions at the basis of the emergence of self, personhood and consciousness. A short detour on this subject can be useful for its relevance to the theoretical clinical approach that will be described later. According to Damasio, consciousness, selfhood and emotions spring ultimately from a single source: the awareness of the current state of the body. He proposes a hierarchy of selves, the lowest level of which is the proto-self. The proto-self is merely a short-term collection of neural patterns of activity that represent the current state of the organism. The core self is a second-order entity which maps the state of the proto-self in rather the same way the proto-self maps the current state of the body: whenever an encounter with an object impinges on the proto-self, the change is registered by activity in the core self. The core self represents the first, lowest level which deserves to be regarded as conscious, though this is the kind of immediate, un-reflecting consciousness presumably possessed by animals in general, not just by human beings. With the next step up, we come to the autobiographical self, which draws on permanent (though modifiable) memories instead of merely the immediate experiences which power the core self. At this point, there is a real, though still pre-linguistic, sense of self. A final layer of development, with greater use of longer-term memory, delivers the kind of foresighted, reflective consciousness which we typically associate with human beings and that is the extended consciousness, with a historical and narrative coherence. Only at this last level could we consider emotions not as isolated, punctual sensory feelings, but as *experiences* in the full sense, located in the plot of all our memories, in our history and – by that – with a *meaning*.

The meaning of an experience, anyway, is not built in isolation, by our own, it spread out, on the contrary, only *in* interaction. As Bowlby (1969, 1973, 1980) or Siegel (1999) or Stern (1998) have written: minds can't be born *but* emerge in interaction. This is the reason why mind is inter-subjective and narrative. This is also the reason why an optimal cognitive/affective development depends mainly on the quality of the relation with attachment figures and with the emotions felt in the attachment experience (Cicchetti & Rogosh, 1997; Ogawa, Sroufe, Weinfeld, Carlson & Egeland, 1997). To summarize: the meaning of each emotion is a *shared co-construction* that continues along the course of life.

Given all that, we might wish that it could be a bit clearer why it is so important for an individual to explore the entire range of his emotional experience, to talk about emotions with someone, to share his inner and private emotional experience with others, to see the variety of coping strategies that others use to face difficult emotions, to see the multiplicity of the human emotional life and not only explore his inner world in solitude. Unfortunately, as we will see in section 4, this easiness with emotional life is not always possible. In some cases the familiar co-construction of meaning for emotional experience is too rigid or too weak; in other cases emotions are perceived as a not-relevant issue in raising a child. Some children feel that there are emotions that they must not feel, because these emotions are bad or wrong. There are children who learn that any emotion must be controlled and not openly expressed and children who learn that only some emotions are acceptable and can be shared. There are also children – as we will see in sections 4 and 5 - who are confused and have great difficulties in understanding what they are feeling. It is then in school, in a safe environment for relational and emotional learning, that children can freely and safely explore and reflect on their emotional experience. If scaffolded by adequately trained teachers, they can more easily detach from the emotional code with which they are familiar and acquire higher degrees of freedom in their emotional competence. This process sometimes takes place in the psychotherapist's office, but it is better for a child to have corrective emotional experiences in a non-medical environment. No less relevant is the fact that school interventions have the advantage of reaching a higher number of target children.

In the next pages an inquiry will be presented on the emotional narratives of children. The inquiry concerns four emotions: happiness, sadness, anger and fear. The aim of the research is to compare narratives of overweight and normal-weight children. The analysis is a bit more complex, because a group of normal-weight children may have a strong body and shape concern: even though they are perfectly normal, they think they're fat and want to be slimmer. This group and the overweight group can be considered similar in their concern about body, weight or shape and – from a clinical viewpoint – they can be considered more vulnerable to the eating/body concerns in pre-adolescence. This vulnerability could easily lead to the development of an Eating Disorder (anorexia, bulimia or binge eating disorder) as consequence in early or late adolescence.

From my point of view, there are two reasons for studying narratives of the emotional experience in children with and without eating or weight and shape concerns: firstly to improve the understanding of the developmental line that leads to the onset of an eating disorder in early adolescence, and secondly to explore the possibility of a new kind of emotion-focused preventive intervention, given the failure of the traditional interventions aimed at modifying only lifestyle and eating habits. I believe that my project is in some way close to the new trends emerging in the field of emotion studies and their application to educational psychology (Izard, 2002; Izard, Fine, Mostow, Trentacosta & Campbell, 2002; Pons, Doudin, Harris & de Rosnay, 2002).

A brief sketch of the cognitive constructive (or cognitive relational) approach to psychotherapy will follow in the next section, but, before beginning, a brief note is needed. In educational psychology *constructivism* is a term that has a precise meaning, but this meaning doesn't correspond entirely to what it is referred to in clinical psychology. In both these fields – educational psychology and psychotherapy – the term *constructivism* refers to "a post-modern paradigm enhancing the centrality of the processes of personal identity development" (Wenger, 1998) and it sees *cognition* as "a situated, socio-cultural and language-mediated activity" (Cole, 1996). By contrast, the concept of *embodied knowledge*, so central in the psychotherapist version of the cognitive constructive paradigm (Varela, Thompson & Rosh, 1991, Johnson, 1987; Glenberg, 1997) partially coincides with the processes of knowledge development proposed by another approach in educational psychology: the *participatory approach* (Lincoln & Guba, 2000). Again, the "learning through immersion" paradigm that requires the presence of a skilled expert (with relational, not just technical, expertise) in the learning environment is basic in the cognitive-constructivist psychotherapist training model, but it is central in the *participatory* approach for teachers training for infant and primary school. It would take us too far to discuss this terminological-conceptual issue here; I wanted just to mention it[2].

3. The clinical background: the cognitive-constructive approach

The cognitive-constructivist approach to psychotherapy (Guidano & Liotti, 1983; Guidano 1987; 1991; Liotti, 2001; Mahoney, 1995; Reda, 1986) is a clinical model that grew out of the tradition of the rational cognitive therapy of Beck and Ellis (Beck, 1976; Beck & Freeman, 1990; Ellis, 1962). In this new framework, one main issue is the central role that emotion awareness and narrative description play in explaining the development of self-continuity. According to Guidano's theory (1987, 1991) emotions are tacit schemata that organize and support personal identity and the feeling of continuity in self-perception. In his latest work (Arciero & Guidano, 2000) personal stability based on the subject's attention to his/her own inner emotional state (inward oriented) is distinguished from that based on the subject's attention to external cues (outward oriented). More recently the theory has been refined by the findings of the evolutionary psychology approach that describe the mind as a set of information-processing machines that were designed, by natural selection, to solve adaptive problems faced by our hunter-gatherer ancestors (Nardi, 2001; Bara, 2005; Liotti, 2005). A central issue in this approach is the adaptive function of cognitive and emotional processes (Barkow, Cosmides & Tooby, 1995; Buss, 1998;

---

[2] For a complete discussion see Varisco (2002).

Crawford & Krebs, 1997; Darwin, 1872; Gaulin & McBurney, 2000; Gilbert 2000; 2001; McGuire & Troisi, 1998; Stevens & Price, 1996). A new impulse was given by the narrative approach mentioned in the section 2.

For cognitive-constructive psychotherapy, knowledge is not passively received either through the senses or by the manner of communication, but instead it is actively built up by the cognizing subject: the function of cognition is an adaptation tending towards fit or *viability*. Cognition serves the subject's organization of the experiential world not the discovery of an objective ontological reality.

Humans are active participants in organizing their experience of themselves and of their worlds. Active ordering processes are primarily tacit and unique to each individual; they are emotion-based, and they are called *core ordering processes* (Mahoney, 1991). The core ordering processes organize experiences and activities along dimensions that include emotional valence, reality status, personal identity and power, as control, efficacy or agency (Mahoney, 2000). Via these processes people can develop their inner feeling of personal identity. Emotional ordering processes are at the very core of the activity of meaning construction because they are the earliest and most powerful distinctions in the emergence of bodily self-regulation (see Damasio's theory in section 2).

Self-permanence perception is built from the sensory activation a baby feels during step-by-step mother-child interaction. The quality of this basic perception (lovable, positive or, on the contrary, unlovable, negative) strictly depends both on the baby's emotional arousal and on the regulation the caregiver provides, that is to say, on the quality of the attachment relation.

Emotions regulate the pattern of interaction with the attachment figures (Lambruschi, 2004). The internal working models of care giving and security of attachment support the core feeling of self, of others and of the world. This basic emotional experience is the original affective grid that operates as a filter on every new incoming experience.

There is a recurrent, never-ending interaction between the immediate perception of our emotional flow, its modifications depending on inner or outer events (affective transitory states), the tacit/explicit core ordering processes and the semantic schemata that filter this immediate experience. As a consequence, full access to consciousness is possible only for that which is coherent with these basic emotive-cognitive structures. For example: the menace/danger/frailty scheme is easily activated in anxious or phobic subjects[3]. Any incoming experience is felt, lived and conceptualized by the *selection* of the elements coherent with this basic scheme among the rich and various sensory, perceptual and cognitive flows of inner states: as heart bumping or pulmonary ventilation, external prompting and cognitive interpretation. They only may have access to full consciousness.

The dynamic of personal identity construction is based on two complementary processes (Guidano, 1987, 1991; Arciero & Guidano 2000): the *tacit* level of immediate experience and its linguistic description or the *explicit* narrative. Only at this second level, with language mastery, can we explain to ourselves and to the others our lived, immediate experience. This explanation is guided by a basic principle, the *coherence principle*, oriented to maintain a stable - *for the subject* - self and world representation. It is one of the most powerful principles in narrative building. Individual differences mainly depend on the way in which the tacit level is transferred to the explicit level and then inserted in the personal narrative. The main transferring principle is to maintain the perceived self-coherence. For example: two students have won a college grant. The first feels joy for what happened, pride for having been good enough to obtain the grant, and excitement for a new life. In thinking toward his new life, he dreams about out how much fun he would have in the new town. The second student lives this experience in a totally different mood. He is unable to activate all the positive emotions the former student had: he feels responsible for the received grant and obliged to show he is doing his best in any occasion. He thinks he must not waste time with social activities when at the college but be a good student who does nothing else but study. Basically he has the feeling that the grant was received by chance and not by virtue. These two students have very different core emotional feelings of themselves and consequently have quite different narratives.

Personal identity develops in the mutual relation between lived experience and the ongoing composition of one's life story. Individual differences and suffering (psychopathology) are the results of these processes of meaning construction.

The acquisition of language is central not only for the development of subjective narratives, but also because it enables the emergence of other basic

---

[3] In some way it states: "something dangerous is happening around me, and I feel in danger, and I feel I'm not able to face this danger, I feel weak, I need help... I need to find protection or I'll perish for my vulnerability" in a mixture of sensory phenomena, bodily experiences, emotional arousal, emotion labeling and cognitive interpretations, connecting causes, consequences and building explanations for what is felt.

processes of experience manipulation: we don't remember an experience in itself, but we remember a re-construction that can sometimes be very different from what was originally experienced.

Personality organizations as individual differences descriptors

According to the cognitive-constructive theory (Guidano & Liotti, 1983) there are four basic personality organizations that correspond to four different strategies of self-coherence construction: phobic, obsessive-compulsive, depressive and eating disordered personalities. Personality organizations were originally labeled by the symptoms that frequently appear as signals of crisis. This classification is a linguistic description that stresses the psychopathological components more than the positive and normal features of each of the four cognitive styles. A different labeling was recently proposed (Rezzonico & Strepparava, 2004). It suggests that the phobic personality would better be described as mainly *will oriented* (easily exemplified by the figure of a leader), the obsessive-compulsive as *rule oriented* (a judge) the depressive as *introspection oriented* (a philosopher) and finally the eating disordered personality as *external recognition oriented* (an actor).

Each organization has its favorite narrative themes and emotions. In the *phobic* or *will-oriented* organization of personality the basic schemata are the dichotomies between freedom and constriction/limitation, between personal strength and felt weakness, and between protection and exploration. For these persons it is not easy to accept that both the polarities can exist and emotions can be a melt of contradictory feelings. For them, self-esteem depends on the feeling of being secure and safe, self-determined, and not controlled by someone else.

In *obsessive-compulsive* or *rule-oriented* personality, the basic emotional-cognitive schemata are the need of being perfect and of being in control, primarily in control over emotions and feelings. Every situation is analyzed by dichotomies: good/bad, right/wrong, true/false, without accepting ambiguity or grey tones. Self-esteem depends on the feeling of being good, right and always aware of what is the true. According to Liotti (2001) another basic core feeling is the connection between responsibility and guilt: the person feels many situations as potentially catastrophic and identifies himself as the only one who could or would prevent a pending catastrophy.

In *depressive-introspection oriented* organization feelings of loss, of personal indignity, of the struggling against an adverse world are predominant. The need for caring (on which self esteem depends) emerges because other people are seen as weaker and more vulnerable than the subject itself.

In an *eating disordered* or *recognition-oriented* personality, the feeling of constantly being judged is predominant; others are perceived as people not to be trusted or, when positively perceived, they are idealized. That is the reason why any relation is easily open to disappointment. Disillusion is the expected feeling when a relation becomes stronger and closer and it is difficult to obtain a true intimacy and closeness. Mood states and feelings in this kind of people depend on and are activated mainly by external events and by problems in relevant relationships.

Interpersonal motivational systems

The Interpersonal Motivational Systems model (Bowlby, 1988; Hinde, 1984; Liotti, 1990, 1994, 2001) has great power as a tool for describing human interaction and for explaining the emotional activation and awareness emerging in social exchanges. The cognitive-constructive clinical approach uses this model to describe and explain the processes in the relational flow (Liotti, 1990, 1996, 2005; Ruberti, 1996).

A motivational system is a set of inherited behaviors and their organizing principles, selected and maintained for the evolutionary advantages they gave and continue to give to the human species. Each motivational system helps an individual to solve a set of problems posed by his physical and relational environment. The biological motivational systems, common also to lower level systems, are the *seeking* behavior, the *feeding* behavior, the *hunting* behavior, and the personal and territory *defense* behavior. The interpersonal motivational systems emerge only in species with high social complexity. These include: attachment, caring, ritual-agonistic, cooperative, sexual, exploration or epistemic systems, and social play. For example, a child at the public garden runs away from her mother to play on the merry-go-round. While playing, she regularly glances back to her mother, to be sure she doesn't move from where she is sitting. The baby's displayed behavior – play and looking – is the result of the oscillation between two systems: the *attachment* and the *exploratory*. The first is telling her "keep yourself close to the one who will protect you" and the second's message is "follow what you feel is interesting and enjoyable". Here is another illustration: an adolescent is boasting about his new PC to his friends. His interactive behavior, aiming to show how cool the new tool he has is, is guided by the *ritual-agonistic* interpersonal motivational system. What he says and what he does are signals of his trial in ascending group hierarchy and being recognized as a leader. Here is a final example: a soccer team has made a golden goal. The strong emotion of joy the players are showing and their embracing of each other reveals the activation of the cooperative motivational system in all of them. As complex as they may be, all human interactions can be analyzed with this classification system.

The emotion a person feels during any interaction is the subjective signal of what motivational system is active and is guiding his behavior. Some behaviors can be apparently different but functionally equivalent when they are the open manifestations of the same underling motivational system: while clearly different, a deep cry or a verbal request for help are functionally equivalent when they are used as the request of help and assistance (attachment system).

The *attachment* motivational system is probably the best known among the interpersonal motivational systems, due to its role in Bowlby's theory. The main goal of the attachment system is to seek physical proximity *to* attachment figures as a means of achieving the goal of felt security. Its function is to elicit care in moments of distress. When proximity and the feeling of security/protection are reached, emotions such as security, joy, consolation and confidence are felt. The failure of the attachment system is the failure to obtain care and proximity. In this case the range of emotions corresponds to the different degrees of subjective suffering due to danger, pain or lack of care: fear, anger, rage, discomfort, sadness, desperation and, as last and worst, emotional detachment.

The *care-giving* system is the complementary system to the attachment system. It is activated by the perception of discomfort or sufferance (physical or psychological) in a con-specific's behavior. Its main relational goal is to stop the suffering of a vulnerable person and to obtain relief signals. The person who is in the caring role will feel tenderness, protection, relief or joy. When the sufferance cannot be reduced, the caregiver feels anxious, feels a deep concern, sympathy, responsibility and finally, when nothing more can be done, he feels guilty.

The *cooperative* system is activated when a person perceives something desirable and available for many people, not only for one. When a resource is perceived as a common goal, when it is seen as useful for all the members of a group, when this goal can be obtained only by the joint action of the group members, interaction becomes cooperative. The need for affiliation to a social group *beyond* the attachment to family members is a basic feature of the human condition. During 99% of the history of our species, human societies were organized in the form of small bands of hunters and gatherers. Selective pressures at the group level may have led the genetic fixation of behavioral adaptations such as cooperation and altruism. The sharing of a common goal and the cooperation for a common aim induce in the group members the feelings of empathy, mutual loyalty, sharing, trust and joy. When the common goal cannot be reached or when someone betrays group loyalty or when someone is kicked out the group, the subjective emotional experience could be: guilt, remorse, isolation, distrust and/or hate.

Ritual-agonistic interactions emerge when a goal – concrete or symbolic, as power – is perceived as available for one person only or by the perception of aggressive signals. The goal of the ritual-agonistic system is to establish rank-dominance and to send submission signals to competitors. Anger is the emotion activated at the beginning of the competition and this accompanies the feeling of being strong enough to win. Pride, a rewarding emotion, is elicited by dominance, while shame is elicited by subordinance. When a person has lost a competition, the emotion of sadness and the depressed mood discourage them from further agonistic encounters, so that they no longer challenge those above them in the hierarchy. On the other hand, the feeling of excitement and pride enjoyed by those who prevail encourages them to further competitive encounters. Mechanisms exist that maintain difference amplification.

The sexual system has as its biological goal reproduction, but in human beings it is much more complicated and became a guarantee for couple stability and newborn survival. Embarrassment, decency, fear of refusal and jealousy are some basic emotions that feature in this interpersonal motivational system.

Core features of self perception in the basic personality organizations

In adulthood a personality organization can be described by a set of parameters:

- *Personal lovableness.* The subjective feeling of lovableness can be positive and unconditioned: "I'm worthy of being loved whatever I do", as in the phobic organization. It can be positive but conditioned: "I'm lovable only if I adjust myself to some rules", as in the obsessive-compulsive organization. It can be instable: "I'm lovable depending on your feedback", as in the eating disorders organization and, finally, it can be absolutely negative: "I'm deeply unlovable 'cause I'm unworthy", as in the depressive organization. It mainly depends on the quality of the relationship with the attachment figures (secure/insecure).
- *Inward/outward organization.* It depends on the preferred channel used for recognizing feelings and emotional states. A person can rely preferentially on the awareness of his internal signals: "I'm always aware of what I feel here and now", as in the depressive and phobic personalities, where differences lie in the quality of the inner perception — that is positive in phobic and deeply negative in depressed. On the contrary, a person can preferentially rely on external information. One powerful source of information can be the

judgment of someone relevant for the subject: "the beloved others are the only ones who can describe my real state and feelings to me" as in the eating disorders personality. The second powerful source of information is common opinion: "there are always rules describing the right way of feeling, thinking or behaving for every occasion, I have just to find out what they are", as in the obsessive-compulsive personality.

- *Dynamic between feeling and explaining.* As stated in section 3, there is mutual interaction between an immediate, tacit experience and its semantic description (the explicit level of knowledge) that involves explanation and interpretation processes. Individual differences emerge from the relative weight given to emotions or to cognitions, to the immediate feelings or to the reflection on them. When the immediate experience has a greater weight, the person can easily feel these emotions, but may have some difficulties in activating the regulatory systems or in building a meta-representation of the felt experiences — for example to clearly identify the causes, effects or consequences of this behavior. When the logical explanation prevails on the lived emotional experience, the person can easily activate detachment mechanisms and reinterpretation processes to modify his experience according to his cognitive expectations. In this case it is harder for the person to have a grip on his immediate feelings.

- *Basic relational schemata.* When entering an interaction, each organization basically "proposes" an interaction schema, the one he found to be the best to regulate interaction with attachment figures and peers. That doesn't mean that the person uses only one of the above-mentioned interpersonal motivational systems each time, but that there is a basic preferred one (or two), and the others are more difficult to activate. As each interpersonal motivational system is connected to a specific range of emotions, the emotional experience of the four organizations of personality is characterized by some prevailing tones — those that are connected to the most relevant (relevant for *each organization*) motivational systems. So, the attachment system and its emotions is the basic interactive strategy of the phobic personality. The caring-system is the interactive basic attitude of the depressed organization of personality. For both of them the cooperative system is easier to activate than for the other two organizations of personality. The agonistic system is the interactive proposal of both the obsessive personality and of the eating disorders personality. This last organization also uses the seductive strategies quite a lot to control an interaction.

4. Eating disorders and emotions

As stated in section 2, my main interest in this chapter is the eating disorders personality (recognition oriented). The self-perception of this organization is ambivalent: the feeling of lovableness fluctuates depending on the approval messages the person receives from the figures whose judgment is perceived as relevant. The main orientation is *outward*, due to the dependence on external judgments. In childhood, the attachment figure was likely to have been *ambivalent*. She usually prevented her baby of freely exploring his physical feeling or emotional states, with an intruding caring style that was mainly food-oriented. Physical sensations and emotional feelings must be felt by the baby, at least for a while, to enable the baby to identify, discriminate and recognize her inner world. The mother's strategy makes it quite difficult for her to recognize, compare, discriminate, and memorize the different internal states and, later, be clearly aware of the whole range of emotions.

As inner feelings are mainly unknown, obscure and unstable, external judgment is perceived as the only channel available to obtain feedback on oneself, the only means for knowing what kind of experience the person is living. Self-esteem and self-worthiness also depend on the positive or negative judgment the person receives. The attention for their image in the other's mind gives to these people a great sensibility to communicative cues. They are constantly oriented to check whether signals of approval are coming during any kind of encounter.

This confusion of personal sensations and feelings, together with the vulnerability to external judgment, generates a basic feeling of being always under examination, of being always confronted by others. The person is highly sensitive to social situations, always comparing her/his status with that of others. Prevalent feelings include embarrassment, shame, defeat, and deception because the subject feels herself/himself to be a loser in the comparison. Rarely does the feeling of pride, the winning emotion, emerge.

The variability and confusion in the emotional flow makes it difficult for these persons to build structured patterns of self-perception, to recognize the links between internal states and external events, and to apply metacognitive processes to their emotional experience. They have a sophisticated "third-person theory of mind", that is to say that they have a highly developed capacity to identify other's mental states (only if they think that those mental states can be relevant for their self-perception and self-esteem). On the contrary they have a very poor "first-person theory of mind", due to their difficulty in recognizing or clearly understanding they own feelings, emotions and desires.

Personal identity is rooted in external recognition and consensus. The person is basically tuned in to other's desires, expectations, and will because receiving approval is equal to being defined, to receiving identity: "I exist only because I am exactly how you want me to be" could be written on their coat of arms.

The learned instability of the attachment figure makes these people sensitive and reactive to the emotion of defeat, that – when felt – usually induces emotional withdrawal, notwithstanding the apparent openness in a particular relationship. The egodistonic emotions of lack of trust or lack of confidence or disappointment arise easily during interactions, inducing retirement, detachment, and isolation. The emotion of true intimacy is rare, because the person is always afraid of being intruded on if someone comes too close.

In a relationship the basic approaching strategy is either seduction or competition. In both cases the goal is to force the other's attention on the person, to receive a regular feedback on self-image and value. The interpersonal motivational systems of sexuality and attachment are interwoven or confused, opening the individual(s) to confusion and ambiguity in relationships.

The winning-losing dynamic is the basic grid for interpreting events. There is a difference between anorexics and bulimics: the first have – in some way – preserved the feeling that they have some possibility of winning (to obtain approval and self esteem and therefore *love*). By contrast, bulimics seem to have given up the battle, and by choosing an avoidant strategy basically have the self-perception of a loser by default. Conflict avoidance is a common attitude in relationships.

Body shape, body weight and physical appearance are main concerns for these subjects. Self-esteem is strongly dependent on body appearance and on positive shape judgment. Body perception tends to be global and not well articulated (Strepparava & Rezzonico, 2005). Body is used as means to control a relation or to avoid closeness. Physical stimuli can be subjectively felt – in many cases – as frightening because they are perceived as too intense. Sometimes a negative emotional activation, even though it may be totally independent from any concern with food or weight, can induce states of sensory and bodily misperception.

5. Overeating or weight and shape concerned children

There are many well-known psychopathological problems in childhood psychology, such as anxiety states, phobias, obsessive-compulsive disorders or depression. There is also a very well known literature on emotion development from infancy to school age or adolescence. In the last decades eating disorders have been widely studied in adolescents as has childhood obesity, the latter having been treated as a problem of overeating or just of having bad eating habits (in essence simply a medical concern). But there are few studies which cross these fields. The topic of emotions in eating disordered children is still an obscure matter. Parents and pediatricians consider childhood obesity to be a less severe problem than adult obesity because children are growing and susceptible to deep and quick changes in their shape and weight. On the other hand, anorexia nervosa is usually seen as a "teenage" trouble, and only very recently has the early onset of this pathology (in some cases as early as 10 years of age) captured clinicians' attention.

A problem in studying emotion awareness in eating disorders is the basic lack of consciousness of inner states these subjects have, that is: the difficulty in recognizing emotions and first person mental states (as seen in section 3). For this reason body and bodily states have increased importance for them and are used as an amplification tool to regulate interpersonal exchanges in childhood and adulthood. When a mother is unstable and inattentive to the *emotional distress* of her baby, a psychosomatic child quickly learns that he/she can keep her attention and be guaranteed of her proximity by various kinds of *physical illness* (Ruggerini, Lambruschi, Neviani, Guaraldi & Manerchia, 2004).

Some relevant information has been reported in the research on the attachment style of eating disordered adults patients (Ward, Ramsay, Turnbull, Benedettini & Treasure, 2000a; Ward, Ramsay & Treasure, 2000b). A high rate of insecure attachment is sometimes reported in eating disordered patients (O'Kearney, 1996; Ward, Ramsay, Turnbull, Benedettini & Treasure, 2000a) as is a relevant percentage of the disorganized/disoriented pattern (Broberg, Hjalmers & Nevonen, 2001). It is less clear is how the two insecure patterns - anxious/ambivalent and avoidant - are distributed in the different diagnostic subgroups of eating disorders: anorexia, bulimia nervosa, Binge Eating Disorder (or BED) and obesity. Many clinical inquiries address a prevalence of the anxious/ambivalent pattern in anorexics, while the avoidant pattern is more common in bulimics, and those with BED or obesity. This last finding is consistent with the well known co-morbidity of depressive symptoms in bulimic and obese people: the link between depression and the avoidant pattern of attachment is widely recognized. Unfortunately results are not homogeneous, and there are data that contradict these observations and in fact show a reverse connection, namely that the anxious/ambivalent pattern seems to be typical in bulimics and the avoidant pattern typical in anorexics (Latzer, Hochdorf, Bachar & Canetti, 2002).

A second problem in working on emotions with eating disordered children is the difficulty of identifying children who are at risk of developing a restrictive eating behavior. With obese or overeating children there is no problem, given their objective weight status, but it is difficult to be sure about the others. Body weight cannot be the only parameter. A strategy for identifying these potentially-at-risk subjects is to assess their body perception. In studies of eating disorders, one of the most important changes has been the modification in diagnostic criteria reported in the DSM-IV (the basic psychopathology manual for clinical psychologists and psychiatrists). One of the most important diagnostic criteria in eating disorders is that abnormal eating patterns and body dissatisfaction are linked to low self-esteem. Usually school-aged children pay little or no attention to their physical appearance nor do their parents draw much attention to topics such as weight and body shape. For children who are overweight, parents, friends or mates can put forth physical appearance or eating habits as an issue of debate, so that it is impossible not to think about it. Such children easily feel inadequate, wrong, and goofy. But sometimes, also for normal weight and normal shape children, one's attention can be oriented to physical appearance. This is especially the case where mothers have this concern about themselves – and such children can say they are overweight when in fact they are absolutely normal, and they can think about dieting or losing weight and have the very same feelings of inadequacy that truly overweight children have. This attitude can be considered as a vulnerability factor for the possible onset of an eating disorder even in primary school. Quite often during psycho-therapeutic sessions eating disordered patients report not only a clinical history being overweight or mild obesity, but also if they were perfectly normal-weight at school age, they remember a strong concern about body shape, about being fat, about eating too much and also feelings of guilt, ineffectiveness, inadequacy and low self-esteem before the onset of pathology. Therefore children who, at a very early age, are unsatisfied with their body or shape can be seen as at risk of a future body image disturbance and eating disorders symptoms.

Given that the standard nutritional and psycho-educational approach to eating disorders prevention has led to few positive results (Vandereycken & Nordenbos, 1998), the Milano-Bicocca Eating Disorders Group[*] has started an emotion-focused project on eating disorders prevention in primary school (Strepparava, Stagnaro, Strozzi & Grimi, 2000; Strepparava, Linguadoro, Notaro, Strozzi & Grimi, 2002). This project aims to develop a multilevel (teach-

---

[*] Research group at the Multimedia Health Communication Laboratory, Medical Faculty

ers, parents, children) intervention. A multidimensional sensory-emotional set of group exercises for children is under development. A side line of research whithin this project is the study of the emotional narrative in eating disordered children. The research question is whether (and if so how) themes appear in their narratives and in particular whether emotions are present that are similar to those present in the clinical narratives of adolescents and adults who suffer from an eating disorder.

6. Children, emotional narrative, eating and weight problems

The study on the emotional narrative in children was done in a small town in the North of Italy. 116 subjects participated in the research, 54 females and 62 males aged 8 to 10 years old (mean age 9,2). Before beginning the collection of narratives, each child filled in a questionnaire on eating habits, dieting attitude, self-perception, perfectionism and relational skills. Two items in this questionnaire concerned body shape – "I think I'm fat" and "I think my belly or my buttocks are fat" - and they were used as grouping variables as follows. Each child was classified as normal or overweight using Cole et al. (2000). Then the coherence between the answers given and the objective weight classification was assessed. Each subject could give an answer *coherent* with his body weight ("Yes, I'm fat" for the overweight and "No, I'm not" for the normal weight) or *incoherent* ("No, I'm not fat" for the overweight as "Yes, I'm" for the normal weight). For the subjects' distribution in the four categories, see Table 1.

For the reasons stated in the previous section, normal-weight children with an *incoherent* body perception can be considered potentially at-risk of developing restrictive eating behaviors or body shape concern in adolescence.

Table 1
Number of children by group and by gender

Gender	Group			
	Normal weight children / Coherent perception (N = 51)	Normal weight children / Incoherent perception (N = 12)	Overweight children / Coherent perception (N = 18)	Overweight children / Incoherent perception (N = 35)
Male	30	4	6	22
Female	21	8	12	13

The psychologist or the teacher who was in charge of the narrative recollection interviewed children in individual sessions. Children were requested to describe events in which they experienced the emotion the experimenter was mentioning. The emotions proposed were: happiness, sadness, anger and fear, and they were presented in a randomized order. There was no time limit or limit to the number of examples a child could produce. The experimenters immediately transcribed the answers during the interview and the interview ended when the child found no more examples. The answers were classified by three independent judges: clinical psychologists and a trainee in cognitive psychotherapy who were well familiar with the cognitive-constructive approach.

Happiness, sadness, anger and fear were chosen as they are basic emotions and are therefore a good starting point for an inquiry on individual differences in cognitive-emotional functioning. Anger and sadness, furthermore, are emotions that can be activated both in the attachment and in the agonistic interpersonal motivational systems.

Narratives classification criteria

The three judges classified the children's answers in a two-step analysis. The first step was to check whether the subject was focused on himself or on a relation. In the first case he described an inner state or feeling, such as: "I feel alone", "I felt bad". In the second, his main focus was the relation between him and someone else "Mum scolded me", "My friends were teasing me". Answers of the first type were labeled *self-focused answers;* the second type received the label *relational answers*. Some answers couldn't be classified, as they described some general or abstract state of the world, not involving or touching the subject itself as, for example, "the war" "AIDS" "poverty in the world". They were therefore classified in a third category.

The second step of narrative analysis was to classify the answers using the interpersonal motivational system theory. Each situation was related to one of the aforementioned interpersonal motivational systems: attachment, caring, cooperative, agonistic, exploratory (see Tables 2a & 2b). In case of persistent disagreement – and after a team discussion – the answers were cut off (three cases only).

Table 2a
Interpersonal Motivational System: Relational-focused answers

Relational-focused answers	Sub-category	Features / Description
Ritual-agonistic	Disagreement	The subject describes a quarrel, discussion, competition with someone or – on the contrary – a disagreement resolution: e.g. to make peace with someone
	Will	The subject describes a situation in which another is opposing to his/her will, desire, goal or, on the contrary, someone is helping to fulfill a subject's goal, desire, will
	Injustice	The subject describes an unfair action against him/her (subject as a victim)
	Intrusion	The subject describes a situation of disrespect for personal, physical, mental boundaries or – on the contrary – he/she feels respected
	Judgment	The subject describes a situation in which he/she is judged or punished: «receiving bad marks» «being scolded by mummy» or the opposite, e.g. «being approved of»
Cooperative	Activity	The subject describes a situation of pleasant action with other people «going to the mountain with daddy»
	Exclusion	The subject describes a situation in which a group of peers excludes him/her or on the contrary receives signals of belongingness to / integration in the group
	Teasing	The subject describes a situation of peers mocking him/her or – on the contrary – he/she feels positively recognized by them
Attachment	Separation	The subject describes a situation of active separation from an attachment figure or reunion/closeness with the attachment figure

Table 2b
Interpersonal Motivational System: Self-focused answers

Self-focused answers	Sub-category	Features / Description
Ritual-agonistic	Judgment	The subject describes a situation of negative or positive self evaluation «I'm good/bad in math»
Attachment	Loneliness	The subject describes a situation of loneliness or isolation «I stayed by myself»
	Action	The subject describes a physical activity done by him/herself «swimming» «dancing disco»
	Mental state	The subject describes a mental activity done alone «I read a book» «I played at the play-station by myself»
	Rewarding	The subject describes a present/a reward received «I received a present»
Exploratory	Novelty	The subject describes a situation in which something new/unexpected happens

Results

Table 3 shows the means of the number of total answers given by the four groups of subjects. There seem to be no relevant differences among the four groups: The normal weight incoherent group gave the highest number, and the obese incoherent group gave the lowest.

Table 3
Number of emotional episodes reported by emotion and by group (means)

Emotion	Group			
	Normal weight / Coherent perception	Normal weight / Incoherent perception	Overweight / Coherent perception	Overweight / Incoherent perception
Happiness	2,7	3,0	2,7	2,3
Sadness	2,3	3,5	2,4	2,3
Anger	2,6	2,5	2,2	1,9
Fear	2,5	3,6	3,0	2,1
Total	10,1	12,6	10,3	8,6

To facilitate a quick comparison among groups, tables 4a to 7b show the percentage for each category of answers. Given the categorical nature of the data, a statistical a chi-square analysis was applied. In some cases, due both to the small size of the sample and to clinical issues, the answers of the two obese groups were grouped together, and sometimes the group typified by normal-weight and coherent self perception was considered the *control* group and the remaining three, together, as the *at risk* group.

Happiness
Children with no weight or body perception problems describe more *relational* situations, while the narrative of the three at risk groups are more *self* focused (50,6%, 49%, 60%), with statistical significance (chi² 11,37, p=0,009, df = 3).

Can we suppose from this finding that happiness is linked to situation of loneliness or, at least, situation in which others are not as relevant for children with weight or shape problems? Some answers are revealed by the second step of analysis.

Table 4a
Happiness – First step categorization: Percentage of answers by focus and by group

Focus	Group			
	Normal weight / Coherent perception (N = 136)	Normal weight / Incoherent perception (N = 36)	Overweight / Coherent perception (N = 50)	Overweight / Incoherent perception (N = 79)
Relation	69.0	50.6	49.0	60.0
Self	31.0	49.4	51.0	40.0

Next step is to check whether the situations referred to are distributed differently among the Interpersonal Motivational System categories (see table 4b)

Table 4b
Narrative of happy episodes - Second step: Interpersonal Motivational System by group

Interpersonal Motivational System		Group			
		Normal weight / Coherent perception	Normal weight / Incoherent perception	Overweight / Coherent perception	Overweight / Incoherent perception
Relational-focused					
Cooperative	Feeling of group integration (not teasing, not exclusion)	22.1	19.4	8.0	17.7
	Activity with other children	11.1	11.1	6.0	4.9
Attachment	Attachment	17.6	16.7	22.0	15.2
Agonistic	Judgment (*positive*)	14.0	5.5	8.0	6.3
	Not competition (agreement, wish fulfillment)	2.2	2.8	2.0	5.1
	Not intrusion (*positive*)	0.7	- -	- -	- -
	Not injustice (*positive*)	0.7	- -	- -	1.3
Self-focused					
Attachment	Physical activity done alone	14.0	11.1	26.0	24.1
	Mental activity done alone	0.7	- -	8.0	5.1
	Reward	7.4	25.0	4.0	8.9
Agonistic	Self-evaluation	6.6	2.8	8.0	5.1
	Physical sensation	0.7	2.8	4.0	3.8
Exploration	Novelty	2.2	2.8	4.0	2.5

There are some commonalities and some differences among the groups. In all four groups, about 25% of subjects told stories concerning the emotions of happiness or joy in situations of positive attachment, but in the two groups of overweight children, happiness is often associated with events in which they are doing something alone – be it mental or physical – such as swimming, disco dancing, reading or drawing (34% overweight-coherent and 29.2% overweight-incoherent, versus 14.7% normal-weight-coherent and 11% normal-weight-incoherent). For normal-weight children happiness is more often linked to cooperative situations, such as playing football, spending time with friends, feeling integrated in their peer group (33.2% and 30.5%). Overweight children pay less attention to cooperative situations as source of positive feelings (14% only). Relating this last observation with the above remark, that doing physical activity in isolation gives joy and the feeling of happiness, a narrative focused on "feeling well when being alone" appears to be typical of overweight children. The statistic analysis done on the macro categories of Interpersonal Motivational Systems was significant (chi^2 = 34,5, p = 0,01, df = 18).

Normal-weight-incoherent children indicate a higher rate of situations (25% compared to 4-8.9% in the other three groups) in which joy is due to a concrete object: receiving a present, a cake or a game, as if the affective need of contact with the attachment figures had to be, in some way, mediated by concreteness and could only be recognized by this means.

In normal-weigh-coherent children, external judgment is reported as a source of happiness more often (14%) than in the other three groups. Tables 5b, 6b, 7b show the degree to which situations evoke opposite emotions (fear, sadness or anger) for overweight children.

Cooperative interactions are much more present in the normal-weight narratives than in the overweight children's stories. From a clinical point of view the difficulty for eating disordered subjects to activate cooperative interactions is very well known.

Sadness
The more extreme variants of sadness, such as grief, bereavement and mourning or disorders derived from sadness, such as depression, have widely been studied in psychology, although their milder everyday variants have received little attention (Power, 1999). This is a pity, as sadness is a transient, normal emotion that, as well all the other emotions, has the function of enabling and motivating subjects to adaptive responses. According to Barr-Zisowitz (2000) sadness can emerge as a response to a goal that is lost or not attained. Sadness emerges when misfortune is caused by something the person cannot control.

Sadness implies that the person has ceased to fight for reaching a goal he was going to lose, unlike anger, which is felt when the person is still battling for the goal. Sadness is a self-focused emotion, and it provides the individual with feedback on how well things were going. The function of sadness is to focus a person inwardly, and probably it is also a signal for the people around that the person needs help. The decreased attention to the outside conserves energy so that the person may focus on solving his problems.

In the Interpersonal Motivational Systems model, sadness is associated both to the agonistic and to the attachment systems. In the first system this emotion accompanies the feeling of a definitive loss in a competition, inducing withdrawal and retirement from social situations. In the attachment system sadness is the feeling of a long-term frustration in reaching proximity and protection and addresses a long-term unsatisfied drive for attachment.

Children's answers are distributed in statistically significant different patterns (chi² = 15.6; $p = 0.01$ df = 6). In narrating episodes of sadness, overweight children are more focused on their internal states (27.2% and 22.4) than are normal-weight children who evoke more relational situations (82.1%). A second point to note is the high rate of normal-weight-incoherent children who report stories concerning events very far from their immediate experience (14.6%), such as African children starving to die, war and bombs in Iraq, or other dramatic environmental events such as the December 2004 Tsunami in Sri Lanka (table 5a). In describing their sad experiences, few subjects mention their internal states; they focus instead on external events. We can hypothesize their use of a diverting strategy: from inside to outside. This strategy can be seen as the antecedent of the much more sophisticated strategies found in anorectic and bulimic adolescents or adults of the removal of painful feelings from consciousness.

Table 5a
Sadness – First step categorization: Percentage of answers by focus and by group

Focus	Group			
	Normal weight / Coherent perception (N = 118)	Normal weight / Incoherent perception (N = 42)	Overweight / Coherent perception (N = 44)	Overweight / Incoherent perception (N = 80)
Relation	82.1	74.9	70.5	72.3
Self	15.3	12.2	27.2	22.4
External event	2.6	14.6	2.3	5.3

As in the case of the happy stories, normal-weight children describe cooperative situations much more than do overweight children (22.9% and 26.8% for NW versus 9.2% and 14.5% for OW). Obviously, in this case, the event causing the emotion (sadness) is any kind of perceived exclusion from the peer group: to be teased by peers, to be excluded from a football team, not to be invited to a birthday party, etc.

Normal-weight-incoherent children describe few situations of attachment as sadness antecedents: only 7.3% reported that they were sad when the mother or any other attachment figure was absent. We can read this result in one of two opposite ways: either separation is not experienced by the child as a moment of sufferance because the caregiver had been good in re-establishing the child's positive mood, or else separation is frequently a bad experience. In this second case, either emotional arousal is not restored by the caregiver or the child is over-aroused through intrusive parenting. The avoidant strategy can therefore emerge as the best solution to manage the relation. Emotional detachment is the most functional way to cope with the sufferance. More research is needed to clarify this point.

The stories whose plot contains events in which either someone judges the child or in which the child evaluates himself are frequently mentioned by the overweight children of both subgroups, coherent (38.6%) and incoherent (25%). This kind of situation is less common in the two normal weight groups: overweight self-perceiver or incoherent (19.5%) and normal self-perceiver or coherent (22.9%). Overweight children often report agonistic events (47.7% and 47.3%) that are less common in the normal-weight children narrative (39.8% and 39%). Rough physical contact (feeling one's hair pulled, being pinched) is mentioned more by overweight children and evokes sadness. The above-mentioned differences in data distribution have statistical significance (chi^2 = 28,4; p = 0,005 df = 18).

Table 5b:
Narrative of sad episodes – Second step: Interpersonal Motivational System by group

Interpersonal Motivational System		Group			
		Normal weight / Coherent perception	Normal weight / Incoherent perception	Overweight / Coherent perception	Overweight / Incoherent perception
Relational-focused					
Cooperative	Exclusion from peers (being teased, excluded)	22.9	26.8	9.2	14.5
Attachment	Attachment (separation)	18.6	7.3	25.0	17.1
Agonistic	Judgment	19.5	17.1	22.7	15.8
	Competition (fighting, will)	14.4	17.1	6.8	18.4
	Intrusion	- -	2.4	- -	1.3
	Injustice	2.5	- -	2.3	2.6
Caring	Perception of suffering in others	4.2	2.4	4.5	2.6
Self-focused					
Attachment	Loneliness	8.5	4.9	4.5	5.3
Agonistic	Self-evaluation	3.4	2.4	15.9	9.2
	Physical sensation	3.4	4.9	4.5	7.9
Exploration	Novelties	- -	- .-	2.3	- -
External events		2.6	14.6	2.3	5.3

Anger

Although emotion theorists do not agree whether anger is a primary human emotion or is just a more generalized distress state, anger serves a variety of adaptive functions (Lemerise & Dodge, 2000) Anger organizes and regulates internal physiological states and psychological processes related to self-defense and mastery. It regulates interpersonal behaviors and comes to be regulated in an interpersonal context through socialization by caregivers, peers, and the larger social context. Anger is felt when an unpleasant adverse event happens and it is possible to identify the source that is responsible of the misfortune. Frustration can sometimes accompany anger. In the Interpersonal Motivational System framework, anger – like sadness – can emerge in two different relational states: as signal of complaint and request for soothing and attention in the attachment system and in the agonistic system as readiness to fight before or during a competition.

Although in our sample most of the stories associated with anger have a plot focused on the relationship (feeling anger for something someone else did), some stories have their main focus on the subjective awareness and internal state of the child. In other cases, the origin of anger is an action, thought or feeling of the subject itself.

Table 6a
Anger – First step categorization: Percentage of answers by focus and by group

Focus	Group			
	Normal weight / Coherent perception (N = 106)	Normal weight / Incoherent perception (N = 30)	Overweight / Coherent perception (N = 40)	Overweight / Incoherent perception (N = 66)
Relation	78.7	76.8	90.2	84.1
Self	21.3	23.2	9.8	15.9

The lowest rate of self-focused answers is found in the overweight-coherent children 9.8% (table 6a) indicating a higher outward attitude (chi = 23.1; p = 0.07; df = 1). An example of this basic outward attitude is the higher sensitivity to situations in which the subject feels confronted by others, such as in injustice situations, reported in this group with a rate of 12.3%, and that is underrepresented in the other three groups (see table 6b).

In remembering sad episodes, overweight children describe many events in which they felt anger while under judgment or because of their own self-evaluation -- 17.2% in overweight-coherent children and 18.9% in overweight-incoherent children, but the highest rate is in normal-weight incoherent children (23.4%). By contrast, in normal weight children anger is activated by judgment in fewer episodes: only in 9.6%. These kinds of events seem to be less relevant for their narrative of sadness. Remember that, for them, judgment was highly correlated with happiness, as shown above in table 4b.

The agonistic motivational system emerges therefore as a relevant narrative topic in the repertoire of overweight and normal-weight-incoherent children: from 64% to more than 68% of the episodes described.

Table 6b
Narrative of anger episodes – Second step: Interpersonal Motivational System by group

Interpersonal Motivational System		Group			
		Normal weight / Coherent perception	Normal weight / Incoherent perception	Overweight / Coherent perception	Overweight / Incoherent perception
Relational-focused					
Cooperative	Exclusion from peers (being teased, excluded)	28.4	20.0	24.4	28.7
Attachment	Attachment (separation)	- -	- -	2.4	2.9
Agonistic	Judgment	1.9	13.4	12.3	7.3
	Competition (fighting, will)	23.7	16.8	19.6	16.6
	Intrusion	21.8	20.0	19.6	25.7
	Injustice	2.9	6.6	12.3	2.9
Self-focused					
Attachment	Loneliness	3.9	6.6	- -	1.4
Agonistic	Self evaluation	7.7	10.0	4.9	11.6
	Physical sensations	9.7	6.6	4.9	2.9

Rough physical contact is an antecedent of anger for normal weight children, while we have just seen that it is an antecedent of sadness in overweight children (see tables 5b and 6b). For normal-weight-incoherent children, the feeling of loneliness is an anger antecedent, while it is rare or absent in the other three groups. When they feel internal discomfort, due for example to temporary separation from their caregivers, they seem to feel a strong activation and reactivity. In fact a deep crying is the first signal of discomfort after separation and fear of loneliness. It is a powerful resource or drawing the caregiver's attention to the child's attachment need, but when this signal is not enough, a higher activation leading to anger is the strategy used for obtaining attention. Therefore the emergence of this emotion in situations of separation signals the hope that the child can be successful in his request of proximity, contact, care, soothing and reassurance. Sadness comes next when these hopes are almost faded away.

Fear

Fear is a widely studied emotion, for its psychopathological implication in anxiety studies. Fear is usually focused on external sources. It is the physical and psychological reaction to a perceived threat or danger, and it has the function of activating aversive or defensive actions and helping the individual to cope with the impending danger.

What kind of narratives did the children have on fear? As expected many stories were on dramatic external events: menacing animals, thieves, earthquakes, diseases, nightmares and darkness. External events were one of the main causes of fear for the children, mostly in the normal-weight group (76.3%) who describe few episodes in which they feel fear due to actions, gestures, or thoughts of people familiar to the child. But in the other three groups, and in particular in the two obese groups, the percentage of episodes in which fear is activated by someone close to the child is significantly higher ($chi^2 = 9,3$; $p = 0,009$; $df = 2$, see table 7a).

Table 7a
Fear – First step categorization: Percentage of answers by focus and by group

Focus	Group			
	Normal weight / Coherent perception (N = 131)	Normal weight / Incoherent perception (N = 43)	Overweight / Coherent perception (N = 54)	Overweight / Incoherent perception (N = 76)
Relation	8.4	13.9	22.2	18.4
Self	15.1	16.3	27.8	14.5
External event	76.5	69.8	50.0	67.1

In the three clinical groups (the two overweight and the normal-weight-incoherent), fear is frequently activated by situations in which the child is criticized by someone – parents or teachers – (table 7b, *Judgment* category). In the two overweight groups it is elicited also by self-evaluation of inefficacy or ineffectiveness: "I'm not good in ... math, reading, play football ...". The association between evaluation and fear is strong for overweight children (20.4% in overweight coherent and 29.1% overweight incoherent), less strong for normal-weight-incoherent (11.6%) and weaker in normal-weight-coherent children (9.8%). These data have statistical significance (chi^2 = 17.07; p = 0.02; df = 8). Again, for overweight children rough physical touch is negatively featured and probably perceived as aggressive and dangerous (14.8%).

Table 7b
Narrative of fear episodes – Second step: Interpersonal Motivational System by group

Interpersonal Motivational System		Group			
		Normal weight / Coherent perception	Normal weight / Incoherent perception	Overweight / Coherent perception	Overweight / Incoherent perception
Relational-focused					
Cooperative	Exclusion from peers (being teased, excluded)	- -	- -	- -	- -
Attachment	Attachment (separation)	0.7	2.3	7.4	1.3
Agonistic	Judgment	7.6	11.6	14.8	17.1
	Competition (fighting, will)	- -	- -	- -	- -
	Intrusion	- -	- -	- -	- -
	Injustice	- -	- -	- -	- -
Self-focused					
Attachment	Loneliness	7.6	7.0	3.7	2.6
Agonistic	Self evaluation	2.2	- -	5.6	12.0
	Physical sensations	5.3	9.3	14.8	4.0
Exploration	Novelties	- -	- -	3.7	- -
External events		76.5	69.8	50.0	63.0

7. Conclusion

As stated in the introduction, individual narratives exemplify a vital process of meaning-making in everyday life. They also reflect individual differences in giving significance to life events as they depend on both the tacit and explicit levels of personality organization. The original nuclear core of self-perception (lovableness or not-lovableness) is generated by the original emotional experience of the attachment relationship. Since its very beginning, this basic inner feeling is enriched and enlarged by the emotional experiences we encounter in our life. Each emotion is a subjective construction, not an objective reality, and since its first appearance it is inserted in an individual, socio-cultural process of meaning-making. Language is a mediator of our subjective experiences by the descriptions our caregivers use to describe us and, on our behalf, our feelings, moods, experience, thoughts and desires. Later it is our own linguistic labeling that creates the meaning of the emotions we experience and share with others.

As stated, every experience is both emotional and cognitive, has a tacit and an explicit level, is immediate, concrete, sensorial and language mediated. Cognition is inextricably connected to one's participation in a shared socio-historical background, to one's personal history and to biological structure. Each event can be an "event" because: it is "for" me, "from "my" point of view, in "my" history, with the meaning "I" give it and because "I" narrate it to myself (I am *conscious* of it) or tell someone else about it. Recurrent emotional states give us the perception of our stability and, as Arciero and Guidano (2000) write "An event is integrated into one's perception through the identification of those properties that match one's sense of personal continuity. This means that the emotional biases that develop provide the coordinates for all subsequent engagement in the world".

As narratives are strictly connected with personality organizations, it is possible, in a sort of *reverse engineering* starting from narratives, to explore the processes of meaning-making: to identify the recurrent emotional themes, the preferred plots, the preferred motivational systems, the inward or outward focus on experience, the prevalence of tacit or explicit memories, the preference for sensory or semantic cues and the language used.

The work described in this chapter analyses individual differences in emotional narratives from a cognitive-constructive point of view and is focused on children with eating and weight concerns due to the relevance of this topic in the field of eating disorders studies. Today the onset of eating disorders appears earlier than in the recent past. The percentage of nine-year old females who desire to be thinner is around 40-55% (Hill, Draper & Stack, 1994; Maloney,

McGuire & Daniels, 1988; Schur, Sanders & Steiner, 2000). 13% of nine-year old children, male and female, are *always* on a diet (Shapiro et al., 1997) and 50% are dieting *sometimes* (Thomas et al., 2000), confirming the oldest observation of the late eighties (Maloney et al., 1989). Equally troubling are the failures of the traditional nutritional and psycho-educational approaches to eating disorders prevention (Smolak, Levine & Striegel-Moore, 1996; Vandereycken & Nordenbos, 1998).

When working in this field it is quite important not to focus directly on the illness and its symptoms (eating, purging, dieting) because there is a risk of inducing the pathology that we aim to prevent (Carter, Stewart, Dunn & Fairburn, 1997). It could be quite helpful to base prevention activity on a better knowledge of the evolutionary path that leads to the onset of eating disorders in adolescence. The cognitive constructive model gives us a hint in this direction, due to the focus it puts on bodily and emotional experiences and on the process of co-construction of the meaning of the emotional experience.

What ideas can we distill from the results shown in section 6? First, children who have different clinical states recall different memories and narrate different stories when asked to describe episodes connected to each of the emotions – happiness, sadness, anger and fear - under inquiry. Differences are qualitative and not quantitative, as the amount of memories the children evoke are similar in the observed groups. The Interpersonal Motivational System model is particularly useful in analyzing and classifying these differences. In the IMS model, to each motivational system corresponds a relational strategy, a self-image, a way of perceiving the events and a "cloud" of emotional states. Each system provides an emotionally-colored perspective of reality. In our research the easiness of recall of the memories that were described in the collected stories was taken as an indicator of the subjective relevance of the motivational system to which each story referred. It was clear that the story patterns of normal-weight children differed from those of overweight children. Within the group of normal-weight, we isolated a subgroup, the normal-weight-incoherent children, who, though they are normal-weight, feel overweight. The stories told by this group were different from the stories that normal-weight subjects told. Stories differed in the motivational systems described and in the foci they showed. In normal-weight-incoherent children the focus of narratives was often not on the self or on relations, but on external events, without any direct involvement of the subject.

Second, the next question of research was whether the differences observed in school-aged children could be found to be coherent with the individual differences observed in adolescents and adults with eating disorders. We found that some of the situations depicted by the interviewed children could be considered as plausible antecedents of emotional and relational schemata that clinicians usually find in their clinical work with older patients.

The body has a central role in eating disorders, due not only to weight and shape concerns but also because, as we saw in section 3, one root of this pathology is a disorganized body experience in early childhood. According to the stories collected, the body is (for children of the clinical groups) something of relevance. As early as the age of 8, as in our sample, the body seems to be used as a means for modulating inner states. For overweight children, joy and happiness are activated in situations in which they do physical activity that does not require specific or complex physical skill or coordination with other players (as in the case of tennis, football or team games). They prefer activities in which body involvement and sensory activation is global, such as swimming or disco dancing which can be done in solitude. More often than normal-weight children, overweight children describe physical punishment from their parents. Many subjects mention the aggressive behavior of mates, but the associated emotions are different for the different groups. In the stories of normal-weight children, being the object of rough physical contact gives rise to an overt aggressive reaction: the anger they feel is the signal of the individual's readiness to fight. In the overweight group, the children's reaction to aggressive behavior is conflict avoidance or withdrawal (feeling sad) or impotence (fear). This can be seen in relation to the conflict avoidance that is known to be typical of eating disordered adults and adolescents.

Overweight children mention much more than normal-weight children the perception of not being respected in their physical or emotional boundaries, the feeling of being *intruded upon*. These situations induce in them either an anger reaction or withdrawal and a sadness response, but basically overweight children seem to have difficulties in reacting. During therapeutic sessions anorexic adolescents often report great problems in containing their mother's intrusive behavior; they usually describe the perception of being intruded upon as a strong feeling that they were familiar with long before the onset of symptoms.

Children in the normal-weight-incoherent group show a clear tendency to give relevance to things as mediators of affective exchange: joy is related to presents, objects or candies. More than the other groups they mention external situations that are far from their immediate and daily experience, as emotion inducers. For example, as regards sadness, emotion antecedents often include violence in the world, AIDS or natural disasters, rather than a specific episode or set of episodes directly experienced by the child. This can be considered to be as a manifestation of a basic attitude of avoiding closeness with others and of avoiding the emotions activated by proximity that we can find in the anorexic relational style. In this group, attachment is under-represented in the narrative of the four emotions. These findings can have different interpretations: (i) good separation experience, (ii) poor experience of separation events because of an anxious, overprotective and constantly present mother, or (iii) as the emergence of a disconnection between the lived experience of sensations and emotions in attachment and separation situations and the conscious emotional experience of distress.

One of the main findings of this research is the over-representation of judgment situations in the narrative plot of overweight and normal-weight-incoherent children. Sensitivity and vulnerability to the feeling of being evaluated or judged is one of the basic individual differences for people with an Eating Disorders Organization of Personality. As we have seen in section 4, these situations and related emotions are described in the narrative of our children: while for normal-weight and unproblematic children judgment or evaluation are mostly linked to positive emotion (happiness), for the other three groups judgment situations are very poorly related to happiness and strongly related to fear, sadness or anger. Therefore, judgment is still perceived as something dangerous, frightening, and low self-esteem inducing. In some cases the expected negative judgment of someone else is anticipated by a self-referred negative evaluation. In the narrative of overweight children the recurrent description of their inability or incapacity in doing something is often colored by the feeling of defeat: a child who is sad thinking about what he cannot do is a child who thinks he has no chance of learning the unknown or improving his performance. He therefore chooses withdrawal from competition and does not see any possibility of changing things. Not by coincidence, happiness emerges for these children during activities that can be done in solitude: drawing, reading, writing or playing on a computer.

Within the overweight group, there seems to be a difference in the main relational concern: while overweight coherent children are more concerned about the situation of attachment/separation with adults, overweight incoherent children appear more concerned about relations with their mates: situations of acceptance or refusal by the peer group, the search for attention or approval by mates, and the suffering that results from being teased or excluded, are highly relevant topics in their narrative. There seems to be a basic difference of focus suggesting, perhaps, two developmental lines that can partially explain some aspects of the high variability in obese adults usually found in clinical and psychotherapeutic work.

Cooperation appears to be easier for normal-weight children than for those who are overweight, and this is consistent with what was stated in section 4 regarding competition and seduction being the preferred interpersonal motivational system in eating disordered subjects.

The observed differences in the emotional narratives of children with different clinical conditions support the two basic assumptions of this work: first, that the construction of the emotional meaning of events is strongly active quite early in life; second that it is guided, from an early age, by different principles of individual meaning-making. As a direct consequence, no therapeutic or educational intervention on emotional awareness can be done without taking into account the main role played by individual differences. The *historical* and *subjective* dimensions of emotional experience are rarely taken adequately into account within the emotion research tradition.

So what further research perspectives emerge from this? First, we need to explore the development of emotional meaning-making in the four Personality Organizations (see section 3) and extend the study to the whole spectrum of emotions. One limitation of the study presented here is not having given attention to self-conscious emotions such as shame, embarrassment, defeat, pride and guilt (Lewis, 2000) which are more directly linked to the judgment-evaluation scheme, and therefore much more relevant for the eating disorders Personality Organization.

Second, this *differential* knowledge of emotion can help to better focus the critical periods in individual development and help teachers, educational psychologists and developmental psychotherapists in setting up more effective educational and preventive strategies. In school the task could be – in my opinion – to open a *window of opportunities* in which the child could experience sensations, feelings and emotions he is not used to in his family environment (for example not being intruded upon, interpreting someone's comment not as a judgment but as a suggestion, being guided by cooperative and not competitive interpersonal schemata). In this way he will learn how not to avoid his sensations, feelings and emotions, but to actively explore them through individual and group exercises and games with the protection of a trained teacher. The subjective flexibility to *inhabit* the world of emotions will be improved, as well as the attitude to share, to communicate, and to compare one's own emotional experiences with others. In this way it will be possible to discover new coping strategies, alternative strategies to those learned in the family. In this way it will be possible to learn how the familiar inherited meaning of the emotional experience is only *one* among many possible meaning attributions. A goal of an emotion-centered prevention program or emotion-centered educational intervention is to increase the general wellbeing, as shown in recent issues within the mainstream of educational psychology (see Cunnigham, Duffy & Knuth, 1991; Knuth & Cunnigham 1993; Black & McClintock, 1996).

Many authors see learning environments as places where people learn how to use one's own culture's tools of knowledge and learn how shared social knowledge is built up (Wilson, 1996b). The process of learning is a social construction of socially-mediated, negotiated and shared meanings (Jonassen & Land, 2000a). Social ability and knowledge are intertwined (Greeno, 1997). The same applies to emotional knowledge. The emotions we feel and we are aware of are deeply stratified objects: they are the here and now pattern of physical activation, the flow of changes and bodily feeling, but they are also the memory of all the times we felt those very same patterns, and the collection of every episode in which we experienced that inner state. And again, the subjective experience of emotions is also the tacit memory of the regulation strategies we learned through the interaction with our attachment figures, the names we were taught to use for labeling them, all names socially shared and at the same time deeply subjective. Having an emotional experience is also experiencing the value we learned to associate with this very same experience. It is the role and value we learned that our culture gives it in a never ending process of meaning construction.

References

Albanese, O., Doudin, P-A., & Martin, D. (2003). *Metacognizione ed educazione.* Milano: Franco Angeli.

Ancona, E., Rezzonico, G., & Strepparava, M.G. (2004). Percorsi di nascita del mondo e del sè : i sogni nelle diverse organizzazioni di significato personale. In G. Rezzonico, & D. Liccione (Eds.), *Sogni e psicoterapia. L'uso del materiale onirico in psicoterapia cognitive* (pp. 127-179). Torino: Bollati Boringhieri.

Arciero, G., & Guidano, V. (2000). Experience, Explanation, and the Quest for Coherence. in R.A. Neimeyer, & J.D. Raskin (Eds.), *Construction of Disorder. Meaning-Making frameworks for psychotherapy* (pp. 91-118). Washington, D.C.: American Psychological Association Books.

Bara, B.G. (1996). *Manuale di psicoterapia cognitive.* Torino: Bollati Boringhieri.

Barkow, J.H., Cosmides, L., & Tooby, J. (1995). *The adapted mind: evolutionary psychology and the generation of culture.* Oxford: Oxford University Press.

Barr-Zisowitz, C. (2000). Sadness. Is there Such a Thing? In M. Lewis, & J.M. Haviland-Jones (Eds.), *Handbook of Emotions, Second edition* (pp. 607-622). New York: Guilford Press.

Beck, A.T. (1976). *Cognitive Therapy and The Emotional Disorders.* New York: International Universities Press.

Beck, A.T., & Freeman, A. (1990). *Cognitive therapy of personality disorders.* New York: Guilford Press.

Black, J.B., & McClintock, R.O. (1996). An Interpretation Construction Approach to Constructivism Design. In B.G. Wilson (Ed.) *Constructivist Learning Environment. Case Studies in Instructional Design* (pp. 25-31). Englewood Cliff: Educational Technology Publications.

Bowlby, J. (1973). *Attachment and Loss. Vol 2, Separation: Anxiety and Anger.* New York: Basic Books.

Bowlby, J. (1980). *Attachment and Loss. Vol 3, Loss.* New York: Basic Books.

Bowlby, J. (1988). *A Secure Base.* London: Routledge.

Bowlby, J. (1969). *Attachment and Loss. Vol 1, Attachment.* New York: Basic Books.

Broberg, A.G., Hjalmers, I., & Nevonen, L. (2001). Eating disorders, attachment and interpersonal difficulties: A comparison between 18 to 24 years old patients and normal controls. *European Eating Disorders Review, 9,* 381-396.

Buss, D.M. (1998). *Evolutionary Psychology: the new science of the mind.* London: Allyn & Bacon.

Cacioppo, J.T., & Gardner, W.L. (1999). Emotion. *Annual Review of Psychology, 50,* 191-214.

Capps, L., & Ochs, E. (1995). Constructing panic: the discourse of agoraphobia. Cambridge, MA: Harvard University Press.

Carter, J.C., Stewart, D.A., Dunn, J.V., & Fairburn, C.G. (1997). Primary prevention of eating disorders: might it do more harm than good? *International Journal of Eating Disorders, 22,* 167-172.

Cicchetti, D., & Rogosh, F.A., (Eds.) (1997). Self-organisation. Special issue of *Development and Psychopathology, 9.*

Cole, T.J., Bellizzi, M.C., Flegal, K.M., & Dietz, W.H. (2000). Establishing a standard definition for child overweight and obesity worldwide: international survey. *British Medical Journal, 320,* 1-6.

Cole, M. (1996). *Cultural Psychology.* Cambridge: Belknap.

Crawford, C. & Krebs, D.L. (1997). *Handbook of Evolutionary Psychology: Ideas, Issues and Application.* London: LEA.

Cunnigham, D.J., Duffy, T.M., & Knuth, R.A. (1991). The Textbook of the future. In C. McKnight, A. Dillon, & R.A. Knuth (Eds.), *Hypertext: A Psychological Perspective* (pp. 19-49). London: Horwood.

Damasio, A.R. (1999). *The Feeling of What Happens. Body and Emotion in the Making of Consciousness.* New York: Harcourt Brace.

Darwin, C, (1872). *The Expression of Emotions in Men and Animals.* Chicago: University of Chicago Press. Trans.It. (1982). *L'espressione delle emozioni,* Torino: Boringhieri.

Ellis, A. (1962). *Reason and Emotion in Psychotherapy.* New York: Stuart.

Emde, R.N. (2003). Early Narratives. In R.N. Emde, D.P. Wolf, & D. Oppenheim (Eds.), *Revealing the Inner Worlds of Young Children* (pp. 3-26). Oxford: Oxford University Press.

Emde, R.N., Wolf, D.P., & Oppenheim, D. (2003). *Revealing the Inner Worlds of Young Children.* Oxford: Oxford University Press.

Gaulin, S.J.C., & McBurney, D. (2000). *Psychology: an Evolutionary Approach.* London: Prentice Hall.

Gilbert, P. (2000). The relationship of shame, social anxiety and depression: the role of the evaluation of social rank. *Clinical Psychology and Psychotherapy, 7,* 174-189.

Gilbert, P. (2001). Evolution and social anxiety, *Social Anxiety Disorder, 24 (4),* 723-751.

Glenberg, A.M., (1997). What memory is for. *Behavioral & Brain Sciences. 20(1),* 1-55.

Goncalves, O.F., Henriques, M.R., & Machado, P.P.P. (2004). Nurturing nature. Cognitive narrative strategies. In L.E. Angus, & J. McLeod (Eds.), *The handbook of narrative and psychotherapy* (pp. 103-117). London: Sage

Goncalves, O.F., Korman, Y. & Angus, L. (2000). Constructing psychopathology from a cognitive narrative perspective. In R.A. Neimeyer, & J.D. Raskin (Eds.), *Constructions of Disorder: Meaning-making Frameworks for Psychotherapy* (pp. 265-284). Washington, D.C.: American Psychological Association Books.

Goncalves, O.F., & Machado, P.P. (1999). Cognitive narrative psychotherapy: research foundations. *Journal of clinical psychology. 55,* 1179-1191.

Gopnik, A. & Melzoff, A.N. (1997). *Words, Thoughts and Theories.* Boston: MIT Press.

Greeno, J. G. (1997). On Claims that Answer the Wrong Question, *Educational Researcher, 26 (1),* 5-17.

Guidano, V. (1987). *The Complexity of Self.* New York: Guilford Press.

Guidano, V. (1991). *The Self in Process. Toward a Post-Rationalist Cognitive Therapy.* New York: Guilford Press.

Guidano, V., & Liotti, G. (1983). *Cognitive Processes and Emotional Disorders.* New York: Guilford Press.

Hill, A.J., Draper, E., & Stack, J. (1994). A weight on children's Mind: body shape dissatisfaction at 9 years. *International Journal of Obesity. 18,* 383-389.

Hinde, R.A. (1982). *Ethology, its Nature and Relations with others Sciences.* Oxford:

Oxford University Press.

Izard, C.E. (2002). Translating emotion theory and research into preventive interventions. *Psychological Bulletin, 128(5)*, 796-824.

Izard, C.E., Fine, S., Mostow, A., Trentacosta, C., & Campbell, J. (2002). Emotion processes in normal and abnormal development and preventive intervention. *Development and Psychopathology, 14*, 761-787.

Johnson, M. (1987). *The Body in the Mind: The Bodily Basis of Meaning, Imagination, and Reason.* Chicago: University of Chicago Press.

Jonassen, D.H., & Land, S.M. (2000). Preface. In D.H. Jonassen, & S.M. Land (Eds.), *Theoretical Foundation of Learning Environments* (pp. III-IX). Mahwah: Erlbaum.

Knuth, R.A., & Cunnigham, D.J. (1993). Tools for Constructivism. In T. Duffy, J. Lowyck, & D. Jonassen (Eds.), *Designing Environment for Constructivistic Learning* (pp.163-187). Berlin: Springer-Verlag.

Lambruschi, F. (2004). *Psicoterapia cognitiva dell'età evolutiva. Procedure di assessment e strategie psicoterapeutiche.* Torino: Bollati-Boringhieri.

Latzer, Y., Hochdorf, Z., Bachar, E., & Canetti, L. (2002). Attachment style and family functioning as discriminating factors in eating disorders. *Contemporary Family Therapy, 24(4)*, 581-599.

Lemerise, E.A., & Dodge, K.A. (2000). The development of anger and Hostile interactions. In M. Lewis, & J.M. Haviland-Jones (Eds.), *Handbook of Emotions, Second edition* (pp. 594-606). New York: Guilford Press.

Lewis, M. (1993). The Emergence of Human Emotions. In M. Lewis, & J.M. Haviland (Eds.), *Handbook of Emotions* (pp.223-235). New York: Guilford Press.

Lewis, M. (2000). Self Conscious Emotions: Embarrassment, Pride, Shame and Guilt. In M. Lewis, & J.M. Haviland-Jones (Eds.), *Handbook of Emotions, Second edition* (pp. 623-636). New York: Guilford Press.

Lewis, M., Sullivan, M.W., Stanger, C., & Weiss, M. (1989). Self development and self-conscious emotions. *Child Development, 60*, 146-156.

Lincoln, Y.G., & Guba, E.G. (2000). Paradigmatic, Controversial, Contradiction and Emerging Confluences. In N.K. Denzin, & Y.S. Lincoln (Eds.), *Handbook of Qualitative Research* (pp. 163-88). Thousand Oaks: Sage.

Liotti, G. (2005). *La dimensione interpersonale della coscienza*, Nuova edizione. Rome: Carocci editore.

Liotti, G. (1990). Il concetto di sistema comportamentale tra etologia e psicologia clinica. *Rivista di Psicologia Clinica, 2*, 176-187.

Liotti, G. (1993). *Le discontinuità della coscienza: etiologia, diagnosi e psicoterapia dei disturbi dissociativi.* Milan: Franco Angeli.

Liotti, G. (1994). *La dimensione interpersonale della coscienza*. Rome: La Nuova Italia Scientifica.

Liotti, G. (1996). L'attaccamento. In B.G. Bara (Ed.), *Manuale di Psicoterapia Cognitiva* (pp. 62-85). Torino: Bollati Boringhieri.

Liotti, G. (2001). *Le opere della coscienza. Psicopatologia e psicoterapia nella prospettiva cognitivo-evoluzionista*. Milan: Raffaello Cortina Editore.

Mahoney, M.J. (1991). *Human Change Processes*. New York: Basic Books.

Mahoney, M.J. (1995). *Cognitive and Constructive Psychotherapies. Theory, Research and Practice*. New York: Springer.

Mahoney, M.J. (2000). Core ordering and disordering processes: a constructive view of psychological development. In R.A. Neimeyer, & J.D. Raskin (Eds.), *Construction of Disorder. Meaning-Making frameworks for psychotherapy* (pp. 43-62). Washington, D.C.: American Psychological Association Books.

Maloney, M.J., McGuire, J., Daniels, S.R., & Specher, B. (1989). Dieting behavior and eating attitude in children. *Pediatrics, 84*, 482–489.

Maloney, M.J., McGuire, J., & Daniels, S.R. (1988). Reliability testing of children's version of the eating attitude test. *Journal of the American Academy of Child and Adolescent Psychiatry. 34*, 1117–1124.

Mancuso, J.C., & Sarbin, T.R. (1983). The self-narrative in the enactment of roles. In T.R. Sarbin, & K. Scheibe (Eds.), *Studies in Social Identity* (pp. 233-253). New York: Praeger.

Mayer, J.D., & Salovey, P. (1997). What is emotional intelligence? In P. Salovey, & J.D. Sluyter (Eds.), *Emotional development and emotional intelligence: implications for educators* (pp. 3-31). New York: Basic Books.

McGuire, M.T., & Troisi, A. (1998). *Darwinian Psychiatry*. Oxford: Oxford University Press.

Nardi, B. (2001). *Processi psichici e psicopatologia nell'approccio cognitivo. Nuove prospettive in psicologia e psichiatria clinica*. Milan: Franco Angeli.

Neimeyer, R.A. (1995). Client-generated Narratives in Psychotherapy. In R.A. Neimeyer, & M.J. Mahoney (Eds.), *Constructivism in Psychotherapy* (pp. 231-246). Washington, D.C.: American Psychological Association.

Neimeyer, R.A., & Stewart, A.E. (2000). Constructivist and narrative psychotherapies. In C.R. Snyder, & R.E. Ingram (Eds.), *Handbook of psychological change: psychotherapy processes and practices for the 21st century* (pp. 337-357). New York: Wiley.

O'Kearney, R. (1996). Attachment disruption in anorexia nervosa and bulimia nervosa: a review of theory and empirical research. *International Journal of Eating Disorders, 20*, 115-127.

Ogawa, D., Sroufe, L.A., Weinfeld, N.S., Carlson, E.A., & Egeland, B. (1997).

Development and the fragmented self. Longitudinal study of dissociative symptomatology in a non clinical sample. *Development and Psychopathology*, 9, 855-880.

Pellerey, M. (2003). Metacognizione e processi affettivi, motivazionali e volitivi. In O. Albanese (Ed.), *Percorsi Metacognitivi* (pp. 57-73). Milan: Franco Angeli.

Pons, F., Doudin, P.A., Harris, P., & de Rosnay, M. (2002). Métaémotion et intégration scolaire. In L. Lafortune, & P. Mongeau (Eds.), *L'Affectivité dans l'apprentissage* (pp. 7-28). Sainte-Foy: Presses de l'Université du Québec.

Power, M. (1999). Sadness and its disorders. In T. Dalgleish, & M. Power (Eds.), *Handbook of cognition and emotion* (pp. 497-520). London: Wiley.

Reda, M.A. (1986). *Sistemi cognitivi complessi e psicoterapia*. Rome: NIS La Nuova Italia Scientifica.

Rezzonico, G., & Strepparava, M.G. (2002). Ansia e psicopatologia. Alcuni aspetti, In B. Nardi, & M. Randoni (Eds.), *Psicopatologia dell'ansia ed epistemologia cognitive* (pp. 37-56).Ancona: Emmepiesse.

Rolls, E.T. (1999). *The Brain and Emotion*. Oxford: Oxford University Press.

Ruberti, S. (1996). *I sistemi motivazionali: l'attaccamento tra psicologia evoluzionistica e psicoterapia*. In G. Rezzonico, & S. Ruberti (Eds.), *L'attaccamento nel lavoro clinico e sociale* (pp. 27-52). Milan: Franco Angeli.

Ruggerini, C., Lambruschi, F., Neviani, V., Guaraldi, G.P., & Manerchia, G. (2004). *Disturbi Somatoformi*. In F. Lambruschi (Ed.), *Psicoterapia Cognitiva dell'Età Evolutiva* (pp. 458-485). Torino: Bollati-Boringhieri.

Saarni, C. (1999). *The development of emotional competence*. New York: Guilford Press.

Shapiro, S., Newcomb, M., & Loeb, T.B., (1997). Fear of fat, disregulate-restrained eating and body esteem: prevalence and gender differences among eight to ten year old children. *Journal of clinical child psychology*. 26, 358 – 365.

Siegel, D.J. (1999). *The Developing Mind*. New York: Guilford Press.

Smolak, L., Levine, M.P., & Striegel-Moore, R. (1996). *The Developmental Psychopathology of Eating Disorders*. New Jersey: Lawrence Erlbaum.

Spelke, E.S. (1994). Initial Knowledge: Six Suggestions. *Cognition*, 50, 431-445.

Sroufe, L.A. (1996). *Emotional Development: the Organisation of Emotional Life in the Early Years*. Cambridge: Cambridge University Press.

Stern, D.N. (1998). *Le interazioni madre-bambino nello sviluppo e nella clinica*. Milan: Raffaello Cortina Editore.

Stevens, A., & Price, J. (1996). *Evolutionary Psychiatry. A new beginning*, Second edition. London and Philadelphia: Routledge, Taylor, Francis Group.

Strepparava, M.G., & Rezzonico, G. (2005). Problematiche dell'immagine corporea e precursori dei disturbi alimentari in adolescenza. *Child Development & Disabilities, 31(3)*, 21-44.

Strepparava, M.G. (2004). La prevenzione dei disturbi alimentari: ricerca sul campo e interventi clinici, In *I disturbi alimentari in eta' evolutiva: integrazione tra pediatria e psicologia* (pp. 39-46). Milan: A.O. San Carlo Borromeo éditeur.

Strepparava, M.G., Grimi, M., Linguadoro, M., Notaro, S., Strozzi, M., & Rezzonico, G. (2003). A Proposal for Assessment of Eating Disorders in Children. Paper, *XIth European Conference on Developmental Psychology*. Milan.

Strepparava, M.G., Linguadoro, M., Notaro, S., Strozzi, M., & Grimi, M. (2002). Disturbi del comportamento alimentare in età evolutiva: sensazioni, emozioni e rappresentazioni cognitive. Paper, *XI Congresso Nazionale SITCC Psicoterapia e scienze cognitive*. Bologna 19-22 September 2002. p. 282.

Strepparava, M.G., Stagnaro, S., Strozzi, M., & Grimi, M. (2000). Disturbi del comportamento alimentare ed indici di rischio in età evolutiva. *X Congresso Nazionale SITCC La psicoterapia fondata sulle evidenze: metodi, protocolli, esiti*. Orvieto 16-19 November, p. 54.

Thomas, K., Ricciardelli, L.A., & William, R.J., (2000). Gender traits and self-concept as indicators of problem eating and body dissatisfaction among children. *Sex roles. 43*, 441–458.

Vandereycken, W., & Nordenbos, G. (1998). *The Prevention of Eating Disorders*. London: The Athlone Press.

Varisco, B.M. (2002). *Costruttivismo Socio-culturale*. Rome: Carocci Editore.

Varela, F.J., Thompson, E., & Rosch, E. (1991). *The Embodied Mind: Cognitive Science and Human Experience*. Cambridge, MA: MIT Press.

Villegas, M. (1994). Costruzione narrativa dell'esperienza e psicoterapia. *Psicobiettivo, 14(1)*, p. 31-41.

Ward, A., Ramsay, R., & Treasure, J. (2000). Attachment research in eating disorders. *British Journal of Medical Psychology, 73(1)*, 35-51.

Ward, A., Ramsay, R., Turnbull, S., Benedettini, M., & Treasure, J. (2000). Attachment patterns in eating disorders: past in the present. *International Journal of Eating Disorders, 28*, 370-376.

Wellman, H.M., & Gelman, S.A. (1992). Cognitive development: foundational theories of core domain. *Annual Review of Psychology, 43*, 337-375.

Wenger, E. (1998). *Communities of practice. Learning, Meaning, Identity*. Cambridge: Cambridge University Press.

Wilson, B.G. (1996). What is a Constructivist Learning Environment? In B.G. Wilson (Ed.), *Constructivist Learning Environment. Case Studies in*

Instructional Design (pp. 3-8). Englewood Cliff: Educational Technology Publications.

Wolf, D.P. (2003). Making Meaning from Emotional Experience in Early Naratives. In R.N. Emde, D.P. Wolf, & D. Oppenheim (Eds.), *Revealing the Inner Worlds of Young Children* (pp. 27-54). Oxford: Oxford University Press.

CHAPTER 6

A reflection on the relationship between emotions and critical thinking[1]

Louise Lafortune and Andrée Robertson

1. Introduction

The Quebec new curriculum (MEQ, 2001, 2003), specifies that pupils exercise their critical judgment as a transversal competency. We consider exercise of critical judgment to be a manifestation of critical thinking, and choose the term "critical thinking" because we believe that emotions can exert an influence beyond critical judgment. We postulate that emotions and critical thinking can influence each other and that intervening on one or the other can favor development of critical thinking or comprehension of emotions. Our intention is therefore to specify the link between emotions and the expression of critical thinking. A line of questioning guides our reflection. For example, can the manifestation of one or many emotions influence – positively or negatively – the expression of critical thinking? Can the development of critical thinking influence the expression or comprehension of emotions? Are there actions or interventions that would make it possible to improve emotion control, and subsequently favor the expression of critical thinking? Can the development of skills linked to critical thinking favor a better control of emotions?

Before providing elements of reflection to these questions, we will briefly define the concepts "emotion" and "critical thinking". We then specify the role of emotions in the expression of critical thinking and that of critical thinking in the expression of emotions. Finally we will suggest possible further actions based on the idea that acting on emotions can favor development of skills linked to critical

---

[1] We thank Nathalie Girardin and Bernard Massé, respectively for the translation and the revisions of the translation of this text.

thinking and that acting on critical thinking can diminish negative influences when learning certain emotions.

2. The role of emotions in the expression of critical thinking

Emotions are characterized by an affective state. Several basic emotions have been recognized in the literature, for example: *fear, sadness, anger, happiness, surprise, disgust,* and *distress* (Martin and Briggs, 1986). Some authors (Gratton, 2001; Guilbert, 1999; Hassel, 2003) uphold that thinking critically helps develop awareness of one's emotions without however being controlled by them. Gut feelings, or feelings from within, and intuition are elements to be considered each time a decision-making process is begun. In fact, according to Hassel (2003), to improve critical thinking skills, one must become aware of personal biases, habits, and "emotional states". Emotions – when expressed without judgment or impulsively – can deceive us, making us think we are right, even when our decision turns out to be ineffective. It could be said that emotions impair the ability to think critically. Critical thinkers do not suppress their emotions nor do emotions overly influence them. The natural response to emotions and feelings can be constructively mitigated by a way of thinking which thrives to be critical. Critical thinking provides room to "select" emotions and feelings and thus recognize those emotions that are most appropriate for a given situation. Seen this way, critical thinking is no longer just a cold and insensitive analytical process but also includes emotions and passions in a positive manner.

According to Leader and Middleton (1999), the emotional reactions a learner experiences when facing a task can greatly influence his attitude toward the same task in a specific context. Generally speaking, people trust their emotional reactions as indicators of their attitudes (Fazio, 1995). Swartz and Perkins (1989) (quoted in Guilbert, 1999) fully agree. In fact, according to the authors, "awareness of feelings, as much as the thinking process that accompanies the accomplishment of a task, are important, precisely to exercise true control over the task" (p. 80). Other studies, particularly those of Schwarz and Clore (1988), show that individuals use their emotional reactions as significant elements in situations where they are required to pass value judgments. Furthermore, the emotional components of memory seem to play an important role in the individual's response to current emotional situations. Middleton and Toluk (1999), quoted in Leader and Middleton (1999), have already brought to light the relevance and the meaning of emotional memory in relation to an individual's evaluation of his participation or involvement in a situation or a specific event. Indeed, when a pupil must participate in an activity, he may experience one or more emotions that were previously experienced during similar activities in which he was once involved. Because these emotions are at the heart of a plethora of conditions from past experiences, emotion serves as a means to free memory, thus revealing potentially important information in regard to the value of the person's participation.

Finally, we note that the role of emotions is characterized as that of "an intelligent interface that would be a mediator between input and output" (Scherer, 1994, p. 127 quoted in Guilbert, 1999). Therefore, emotions enable individuals to evaluate the relative importance of new information in relation to an event, with the purpose of adapting themselves, according to context and to their needs and goals.

3. The role of critical thinking in the expression of emotions

In the previous section, and although studies in this field do not abound, we described the relationship between expression of emotions and critical thinking by emphasizing the individual's response in relation to emotions experienced. In a similar perspective, it can also be said that research into the influence of critical thinking on emotion expression is scarce. To provide elements of reflection on this subject, we have examined what has already been said on the role of emotions in relation to the expression of critical thinking and have tried to think about the opposite process, that is to say, into the role of critical thinking on emotion expression. However, beforehand, we will look into critical thinking and its components and we will observe how affective strategies can be linked to the control or expression of emotions.

In general terms, critical thinking is associated with cognitive skills such as analyzing, interpreting, and evaluating (Ennis, 1987; Facione, Facione & Giancarlo, 2000; Facione 2004; Lipman, 1995); and with attitudes or dispositions, in particular, being surprised, showing open-mindness, and manifesting analytical judgment, to name just a few (Ennis, 1987; Facione, Facione & Giancarlo, 2000). Ennis, who defines critical thinking as "reasonable, rational thinking that helps us decide what to believe or what to do" (1985, p. 180), refines his definition adding twelve abilities such as "analyzing arguments" or "judging the credibility of a source" and with fourteen dispositions, among others, "searching for reasons" and "trying to be well-informed" which, according to him, describe a person who has developed critical thinking. Likewise for Lipman (1995) who also works from cognitive abilities (to reason, research, define, and interpret), which are inseparable from the dispositions and attitudes the child develops in a philosophical community of inquiry.

In their search for a better comprehension of the various components of critical thinking, Paul, Binker, Jensen and Kreklau (1990) suggest 35 strategies associated with critical thinking, including nine affective strategies. One of these, "exploring the thoughts that underlie emotions and the emotions that underlie thoughts" can help to understand the relationship between critical thinking and the expression of emotions.

Although it is common to separate thought and emotions, as though these entities were independent, the fact is that practically all human feelings or emotions rest on a certain form of thought. Together with Paul, Binker, Jensen and Kreklau (1990), we could say that, to a certain extent, our thoughts result from our emotions. Reflecting, thinking with a certain degree of introspection and self-comprehension, requires reconciliation of the close ties that exist between thought and emotions and between reason and emotions. Critical thinkers become aware that their feelings or their emotions in fact constitute an answer (not the only one possible or necessarily the most reasonable) to a given situation. They recognize that their emotions might be different if they had an understanding or a different interpretation of the situation. They also admit that thoughts or emotions, far from being isolated or different "things or elements", are in fact two intrinsically linked aspects, issued from their own interpretations. On the other hand, "non critical" thinkers see little or no relationship between their emotions and the expression of their thought. Unfortunately, in doing so, they shun their responsibility toward their own thoughts, emotions and actions. Moreover, their emotions often seem unintelligible to them.

Paul (1982), quoted in Guilbert (1999), also suggests a model that characterizes the interaction between the affective and the cognitive, in relation to critical thinking. The author presents two levels, which he refers to as the "weak sense of critical thinking" and the "strong sense of critical thinking" (p. 83). The first level represents "the person with numerous critical thinking skills, who uses them to defend his own interests or point of view; in other words, simple control of intellectual critical thinking skills with no concern for others, with no intellectual empathy" (p. 83). In the second level, in addition to intellectual critical thinking skills, there is "a concern for others, a decentering that allows comprehension of others, of their values, and thus enables a more informed, more global decision, less tainted with personal values" (p. 83).

In reflecting upon the significance of these two levels, it can be said that the development of critical thinking involves two facets: command of intellectual abilities with little intellectual empathy or with the same command associated with a limited understanding of others and of their values. At the first level, it could be said that the development of critical thinking would have little influence or a negative influence on the expression of emotions or on affective development. For example, if there is little intellectual empathy, it can be difficult to adapt one's explanations or justifications to a particular situation and thus, have a profitable exchange. At the second level, it can be understood that concern for others, in the expression of one's critical thinking, can help develop healthy and harmonious interpersonal relationships. This does not mean confrontations cannot exist. However, they take into account a series of factors in relationships between oneself and others. To this effect, Daniel, Lafortune, Pallascio, Splitter, Slade and De la Garza (2005) include "responsible thinking" as a component of critical thinking.

There is a concept linked to the emotional component of critical thinking that Gould and Kolb (1965) refer to as "ego involvement" (p. 83). For her part, Guilbert (1999) relates it to "emotional involvement" (which she names "emotional implication"). Her works have greatly helped us understand the role of the development of critical thinking on emotion control. Guilbert (1999) uses the concept *emotional implication*, which, according to her, helps clarify the concept of the emotional component in critical thinking. Gould and Kolb (1965) uphold that the intense behavior of an extremely emotionally involved person can take the shape of increased intellectual and physical efforts to defend a point of view or reasoning troubles when facing arguments expressed by a person defending an opposite point of view.

Basing ourselves on the work of Guilbert (1999) and keeping in mind that our intention is to explore the role of critical thinking on the expression of emotions, we state the following ideas:

- Thought and emotion are closely related. Becoming aware that expression of thought results in part from our emotions can help us understand that emotions can be different, inasmuch as our interpretation of the situation is more "critical".
- Development of critical thinking is helpful in taking an external look and brings a certain form of objectivity. This could mean that critical thinking may reduce the influence of emotions on our judgments of ideas, opinions, persons, and events ... Critical thinking could help improve awareness of the role of emotions when listening to the ideas of others.
- If emotional implication is too great, the development of critical thinking could encourage more informed judgments regarding differences between one's own ideas and those of others. Critical thinking will guide and shed light on our own emotions.

- Development of critical thinking presupposes judgment abilities regarding, for example, the quality of a text even if it goes against our ideas. In this case, critical thinking skills help us limit the influence of emotions. This in turn can help us control emotions in other circumstances.
- One can wonder whether the development of critical thinking exerts an influence on the degree of control over an emotion. Critical thinking skills could favor the control of emotions. However, it is important to make sure that this control does not limit intellectual empathy (see the first level of Paul, 1982).

Paul's concept of intellectual empathy (1982) could be related to what Lipman (1991, 1995) refers to as "caring thinking" which is centered on comprehension, respect and acceptance of others. Daniel, Lafortune, Pallascio, Splitter, Slade and De la Garza (2005) consider that caring thinking stems from the relationship between behavior and moral rules or ethical principles with the intent of improving personal and social experience. It would then appear that pupils put a lot of effort in an increasingly complex reflection, first on human behavior, then on moral rules (categorization of specific actions), and finally on ethical principles (reflection on the foundations of these categories). This component of dialogical critical thinking, defined by the previously mentioned authors, could influence the expression of emotions, stemming from a reflection process associated with the understanding of emotions.

Based on our reflection, we believe that the influence of critical thinking on the expression of emotions could be tied to the concept of meta-emotion, which, according to Pons, Doudin, Harris and de Rosnay (2002, p. 9) is "the subject's *comprehension* of the nature, causes and possibilities of the control of emotions. In other words, it is the individual's conscious and explicit knowledge of emotions (for example, understanding it is possible to hide emotions or understanding the incidence of moral rules on emotions). Moreover, meta-emotion refers to the subject's capacity to *regulate* the expression of an emotion and the emotional experience, more or less consciously and implicitly (for example, pretending to be happy or sad, or feeling guilty or proud)" (Authors' italics).

At this stage of the reflection on the inter-influence of emotions and critical thinking, we will explore ways to interact with pupils while taking into account this mutual influence.

4. Actions which favor intervention

Among the actions which favor intervention, some use reflection on emotions (or beliefs) to foster the development of critical thinking whereas others encourage the development of critical thinking skills for an improved control of emotions.

Intervening on emotions in order to favor the development of critical thinking

Intervening on emotions in order to favor the development of critical thinking could be achieved in three ways: 1) by encouraging the expression of emotions experienced during learning to encourage pupils who need to speak of their emotions before entering a learning position; 2) by facilitating comprehension of emotions to help pupils transpose their emotional experience in a given situation to another context; 3) by taking a philosophical look at emotions to favor a more conceptual discussion on the role of emotions in learning.

Inciting the expression of emotions

In a project of Lafortune and Massé (2002) and another of Lafortune and Lafortune (2002), pupils were encouraged to express their emotions regarding mathematics. Through activities of reflection and three-minute videos, pupils were encouraged to express their emotions regarding mathematics and to find solutions to counter negative reactions.

With material developed for this project, the authors attempted to foster awareness of the emotions that can be experienced in mathematics, to counter beliefs and prejudices, and to develop positive attitudes toward this discipline. In particular, the objectives were:

- Showing that it is possible and normal to feel emotions regarding mathematics;
- Showing that many people either experience anxiety toward this discipline or lack the necessary confidence to succeed in this field;
- Developing awareness that certain beliefs are unfounded and can stem from prejudices;
- Developing awareness that there are solutions to come to grips with or overcome negative affective reactions regarding mathematics.

It should therefore be noted that the objectives are double: some are directly associated with emotions whereas others concern pupils' beliefs regarding mathematics, in order to reach the affective dimension. Lafortune and Fennema (2003) consider that a belief is a statement or an opinion that is considered real, plausible or possible. A belief can be a notion or a conviction. If it is a notion, it refers much more to the cognitive dimension, and if it is a conviction, it falls in the domain of the affective dimension. A critical look at beliefs and prejudices regarding mathematics can influence emotions concerning this discipline. It is from this presupposition that the authors developed certain reflective questions and activities to foster class discussion. In the next section are some examples associated with the belief in a "gift for math" and the uselessness of this discipline.

The "Gift for Math"
The "gift for math" is often associated with a special or superior talent for success in mathematics. This belief influences the affective reactions of certain pupils in mathematics, inasmuch as mathematics' supposed inaccessibility provides pupils with an excuse to fail due to their lack of this famous "gift for math". This is an excellent pretext to avoid making the necessary efforts to succeed. Pupils that entertain this belief in a "gift for math" rely too much on their memory when learning mathematics. Because they do not think they can understand, they end up integrating the idea that mathematics must be learnt by heart. Reflection questions, associated with this belief in a "gift for math" might take the following form:
- Is there such a thing as a "gift for math"? Why do you say that? How do you justify this opinion?
- What characteristics could you associate with the supposed "brainers" in mathematics? Do you know any "brainers" that are tired of being treated differently from others?

We assume that the search for answers to these questions comes within the scope of critical thinking skills and that the exchanges will have an impact on the "gift for math" belief. According to us, questioning this belief may bring pupils who associate their difficulties in mathematics to their lack of this special or superior talent, to reflect, and to make an effort in mathematics. This in turn would help them increase their self-confidence regarding their possibilities of success in this discipline. The following questions could help pursue the reflection:
- What could you say to a pupil who wonders whether a special talent is needed to succeed in mathematics?
- What are the secrets to success in mathematics?
- What could you do to help a person who has trouble with mathematics and claims a lack of this special talent?

"Math, what is it good for?"
Pupils often ask the question "Math, what is it good for?" Perhaps this question is related to the fact that mathematics is often presented as very abstract. This image of abstraction often brings pupils to think that mathematics is useless, since they do not realize they use it on a daily basis. This belief in the uselessness of mathematics is very difficult to counter. It helps pupils justify their lack of interest and their lack of motivation in this discipline. Just as with the "gift for math", we believe that countering this belief, by looking at it critically, can influence pupils' emotions regarding this discipline. Questions such as the following can serve to foster a reflection to counter this belief by looking at it critically:
- What would be the characteristics of a world without mathematics?
- What do you think of a pupil who believes mathematics is unnecessary for his future work as an architect or as a graphic designer?
- What questions do you have regarding the usefulness of mathematics?
- What is the place of mathematics in your surroundings?

Such a reflection concerning the belief that mathematics is useless may have an effect on pupil motivation or at the very least help teachers react when pupils assert that mathematics is useless.

Favoring comprehension of emotions

As previously mentioned, the role of critical thinking on the expression of emotions could favor the comprehension of emotions. Pons, Doudin, Harris and de Rosnay (2002) refer to this comprehension of emotions as *meta-emotion*. These authors evaluated the SMILE (*School Matters in Lifeskills Education*) program which suggests a number of activities to develop pupils' meta-emotion. These activities use reading, discussions or role-play and consist in: 1) relating past and present emotions and attempting to understand their origin; 2) naming persons that are liked or disliked; 3) understanding what is a real friend and an imaginary friend; 4) recognizing and expressing positive and negative emotions (with and without words or images); 5) understanding their origin; 6) understanding the distinction between apparent emotion and experienced emotion as well as anger and fear, and learning to control them; 7) recognizing the origins of sadness, anger, and fear, and learning to control them; 8) recognizing emotions in situations of loss, separation, abandonment, exclusion and harassment, and learning to control them; 9) recognizing and understanding the origins of pride and guilt; defining what they like or dislike in themselves, in others; 10) determining the similarities and differences in emotions experienced by various people and understanding the origin of these differences; 11) pretending to be a mistreated person and describing what this person feels; 12) recognizing the influences and consequences of drugs on emotions; 13) understanding how adolescence can influence emotions (desires, depression, rage, all-mightiness, etc.) and how to deal with this change.

In this type of intervention, because pupils take a cognitive look at emotions, recognizing positive and negative emotions (4), apparent and experienced emotions (6), and their origin (5), may help favor the development of critical thinking. Pupils are not only in a position to express their emotions, but also to study and understand them. They end up taking an external look at what they are experiencing, which helps improve their critical thinking.

Among other similar solutions, Guilbert (1999) implies that inciting awareness can favor cognitive links between critical thinking and emotions. Awareness encourages learning to control the influence of emotions on critical thinking. The development of critical thinking makes it possible to better organize thinking so as to limit the "harmful" influence of emotions. This author gives the example of judges who must attempt to limit the influence of their emotions on the judgments they make in court.

Philosophizing about emotions

In "Philosophy for Children Adapted to Mathematics", Daniel, Lafortune, Pallascio and Sykes (1996) developed discussion plans and philosophical-mathematical activities that enable youngsters to take a philosophical look at emotions regarding mathematics. In these discussion plans and activities, pupils are encouraged to express themselves conceptually about emotions and to distance themselves from their feelings. Even if this external perspective presupposes that the pupils express themselves about their own emotions, it is likely that some pupils will feel more comfortable about expressing themselves in a discussion of this type. Furthermore, they will put their critical thinking to the test, since they will have to present ideas that are justified in an organized manner, not just emotionally as some youngsters would if directly questioned about their emotions.

The following section contains two examples of discussion plans: one is called "Hating Math" and the other concerns "Fear of Failing" (Daniel, Lafortune, Pallascio & Sykes, 1996).

"Hating Math"
Discussion plan:
- What emotions are brought into play when you hate someone or something?

- Can a feeling about mathematics change over time or according to experience? Why?
- Are you always aware of your feelings when you try to solve a difficult problem? Why?
- Why do you like or dislike mathematics? (p. 96-97).

"Fear of Failing"
Discussion plan:
- Is fear positive or negative? Why?
- Is the fear you experience during a horror movie the same as a fear of failing in mathematics? Why?
- Can a fear of failing mathematics be compared to a fear of spiders or a fear of the dark, for example? To what can you compare fear of failing in mathematics?
- Can tension felt in mathematics help you solve a math problem? (p. 184-185).

These examples show how emotions can be discussed in a manner that is conceptual (philosophical and cognitive). Even though pupils speak about themselves in the discussions, many may feel more comfortable doing it this way.

Using emotions as a basis for a philosophical community of inquiry (a moment when pupils philosophize about concepts related to learning) includes two parts. It can be difficult for some pupils to distance themselves from their own emotions in order to consider them philosophically. However, this may be a way to get certain pupils, who avoid showing their personal emotions, to reflect on these emotions. No matter what a person's situation is, this philosophical perspective can favor the development of skills related to critical thinking. Since emotions have a meaning for all pupils, they can participate in such an exchange. Moreover, pupils will learn to differentiate emotionally-laden arguments from arguments that are more critical.

Emotions and meta-cognition to develop critical thinking

In a text relating meta-cognition to critical thinking, Lafortune and Robertson (2004) noted that current research mostly suggests means or models to favor critical thinking through the development of metacognition. The opposite perspective, in other words that the development of critical thinking helps metacognition, has not been fully exploited. For their part, Lafortune and St-Pierre (1996) show that emotions experienced during learning influence mental activity control. This means that in a process of learning, emotions that influence the mental process (either positively through motivation or self-confidence or negatively through anxiety or lack of interest) must be taken into account. Meta-cognition, seen as a supervision of one's own mental functioning to better plan actions and control the learning process, brings pupils to become aware of their mental processes. They can therefore take action and choose the strategies that seem most adequate to control mental activity when accomplishing a specific task.

With regard to critical thinking, Lipman (1995) stresses that pupils resort to fundamental cognitive activities, such as reasoning, searching, and organizing to help them separate the most relevant information from that which is less relevant given the information they receive.

It is likely that the transition from emotions to meta-cognition favors the development of critical thinking. Indeed, to become efficient and effective thinkers, pupils must control their level of comprehension of the subject studied, be sensitive to the knowledge they are building, and be aware not only of the task required, but also of the manner in which the strategies used facilitate their thinking process. Today, pupils are encouraged to reflect, to think beyond the subject studied. Involvement is required of them; this translates into an active participation in the construction of their knowledge: pupils have a critical look at their learning, uphold their opinions, ask questions, and make the necessary connections between new learning and their current knowledge. If this process presupposes a certain ease in the practice of self-reflection, in the use of strategies most helpful in reaching the objectives pursued, it also commands a process of critical reflection that calls upon evaluation, analysis and synthesis skills (Lafortune & Robertson, 2004). To this effect, Kuhn (1999) reinforces the idea that critical thinking, more that simply a cognitive ability, should also be perceived as a meta-cognitive ability. Along the same lines, Daniel, Lafortune, Pallascio, Splitter, Slade, De la Garza (accepted) consider that dialogical critical thinking includes logical, critical, caring and meta-cognitive thinking.

In sum, the more the pupils use meta-cognitive skills, the more they have opportunities to "be in contact" with their thoughts and with the progression of their thinking process. They will also be in a better position to strategically choose the specific skills related to critical thinking that will help them progress in their learning.

These thoughts bring us to consider the inverse process. In other words, is it possible to organize interventions to develop critical thinking with the specific purpose of improving understanding of emotions, and thus, control them better?

Developing critical thinking to help control emotions

Research on strategies used to develop critical thinking to improve control of emotions is scarce. As explained by Paul, Binker, Jensen and Kreklau (1990), we sometimes feel sad or depressed because we interpret a situation that affects us in an excessively negative or pessimistic manner. Perhaps we have forgotten to consider other dimensions or aspects that might positively influence our analysis. A way to better understand our emotions is to question ourselves critically: How come I feel so sad? How am I analyzing the situation? What conclusion have I reached? What are my deductions? Are they "realistic"? Are there other ways of interpreting the situation? In this way, we can learn to identify "recurrent models" in our interpretations and, thus, begin to see what stimulates our thoughts. Without a doubt, understanding ourselves constitutes the first step towards self-control, or self-regulation, and self-improvement, strategies that require another type of outlook on our emotions and on their relationship with our thoughts, our ideas, and our general interpretation of the world.

Along the same lines, our attention is drawn to research that emphasizes the "educational challenges" related to teaching critical thinking (Gratton, 2001). This research suggests a different approach, which is to teach pupils how to apply critical thinking skills to self-perception (the author refers to this perception as "beliefs"), which would, to a great extent, account for the expression of emotions.

Regarding the relation that seems to exist between belief and emotion, the literature clearly shows the difficulty in defining and operationalizing the concept of belief. Goodenough (1963), taken up in Doudin, Pons, Martin and Lafortune (2003) defines belief "as an assertion considered to be true; it is essentially of an individual, idiosyncratic nature, for it stems from personal experience, and includes an emotional or judgmental dimension" (p.10). Lafortune and Fennema (2003) have defined the concept of belief as "a statement considered to be true, plausible or possible" (p. 34). These authors consider that a belief can be either a conception, it then refers to a cognitive dimension, or a conviction, in which case it is closer to the affective dimension. Gratton (2001) does not provide a definition for the concept of belief; nevertheless, his works show that he associates the concept of belief to a person's self-perception: "I feel ridiculous", "I'm no good". This perception refers to concept of self. With respect to this author and to ensure coherence with the present text, we will adopt the expression of self-perception in relation to the remarks of Gratton (2001) and will adjust these remarks to our concept of belief (Lafortune & Fennema, 2003).

Gratton (2001) upholds that applying skills related to critical thinking could be a valid strategy for the development of positive self-perception. Therefore, it would be possible to show pupils how to use critical thinking skills to favor "emotional well-being". For this author, it is important to remember that emotions stem in part from the way people perceive themselves when accomplishing a task, for example. If these perceptions greatly deform reality, they are conducive to the expression of inadequate and disturbing emotions (fear, sadness, ...), which could bring pupils to act inadequately. The following example illustrates this: a pupil, who exaggerates the consequences of failing a class, could experience fear, which will discourage him to repeat the class or which will lessen his ability to succeed in this class or in another. This example shows that when emotions arise from negative or inadequate self-perception, other disturbing emotions emerge and may lead to behavior or attitudes that are harmful to learning. Generally speaking, the critical thinker tries to act more constructively in his day-to-day actions.

Gratton (2001) gives two reasons why thinking critically is a relevant strategy to sustain a person's emotional well-being. The author upholds that critical thinking provides individuals with tools to help them adjust their self-perception and thus give them the power to avoid or eliminate unpleasant emotions or lessen their intensity, duration or frequency. Needless to say the purpose of practicing skills related to critical thinking is not the elimination of all unpleasant emotions. It is sometimes healthy and necessary to experience this type of emotion (Lafortune & Pons, 2004): for example, sadness when mourning or grieving over the loss a loved one, or anger when faced with an obvious injustice. Neither will practice of these skills lessen or eliminate certain pleasant and enjoyable emotions, especially since some pleasant emotions may also be based on inadequate perceptions. Eliminating them would amount to lessening or eliminating the pleasant emotions that are linked to them. In one case or the other, ignorance or irrationality may at times be beneficial and at other times harmful. Perhaps it is a question of helping the individual, who is discovering things about himself and about others, to become aware of the elements that are beneficial or harmful to his "emotional well-being" with an approach that is more respectful of his pace (Ennis, 1987; Facione, 2004). Gratton's remarks lead us to believe that the development of skills related to critical thinking may encourage individuals to take a reflective look at their ways of thinking and acting and thus adjust their perception of themselves. In this sense, the development of such skills would help a person attain a certain objectivity when faced with situations that produce emotions.

The objective pursued by Gratton (2001) is mainly to provide tools for pupils, so they can obtain the benefits of a strategy focused on the development of critical thinking to help define the irrational perspectives underlying their emotional reactions. Within this perspective, expression of critical thinking brings to mind that "Men are disturbed, not by the things that happen, but by the opinions generated by the things that happen" (Epictetus, 1991, p. 14, quoted by Gratton, 2001, p. 40).

Educational considerations

Thinking critically helps pupils evaluate a situation after examining several possibilities. Teaching critical thinking skills to learn how to control emotions inevitably leads to consequences of an educational nature. Interested by the educational application of a theory of emotions in teaching critical thinking, Gratton (2001) created a process based on a cognitive-behavioral approach. Although pupils for whom the approach was intended perceived the development of critical thinking classes as "useless mind gymnastics", the author noted that they were still willing to be taught the skills and attitudes a critical thinker must command. Moreover, given the clear advantages that this strategy allows them to apply to their "emotional life", pupils were encouraged to adapt these skills to other disciplines or fields of study as well as to their day-to-day activities. Finally, more pupils developed the intellectual ability to seriously evaluate their own judgments and interpretations. Following the adequate application of the strategy, they became aware that the fear or discomfort of experiencing certain educational situations, such as being evaluated by their peers, lessened.

Interventions

To Gratton's approach (2001), inspired from cognitive-behavioral trends, we have chosen to add elements of our socio-constructivist conception of learning and, in doing so, to make adjustments to what the author proposed. Among these changes, instead of speaking of steps to be achieved, we focus our intervention as an integrated entity; the theoretical aspect will be oriented towards discovery. Although based on the proposed model, the changes we make are important and take into account our concept of beliefs (beliefs refer to concepts and convictions). With this approach, it is important to bring pupils to construct a comprehension of the emotions (meta-emotion) at stake in different contexts and to expose the theoretical and applied aspects of the place of emotions in self-perception and beliefs.

Emotions and Self-Perception

Generally speaking, when we experience an emotion (consciously or not), it is because we have specifically thought of something. Here, the verb "to think" is used in its general sense, which includes concepts such as believing, inferring, explaining, judging, interpreting, and several others. For emotions such as fear (horror, terror, worry), a person may perceive some sort of threat. If the person becomes aware of this perception, its influence can be limited and fear considerably lessened. For example, a person who is afraid of giving a lecture may either avoid the situation or experience a great deal of stress. Simply demonstrating that the activity does not represent any danger is probably not enough for this person to counter his fear. However, the person who, in spite of apparent unease, persists in countering the irrational thoughts that sustain the fear associated with lecturing may come to realize that the emotions associated with fear lose their intensity, are less frequent or may almost disappear. Comprehension of emotions accompanied by positive experiences may lead to justification of possible occurrences and help a person circumvent the influence of irrational thoughts of fear or even of anxiety.

Critical thinking, self-perception and beliefs
If we deem that a belief is a necessary condition for expressing an emotion and that self-perception affects the existence, the intensity, the frequency or the duration of an emotion, then countering or rejecting this belief would be enough to greatly lessen the influence of this emotion. However, if we deem that a belief is sufficient for an emotion to be manifested, rejecting it is not enough to eliminate the negative influence of the emotion.

Gratton (2001) suggests an exercise that we adapted into our socio-constructive perspective. Using an event, an underlying belief and its resulting self-perception, pupils are asked to recognize the emotion at stake and provide an explanation that favors its understanding. This reflection helps to understand the relationships between emotions, beliefs and self-perception in a given situation.

Event	Belief	Perception of self	Emotion	Explanation
I have to give an oral presentation in class.	A person giving an oral presentation is ridiculous.	I feel ridiculous.	Embarrassment	
I have to give an oral presentation in class.	An oral presentation allows one to share ideas and can be pleasant.	I feel comfortable, and I feel like sharing my ideas.	Pleasure	
I have to give an oral presentation in class.	In an oral presentation, people always ask difficult questions.	I hope the pupils won't ask too many difficult questions.	Worry	
I failed the English test.	English tests are always difficult.	It's not my fault; the test was too difficult.	Frustration	
I failed the English test.	If you fail, you're no good.	I'm worthless.	Loss of self-worth	

The accomplishment of such a task not only provides a representation of beliefs, of self-perception, and of emotions linked to an event, but also provides explanations of the relationships worked out. Such a reflection, achieved in a development of critical thinking context, encourages pupils to adjust their perceptions. This in turn may influence the intensity of their emotions in subsequent and similar situations. This activity provides the opportunity for pupils to further their comprehension of the complexity of emotions and to explore questions such as "What beliefs are likely to sustain this emotion?" or "What could explain the emotions involved?"

Sometimes pupils rush their explanations or put forward interpretations characterized by a lack of reflection; emotions associated with these judgments or interpretations may then surface and exert a negative effect on learning and on communication. In another phase, and to further comprehension of the emotions at stake, the eight components of emotional competence, as defined by Saarni (1999), could be taken into account. This would better delimit the beliefs, self-perception, and emotions involved, and thus provide more elaborate explanations of what is happening.

1. The awareness of one's emotional states refers to recognition of emotions experienced and to their connection to the events that cause them.
2. The ability to recognize and understand other people's emotions is complementary to understanding one's own emotions.
3. The ability to use the language associated with emotions with words, images, symbols, makes it possible to communicate one's own emotional experience to others.
4. Capacity for empathy is a necessary component to create relationships with others.
5. The ability to differentiate internal subjective emotional experience from its external expression refers to the fact that a person does not always outwardly express emotions.
6. The capacity to control emotions of disgust or of distress by using self-regulation strategies helps bear high intensity emotions, over quite a long period.
7. Awareness of the nature of relationships or of communication depends on emotions and particularly on the degree of reciprocity and of symmetry in the relationship.
8. The capacity to accept emotional experiences and to develop a feeling of self-efficiency is tied to the personal belief in a socially acceptable emotional balance.

Thus, emotions are a precious source of information. For example, when we meet a person for the first time, we may feel distrust towards her without being aware that we had made a hasty judgment. Being able to recognize the emotion we experience at a specific time can help us become aware of "irrational" judgments, reevaluate a situation and, consequently adjust our interpretation or actions.

Evaluation
Through this process, it is important to bring pupils to use their critical thinking skills and evaluate beliefs that show relevant causality links. The task consists in identifying unfounded beliefs, to reject them or not, and to justify the fact that they are remote. This reflection helps pupils avoid overcoming emotions they believe are inappropriate or disturbing by using pretexts that stem from more or less justified beliefs.

Along the same lines, if the use of skills related to critical thinking aim to significantly improve "emotional well-being", learning to recognize and evaluate certain statements is essential. These statements stem from specific beliefs in various contexts. These statements entail practice or appeal to moral rules that bring to mind "what we should believe, do or evaluate in specific situations" (Gratton, 2001, p. 45). These statements refer to self-perception ("If I fail a test, I'm not worth much") or confine or limit a person's personal philosophy of life ("If I want to be happy, I have to be financially successful"). These statements have underlying emotions that influence choices and actions. More specifically, an unfounded statement might lead, in similar contexts, to the expression of inappropriate or disturbing emotions – to the extent that a person attaching importance to these statements – might end up in a vulnerable position in relation to these same emotions.

Situation	Belief	Statement	Emotion	Explanation
My friends didn't congratulate me on my success.	You have to congratulate a person that succeeds.	My friends should have congratulated me.	Anger/ Deception	
My teacher doesn't pay much attention to me.	A teacher ought to pay attention to all pupils.	My teacher should pay more attention to me.	Deception/ Frustration	

An incorrect evaluation or analysis of the situation might increase the person's vulnerability and bring out anger and frustration. The person might not receive the desired attention in similar situations and his "emotional well-being" might suffer.

5. Conclusion: Discussion and perspectives

In this chapter, we attempted to clarify the correlation between emotions and the expression of critical thinking. A line of questioning guided our reflection, such as: Can the manifestation of emotion or emotions influence – positively or negatively – the expression of critical thinking? Can the development of critical thinking influence expression or comprehension of emotions? Are there actions or interventions that would make it possible to improve emotion control, and subsequently favor the expression of critical thinking? Can the development of skills linked to critical thinking favor better control of emotions?

In regard to interventions, we observed that some authors rely on actions that encourage the expression of emotions whereas other actions focus on comprehension of emotions to learn to control them better. Comprehension of emotions is linked to an evaluation of the situation, to explanations and interpretations that rest on critical thinking. There may therefore exist a more emotional pathway (eliciting expression of emotions) and a more cognitive pathway to awareness of emotions (favoring comprehension of emotions: meta-emotion and emotional competence).

We believe that depending on the circumstances, either way can be valid. It may be necessary to bring emotions to the surface to get to know them and to foster pupils' awareness (becoming aware that emotions are involved); at other times, it may be necessary to understand the emotions involved and take a rather cognitive look at what is occurring. In a recently completed project, Lafortune (2004a; see also Lafortune, St-Pierre & Martin, 2005) conducted some exploratory research that suggests that persons intervening with pupils tend to choose either one of these options (bringing forth or understanding the emotions involved). We believe both options must be explored to make an informed decision, according to circumstances. We also feel that favoring comprehension of emotions and developing a critical perspective on the emotions involved is a means to refine the language of emotions used by persons in contact with pupils and the pupils themselves.

As a research perspective, we suggest researching the links between emotions and critical thinking in regard to interventions, so as to extend the idea that critical thinking is only about ideas and opinions, but also that it can help control emotions. To study the influence of interventions on the teaching/learning process, long-term research must be considered. Finally, the fact that development of critical thinking is linked to development of emotional competence, and vice versa, could provide food for thought.

References

Daniel, M.-F. (1998). *La philosophie et les enfants.* Montreal: Logiques.

Daniel, M.-F., Lafortune, L., Pallascio, R., Splitter, L., Slade, C., & De la Garza, T. (2005). Modeling the development process of dialogical critical thinking in pupils aged 10 to 12 years. *Communication Education,* 54(4), 334-354.

Daniel, M.-F., Lafortune, L., Pallascio, R., & Sykes, P. (1996). *Philosopher sur les mathématiques et les sciences.* Quebec: Le Loup de Gouttière.

Doudin, P.-A., & Martin, D. (1992). *De l'intérêt de l'approche métacognitive en pédagogie.* Lausanne: CVRP.

Ennis, R. (1985). *Critical thinking.* Upper Saddle River, NJ: Prentice-Hall.

Ennis, R. (1987). A Taxonomy of critical thinking dispositions and abilities. In J. Baron, & R. Sternberg (Eds.), *Teaching critical thinking skills: Theory and practice* (pp. 9-26). New York: W.H. Freeman.

Facione, P. (2004). *Critical thinking: What it is and why it counts?* California Academic Press, updated 2004, (http://www.insightassessment.com/pdf files/what&why2004.pdf) (consulted during the summer of 2004).

Facione, P., Facione, N., & Giancarlo, P. (2000). The Disposition Toward Critical Thinking: Its Character, Measurement, and Relationship to Critical Thinking Skill. *Informal Logic, 20 (1)*, 61-84.

Fazio, R.H. (1995). Attitudes as object-evaluation associations: Determinants, consequences, and correlates of attitude accessibility. In R.E. Petty, & J.A. Krosnick (Eds.), *Attitude Strength: antecedents and consequences* (pp. 247-282). Mahwah, NJ: Lawrence Erlbaum.

Gonzalez, V. (1997). Using critical thinking to stimulate in-service teachers's cognitive growth in multicultural education. *NYSABE Journal*, University of Arizona.

Gould, J., & Kolb, W. (1965). *A Dictionary of the Social Sciences* p. 232 (*Ego-Involvement*). New York: Free Press.

Gratton, C. (2001). Critical thinking and emotional well-being. *Inquiry: Critical thinking across the disciplines*, Spring, 20(3), 39-51.

Guilbert, L. (1999). La relation cognitivo-affective de la pensée critique: vers un modèle d'évaluation. In L. Guilbert, J. Boisvert, & N. Ferguson (Eds.), *Enseigner et comprendre* (pp. 81-98). Ste-Foy: Presses de l'Université Laval.

Hassel, C. (2003). Why Critical thinking? Minnesota, Regents of the University of Minnesota.

Khun, D. (1999). A developmental model of critical thinking. *Educational research, 28(2)*, 16-26.

Lafortune, L. with the collaboration of S. Cyr, S., & Massé, B., and the participation of Milot, G., and Milot, K. (2004a). *Travailler en équipe-cycle. Entre collègues d'une école.* Ste-Foy: Presses de l'Université du Québec.

Lafortune, L., & Fennema, E. (2003). Croyances et pratiques dans l'enseignement des mathématiques. In L. Lafortune, C. Deaudelin, P.-A. Doudin, & D. Martin (Eds.), *Croyances à l'égard des mathématiques, des sciences et des technologies* (pp. 29-55). Ste-Foy: Presses de l'Université du Québec.

Lafortune, L., & Lafortune, S. (2002). *Chères mathématiques. Susciter l'expression des émotions en mathématiques: Huit capsules video.* Ste-Foy: Presses de l'Université du Québec.

Lafortune, L., & Massé, B. with the collaboration of Lafortune, S. (2002). *Chères mathématiques. Des stratégies pour favoriser l'expression des émotions en mathématiques.* Ste-Foy: Presses de l'Université du Québec.

Lafortune, L., & Pons, F. (2004). Le rôle de l'anxiété dans la métacognition. In L.

Lafortune, P.-A. Doudin, F. Pons, & D.R. Hancock (Eds.), *Les émotions à l'école* (pp. 145-169). Ste-Foy: Les Presses de l'Université du Québec.

Lafortune, L., & Robertson, A. (2004). Métacognition et pensée critique: une démarche de mise en relation pour l'intervention. In R. Pallascio, M.-F. Daniel, & L. Lafortune (Eds.), *Pensée et réflexivité* (pp. 107-128). Ste-Foy: Presses de l'Université du Québec.

Lafortune, L., & St-Pierre, L. (1996). *L'affectivité et la métacognition dans la classe*. Montreal: Logiques.

Lafortune, L., St-Pierre, L., & Martin, D. (2005). Compétence émotionnelle dans l'accompagnement et l'analyse des manifestations des émotions dans un contexte de changement. In L. Lafortune, M.-F. Daniel, P.-A. Doudin, F. Pons, & O. Albanese (Eds.), *Pédagogie et psychologie des emotions* (pp. 87-118). Ste-Foy: Presses de l'Université du Québec.

Leader, L., & Middleton, J. (1999). From ability to actions: Designing instructional for critical thinking dispositions. Presentation at the *National Convention of the Association for Educational communications and technology*. 10-14 February. Houston.

Lipman, M. (1995). *À l'école de la pensée*. Brussels: De Boeck University Press.

Lipman, M. (1991). *Caring Thinking*. Presentation at the 6e conférence internationale sur la pensée. Boston, Massachusetts Institute of Technology.

Martin, B.L., & Briggs, L.J. (1986). *The Affective and Cognitive Domains: Integration for Instruction and Research*. New Jersey: Educational Technology Publications.

Middleton, J., & Toluk, Z. (1999). First steps in the development of an adaptive theory of motivation. *Educational psychologist, 34*, 37-49.

Ministère de l'Éducation. (2001). *Programme de formation de l'école québécoise : Éducation préscolaire, enseignement primaire*. Quebec: Gouvernement du Québec, Ministère de l'Éducation.

Ministère de l'Éducation. (2003). *Programme de formation de l'école québécoise: Enseignement secondaire, 1er cycle*. Quebec: Gouvernement du Québec, Ministère de l'Éducation.

Paul, R., Binker, A., Jensen, K., & Kreklau, H. (1990). *Critical thinking handbook: A guide for remodeling lesson plans in language arts, social studies and science*. Rohnert Park, CA: Foundation for Critical Thinking.

Pons, F., Doudin, P.-A., Harris, P.L., & de Rosnay, M. (2002). Métaémotion et intégration scolaire. In L. Lafortune, & P. Mongeau (Eds.), *L'affectivité dans l'apprentissage* (pp. 7-28). Ste-Foy: Presses de l'Université du Québec.

Saarni, C. (1999). *The Development of Emotional Competence*. New York: Guilford Press.

Scherer, K.R. (1994). Emotional control: variation and consequences. In P. Ekman, & R.J. Davidson (Eds.), *The nature of emotion* (pp. 273-279). New York: Oxford University Press.

Schwarz, N., & Clore, G.L. (1988). How do I feel about it? The informative function of affective states. In K. Fiedler, & J. Forgas (Eds.), *Affect, Cognition and Social Behavior* (pp. 44-62). Toronto: C.J. Hogrefe.

Swartz, R., & Perkins, D. (1989). *Teaching thinking: Issues and approaches*, Pacific Grove, CA: Midwest Publications.

CHAPTER 7

The development of emotional competency: Using interactive-reflexive activities as a family assistance program in mathematics[1]

Louise Lafortune

1. Introduction

The present Educational Reform in Quebec[2] (MEQ, 2001, 2003) is notably based on socio-constructivism and a program defined in terms of competency. This reform puts forward fundamental changes on both didactic and pedagogical levels which will not only influence pupil-teacher relationships in the classroom but also parental follow-up at home. Dodd and Konzal (1999) highlight the importance of fostering parents' awareness of the aims of these types of changes, while allowing them to participate in the actualization of the spirit of this reform. Parent involvement is particularly important when learning mathematics, since parents often feel helpless when faced with their children's mathematics homework. As significant contexts and complex tasks favor competency development, it is by understanding the meaning of these changes that parents will be able to help their children get involved in the mathematical activity and work with them rather than for them. For a number of parents, this means a change in the way they intervene in their child's homework. However, for the reform to take place in school, coherence between what is done in the classroom and the manner in which parents intervene is necessary (Dauber & Epstein, 1993; Hoover-Dempsey & Sandler, 1997). This coherence stimulates learning since youngsters do not feel compelled to defend their school methods when at home and vice-versa.

---

[1] We thank Nathalie Girardin and Bernard Massé, respectively for the translation and the revisions of the translation of this text.
[2] This Educational Reform in Quebec was initiated in September of 1999.

Although youngsters' difficulties in mathematics may stem from cognitive, metacognitive, or emotional aspects, we believe that parents can help their children develop positive attitudes toward mathematics without too much mathematical knowledge. For example, they can avoid using negative comments regarding mathematics, such as, "math is useless," or referring to their "supposed" inability to solve math problems with comments such as, "math just isn't for me" or "I don't have that kind of logic." We think parents can contribute to the development of their child's emotional competency in mathematics through their interventions, their non-verbal support, their encouragements, and also by understanding their children's emotions regarding this discipline. Previous works leads us to suppose that pupils are too often influenced by the beliefs they maintain toward mathematics, such as: "there is such a thing as a gift for math, and it is hereditary" (Lafortune, 1994, 2003a & b). Our interest in studying emotional competency in the relationship between parents and children concerning mathematics comes from a wish to understand youngsters' emotions regarding mathematics (a cognitive dimension) rather than simply encouraging them to express emotions towards mathematics. In our opinion, the latter choice limits the actions of teachers or parents. The motivation to treat emotional aspects according to a cognitive perspective comes from the works of Saarni (1999) and Pons, Doudin, Harris, and de Rosnay (2002). Our contribution consists in transposing their work to the field of mathematics learning.

In order to pursue the exploration of this problem, we will begin by summarizing the results[3] of a first research stage that attempts to validate Interactive-Reflexive Activities in mathematics to ensure a follow-up of school mathematics at home. Then, we will explain the three main concepts that underlie our chapter: emotions, meta-emotion, and emotional competency, while attaching particular importance to the third concept. We will also address the results of implementation as well as the evaluation of the implementation of Interactive-Reflexive Activities at home while specifically examining activities that deal with the emotional dimension in order to establish links with emotional competency. To pursue this reflection, we will address results of an exploratory study[4] that deals with pupil perceptions regarding what they suppose are their parent's beliefs regarding mathematics. The results of this exploration will serve to provide possible solutions and directions for future research.

---

[3] The Social Sciences and Humanities Research Council of Canada (SSHRC) (Lafortune and Deslandes, 2000-2003) has subsidized this research.
[4] This research has been subsidized by the Assistance for the Upcoming Generation of Students in Science and Technology (AUGSST) program of the *Ministère du Développement économique et régional* (MDER) (Lafortune, 2001-2003).

2. Validation of interactive-reflexive activities in mathematics

To better understand what teachers are willing to suggest to their pupils, what parents will agree to do with their children, and what youngsters would appreciate, we suggested some Interactive-Reflexive Activities (IRA) to teachers, parents and pupils in order to subsequently proceed to an experimentation stage (see Lafortune, 2003a & b for more details on this stage of research). During interviews, we consequently met with 16 parents from four different schools, their children, and 10 teachers (2 men and 8 women) who intervened with these children. The suggested activities were related to the following aspects: beliefs and prejudices, consideration of the emotional dimension, awareness of mental processes, practice of philosophical discussions in mathematics, creation of links between mathematics and daily activities, as well as integrative projects.

As a result of this validation process, teachers pointed out that classroom preparation is essential and that the activity completed at home must be followed up in class, to show the pupils that work done at home is just as important as work done in school. Furthermore, the teachers found it difficult to remember that the activities suggested were in keeping with a parental follow-up and implication. They were readily interested in using the activities in class, rather than keeping in mind that parents could contribute to the activities' success at home. The concern for homework to become the continuation of a reflection begun in the classroom, rather than simple practice of what was learned in class, has yet to be developed. In spite of the difficulty of keeping a parental perspective, the teachers we met were open to using innovative activities.

The parents we met were very open to this type of at-home activity, even if lack of time was often mentioned as a disincentive. Nevertheless, these parents felt that they must be given explanations in order to carry out this type of activity correctly. For them, this differs from usual practice, and they can hardly picture themselves, for example, starting up a philosophical-mathematical discussion with their child without having any reflection elements to sustain their ideas on a given subject. They do not wish to feel disadvantaged, if ever they are faced with situations that are either embarrassing or too different from what they are used to.

Several parents seemed at times to be unaware of their child's difficulties; and yet, youngsters would like to be heard-out by their parents, but without being told "well come on, I don't understand why you feel so stressed out, you're well prepared". They prefer to not say anything rather than hear this type of comment.

Youngsters are ambivalent towards their parents' interventions when they have to complete work at home. Parents are mistaken if they think they are being helpful by giving answers; youngsters do not want this kind of help. They prefer being given clues or a starting point to help them get "unstuck" and continue solving their math problems on their own. They do not want their parents to help by doing everything for them. They are well aware that this is not going to help them learn.

Our validation process showed the necessity of creating comprehension links between teachers, pupils, and parents. This comprehension could just as well concern the cognitive, meta-cognitive, or emotional dimensions. In this chapter, we choose to explore elements linked to the emotional dimension because of the negative attitudes of several pupils and parents regarding mathematics. Moreover, we believe that considering this dimension will have a positive influence on school-family interactions in learning mathematics in all the dimensions of learning. We therefore approach different concepts linked to the emotional dimension that will enable a better comprehension of the role of emotions in mathematics.

3. Theoretical concepts: Emotion, meta-emotion, and emotional competency

Difficulties experienced by pupils in mathematics may stem from various factors such as weaknesses in their knowledge of mathematics, different meanings given to problem statements (Baruk, 1973, 1977, 1985), language problems (natural, symbolic and graphic language) (De Serres & Groleau, 1997), beliefs and prejudices (Lafortune, Mongeau & Pallascio, 2000; Dehaene, 1997), as well as attitudes adopted toward mathematics (Anthony, 1996; Ma & Kishor, 1997; Fennema & Sherman, 1976; Goos & Galbraith, 1996; Jitendra & Xin, 1997; Lafortune, Mongeau, Daniel & Pallascio, 2000; McLeod, 1994; Meravech & Kramarski, 1997; Petit & Zawojwoski, 1997). These attitudes are linked to the emotions pupils feel toward this discipline.

Emotion

An emotion is an affective reaction, happy or painful, that appears in a number of ways (Sillamy, 1980). Several basic emotions have been identified, such as *fear, anger, joy, sadness, surprise, disgust,* and *distress* (among others, see Martin & Briggs, 1986). The emotions studied in the works of Lafortune (1992a and b) were anxiety, motivation and self-confidence. Among these elements, the emotion most studied in relation to learning mathematics is anxiety (Hatchuel, 2000; Kogelman & Warren, 1978; Lafortune, 1990, 1992a & b; Lafortune, Mongeau, Daniel & Pallascio, 2002a & b; Lafortune & Massé, 2002; Nimier, 1976, 1985;

Tobias, 1978, 1987, 1990; Weyl-Kailey, 1985; Zaslavsky, 1996). Lafortune and Pons (2004) suggest a perspective of anxiety towards mathematics that allows one to perceive this emotion as having an equally negative or positive influence. Parents who wish to help their children during evaluation situations could thus be made aware of this perspective. The fact that anxiety is the most studied emotion with regard to learning mathematics will influence the examples provided in a later section to explain the components of emotional competency.

Meta-emotion

According to Pons, Doudin, Harris, and de Rosnay (2002, p. 9), meta-emotion refers to "a subject's *comprehension* of the nature, the cause and the possibilities of controlling emotions. [. . . , as well as] the subject's capability to *regulate* the expression of an emotion and his or her emotional experience in a more or less unconscious and implicit manner". These authors consider the relationship between the comprehension of emotions and the ability to control them as fundamental. Even though we do not know of any studies regarding the development of meta-emotion when learning mathematics, we believe that if pupils understand the nature and the cause of their anxiety toward mathematics, they will be better prepared to ensure that these emotions do not keep them from succeeding in the mathematical activity according to their capabilities and abilities. Furthermore, understanding the source of anxiety will diminish the influence of causal attributions related to the belief that success in mathematics stems from superior talent or parental genetics. Beliefs such as these are excellent pretexts to avoid making the efforts necessary to succeed.

Meta-emotion is, according to us, a component of emotional competency that attaches as much importance to understanding one's emotions as to understanding the emotions of others. Since we consider learning in a socio-constructivist perspective (Jonnaert & van der Broght, 1999; Lafortune and Deaudelin, 2001), and since our research places learners in interaction with others, we approach the problem of parental assistance in mathematics at home using the framework of emotional competency. We feel this aspect must be considered in a socio-constructivist perspective because emotional competency equally emphasizes recognition and comprehension of ones emotions in interrelation and interaction with those of others.

Emotional competency

Saarni (1999) is the author who provides the most comprehensive explanation concerning emotional competency by explicitly defining eight components which we will clarify by formulating and then explaining each component. We will also specify the meaning of each component for parents' interventions in mathematics and for pupils learning this discipline. Few authors treat this concept (Webster-Stratton, 1999); however, our readings and our previous research shows that explanations of emotional competency are closely tied to what Harris (1985, 1989, 1995) reports on the comprehension of children's emotions. According to these authors, the development of emotional competency is not only reserved for teachers; it also concerns the parental relationship.

First component
The awareness of one's own emotional states refers to awareness of one's emotions and to the ties between the emotions and the events that cause them. This awareness relates to meta-emotion, which requires awareness to comprehend emotions and to make adjustments that consider this comprehension. Mongeau and Tremblay (2002) speak of conscious attention, which may be linked to awareness of one's own emotional states. According to them, this conscious attention produces a desire to act to get rid of any uneasiness, such as discomfort. In spite of the fact that these authors refer to conscious attention, they consider that the reaction towards discomfort can be instantaneous, unconscious and reflex-triggered, or it can stem from a well-thought-out and differed analysis.

We believe that parents must become aware of the emotions that mathematics trigger in them to better recognize their source. This awareness can help them avoid perpetuating in their children the idea that their troubles with math stem from genetic problems and, thus, help them avoid telling their children, "it is normal for you to find mathematics difficult, I had as much trouble as you when I was in school" or "failing math is a family problem". In addition, youngsters who are aware of the emotions they feel towards mathematics may consider it normal to feel emotions even if they believe mathematics to be a neutral, objective, and rational discipline. According to us, when solving problems, awareness of one's own emotions in mathematics is essential. Thus, this ability is central to emotional competency.

Second component
The ability to discern and understand others' emotions is complementary to understanding one's own emotions. The more we know about others' emotions, the more it is possible to understand what is happening emotionally in ourselves. This component of emotional competency demonstrates the importance of looking into the construction process of emotions in order to accept not only the limits of one's own emotions, but also those of others (Lafortune, 2004a). Moreover, this component of emotional competency is tied to transversal

competencies of the personal and social order, whose purpose is actualizing one's potential and co-operating, which means knowledge of self as well as knowledge of others (MEQ, 2004).

This component of emotional competency is important for parents who want to know and understand their children's emotions. This aspect is particularly important when learning mathematics; for parents tend not to recognize the stress this discipline may cause in their children (Lafortune, 2003a and b). Recognizing that one's child can feel emotions towards mathematics has a positive impact on communication and can diminish the negative impact of emotions such as anxiety. Knowing and understanding the emotions of others can help pupils compare themselves to others and thus feel less isolated in their experience of mathematics. However, in order for comparisons with the emotions of others to be relevant and not to give rise to low self-esteem, a better awareness of one's own emotions (first component) is essential.

Third component
The ability to use the vocabulary linked to emotions especially using words, images, and symbols enables one to communicate one's personal emotional experience to others and to access representations of one's own emotional experiences. This in turn makes it possible to place them in a context and to compare them with the representations of others.

Within the parent-child relationship, this component of emotional competency fosters discussions and emotion sharing; it is not limited to putting a name to the experienced emotions but rather attempts to explain or justify them. Lafortune and Massé (2002), and Lafortune and Lafortune (2002) suggest means to foster the expression of pupils' emotions regarding mathematics; these means are presented in grids of reflection, subjects of discussion, mathematical tasks, process-sharing, and video briefs. Lafortune and Mongeau (2003a and b) suggest an approach through drawing, whereby pupils express their emotions by drawing mathematics. These means are directly associated to pupils' emotions. Finally, Lafortune, Mongeau, Daniel, and Pallascio (2002a and b) encourage pupils to speak of emotions in mathematics by using a philosophical approach. This approach encourages pupils to visualize emotions and thus address them in a conceptual manner.

Fourth component
The capacity for empathy is the component that is necessary to establish relationships with others. According to Saarni (1999), empathy refers to feeling *with* others and sympathy refers to feeling *for* others; these states of affection enable

one to communicate with others. According to Legendre (1993, p. 488), empathy is the "capacity to identify the emotions and representations of others"; since it is a capacity, it can be developed and learnt.

Parents' empathy regarding their children's emotions towards mathematics entails that they are aware that their child can feel and explain their emotions. Hence, the parent will be sensitive to the explanations of a child following a failure in mathematics. The child feels he or she is seen as a person that may have failed not because of lack of potential, but rather because of his or her emotions. This empathy can also be useful to pupils with respect to understanding and helping each other out when having trouble in mathematics. This empathy helps establish links between one's experience and that of others.

Fifth component
The ability to differentiate internal subjective emotional experience from its external expression refers to the fact that a person does not always express emotions outwardly for fear of the negative effect the reaction of others might produce on his or herself. Understanding this phenomenon greatly improves relationships with others. Developing this aspect of emotional competency fosters causal attributions that are relevant to the situation and lead to increased coherence between thoughts and actions (Thagard, 2000).

With regard to learning mathematics, parents ought to pay attention to the difference between what their children express and what they feel. Lafortune (2003a) notes research results where youngsters prefer telling their parents they do not feel any stress during math evaluations, because, too often, their parents answer, "How come you feel stressed if you're well prepared?" Youngsters feel misunderstood and on subsequent occasions will choose to remain quiet. We have noticed that, generally, boys prefer to show indifference and girls show anxiety (Lafortune, Mongeau, Daniel and Pallascio, 2002a; Lafortune and Fennema, 2002, 2003). We now question ourselves as to the purport of these emotions. Are they exaggerated? Do they correspond to what is being felt? Are they a social construct associated to either gender?

Sixth component
The capacity for self-regulation when coping with aversive emotions and distressing circumstances makes it possible to withstand emotions of great intensity for quite a long period. This capacity presupposes the development of self-regulating strategies that induce adjustments while emotions are felt. It may be that using a "meta outlook" during emotional experiences is necessary to understand what is happening. This "meta outlook" enables one to see what is happening as it is

happening and to act accordingly (Lafortune and Martin, 2004). This capacity can develop the ability to highlight positive aspects of supposedly negative emotions such as anxiety towards mathematics (Lafortune and Pons, 2004).

When helping their children with mathematics, parents could avoid showing negative reactions towards mathematics, as these reactions may cause youngsters to think that mathematics should be avoided because of resulting fears, uneasiness, or tension. One way of doing this is agreeing to search for solutions with the child and getting involved in the mathematical activity. As for pupils, they would benefit from exchanging on their strategies in situations where negative emotions arise, since these emotions deprive them of the means to solve mathematical problems (Lafortune and Massé, 2002).

Seventh component
Awareness of the nature of relationships or communications depends on emotions and particularly on the degree of reciprocity and symmetry in the relationship. This component integrates previously described components and encourages the person to become aware that not everyone communicates emotions in the same manner, which influences relationships with others. This component can be associated with the transversal competency "communicating appropriately" of the Quebec School Training Program (MEQ, 2001, 2003). This competency presupposes, for example, that managing communication leads to the consideration of factors (such as emotions) that facilitate or hinder communication and thus to an adjustment according to the listeners' reactions.

This awareness is important for parents who wish to help their children learn mathematics; it enables them to listen to their children in a manner that encourages communication, since youngsters may come to avoid communicating their emotions or asking for help if they sense their parents' aversion towards mathematics.

Eighth component
The capacity to accept one's emotional experiences and to develop a feeling of self-efficiency is linked to personal beliefs in a socially acceptable emotional balance. This means that we build our own theory of emotions, which develops our feeling of emotional self-efficiency.

Parents who look into their own emotional experiences in mathematics can improve their feeling of competency in supporting their children. Bouffard and Bordeleau (2002, p. 199) show that "the more the parents' feeling of self-efficiency is high and the more they believe in the role the parents play in the development of the child, the more their educational practices are positive".

The development of this component of emotional competency is important for parents. For youngsters, accepting that mathematics can bring out emotions such as anxiety or pleasure can contribute to increasing self-esteem and to valuing the process used in solving math problems.

Prior to demonstrating how emotional competency can be linked to the use of Interactive-Reflexive Activities at home, we present the result of the implementation of such activities in intervention programs developed by teachers participating in the research.

4. Implementation and evaluation of the implementation of interactive-reflexive activities: description and results

The teachers who participated in the implementation of Interactive-Reflexive Activities (IRA) promoting assistance with school mathematics at home created their own intervention program (comprising 5 to 8 activities) from 29 activities developed following the validation process described in section 1 (Lafortune, 2002). The majority of teachers that participated in this stage of the research had collaborated in the validation stage. Pupils and parents who collaborated came from these teachers' classrooms. The pupils were between 8 and 15 years old.[5] The activities came within the scope of three categories: 1) beliefs and prejudices, 2) meta-cognition and reflection, and 3) the emotional dimension (see Lafortune 2003 a and b for more details.) Here, we will study some results of the implementation of IRA in the "emotional dimension" category.

The IRA that fall within the direct scope of the emotional dimension develop the following activities:
- Highlighting the positive and negative aspects associated with mathematics and reflecting upon them, within the framework of parent-child communication;
- Writing a text on personal advancement in mathematics or on perceptions about this discipline (boredom, uselessness, …) so that these can be discussed within the family;
- Giving parents reflection sheets regarding interventions with their children which touch on the emotional dimension (relating to progress, to questions asked, to emotional reactions . . .);

---

[5] The teachers who participated in the previous stage sometimes changed teaching levels. Moreover, other teachers joined in, because of interest or because they believed, from their knowledge of the material (even if minimal), that they could adapt the activities to the pupils in their level.

- Providing parents with the means to discuss their children's stress during math exams, in order to better manage it;
- Learning that making mistakes can be less alarming by trying to understand their source through reflection at home;
- As a family, exploring the place of mathematics in games (board, card, dice…).

Some parents were interviewed by the teachers and transcripts of these interviews were analyzed. This analysis led to certain results. In the present text, we present some of the results that concern the emotional dimension. For example, in a process of reflection and writing, a teacher asked pupils to write a text based on the characteristics that they felt distinguished a successful pupil from a pupil that who does not feel like succeeding. According to a parent, this activity enabled his child to have *a better perception of stress in math*; another adds that *it enables a child to question his (or her) success*. As such, this type of activity seems to foster awareness. The majority of pupils appreciated doing this activity at home; as mentioned by a pupil, *it gave [him] a good idea of what a person who is successful in mathematics is like* and another adds that he *likes to participate in activities with [his] parents*.

A teacher met the parents (10) whose children had the most negative emotional reactions towards mathematics. After discussing with these parents, she handed out some explanation sheets to help them improve their interventions with their children. The explanation sheets dealt with "showing there is progress even in the absence of success"; with "repeating over and over that solutions do not spontaneously appear in one's mind"; with "getting youngsters to talk about their emotional reactions" and finally, with "believing in the child's capacity to succeed." Seven parents out of ten held discussions with their children. According to this teacher, the pupils *were given an opportunity to discuss their feelings with their parents; [. . .] noted that they are not alone in experiencing [negative feelings]; [. . . realized] that by speaking out, they can find help and comfort; [. . .] found solutions to their problems*. According to her, they started developing better self-confidence and self-esteem. She adds that parents came *to know their children better; to communicate [with their child and to develop] a new way of encouraging their child*. The parents on their part *believe that these activities can help their child adopt a positive attitude*.

Two teachers encouraged pupils to discuss the stress they experience during math evaluations. A teacher allowed the pupils to begin a discussion, as a group, in class, about the manifestations of stress: the moment in which it arises and the means used to manage it. Subsequently, a questionnaire was completed at home to initiate a family discussion; its content was then used in class for a follow-up. Another teacher gave a letter to parents that contained questions to elicit a reflection regarding what their child experiences in mathematics. Discussions were then carried out, both in class and at home. This experience led a teacher to underline the fact that she was surprised to hear parents say their children were not talkative on the subject, because in the classroom, *pupils had much to say*. A teacher adds: *This made me realize how much stress the children experience, whether in sports activities, at home or in school. This activity also allowed parents to consider lessening their demands, since they had a tendency to ask for too much. The pupils and I were able to find sources of stress, symptoms, and means to help them out. Once again, parents enjoyed discussing with their child. As such, they were able to increase their understanding of their child's stress. In addition, the realization that mom and dad also experience stress made the situation less awesome.*

Solving mathematical problems at home and discussing causes of errors led parents to make three types of comments. This activity brought out feelings of insecurity in parents that had to find errors in previously solved problems. It also made them think of causes of errors, such as distraction, a false sense of simplicity, or speed. Parents were appreciative; they said they had a better understanding of how teaching mathematics evolved.

By searching for mathematical aspects found in some games, according to a teacher, youngsters were able to think about the strategies they use. *Parents enjoyed participating* in this activity and both children and *parents realized that there are a lot of mathematics in games*. According to parents, this exchange enabled them to draw closer to their children with regard to their experiences in class; some parents added that this activity was much *more motivating than paper-and-pencil homework.*

5. Links with emotional competency

In the results of the implementation of IRA, we note that some parents and pupils became aware of the existence of emotions related to mathematics, for example that mathematics can cause tension (success, errors and stress during exams) but also pleasure (board games). These realizations are linked to the first and third components of emotional competency that show the importance of being aware of one's own emotions, and of having words to express these emotions. By discerning their child's emotions in mathematics (2nd component), parents were able to put their capacity for empathic involvement to the test (4th component). However, during the validation phase, some youngsters indicated that parents had to evolve in their understanding of their child. The majority of pupils questioned seemed to say that parents exaggerate in their attempts to support them in their studies at home. One boy related that *[it is] not that I enjoy not studying with [my parents], but it's because my mother wants us to succeed so much. . . She pretty much exaggerates. Every two minutes, she would ask me to study. Instead, I don't talk to her about it and I study a little bit every day and I tell her "Yes, yes. I studied very, very, very much." Actually, I just studied a little bit. Because before, I tried telling her "No, I haven't really studied" and she said, "OK, let's go." We spent almost half an hour studying the same thing. It's not very pleasant.*

Along the same lines, in a study in which we asked some youngsters to "Draw math," in an explanatory sentence of his drawing, a youngster wrote, "Math is like my mom: bothersome." These comments from youngsters show that parent-child communication can be improved with regard to school follow-up at home.

In this project, we believe that parent and child awareness has begun to develop (components 5 to 8) regarding the place of emotions in learning mathematics and in the parental relationship at the school level. However, we think that the implementation of such activities should be pursued beyond the use of 5 to 8 activities. Homework could be adapted in order for parental follow-up at home to contribute to the development of emotional competency, especially regarding learning mathematics.

This reflection on the development of parents' emotional competency to help their children in mathematics is completed by the children's perception of their parents' beliefs regarding this discipline. This perception shows that parent-child communication concerning the learning of mathematics must be improved, mostly with regard to the development of emotional competency in both youngsters and adults.

6. Pupil perceptions regarding parent beliefs toward mathematics

On an exploratory basis, in order to sustain our reflection concerning beliefs about mathematics and emotions towards this discipline, we asked youngsters in their last year of elementary school what they thought their parents would draw if asked to *Draw Mathematics* (see Lafortune and Mongeau 2003a, for more details). The following questions were used as a starting point to collect data: "If your parents were asked to draw mathematics, what would they draw? Why would they have done those drawings?" and "What do your parents say about mathematics at home?" The results of this exploration could provide clues to possible interventions with pupils for discussions at home.

We note that several youngsters think their mother would draw a rather negative image of mathematics. They would express this as follows: *I am pretty sure that [. . .my mother would draw herself] helping me out because she finds it very [difficult] to help me. She doesn't understand anything [...] because she didn't learn the same method. My mother would draw someone that has [trouble]. A balloon, [...] a question mark, a question mark, a question mark. Because my mother didn't learn math very much. She finds it hard. She would draw a big black cloud because she doesn't like math and problems really aren't her strong point. My mother, I think it would be muddled because she works a little with numbers, but I don't know if she likes to.*

Some mothers' perceptions would be positive either because they studied in the field of mathematics or sciences or simply because they like mathematics. For example, a youngster suggests that his mother would draw *a big heart with math written inside*.

According to the pupils, some fathers seem to have a negative representation. For example, one father would draw *a big grey cloud with lightning inside* and another *draw [something] muddled*. However, other fathers are perceived as having a rather positive image of math. In this sense, a youngster emphasizes that *[his] father would draw someone doing a problem [...] He would be concentrated* and another adds that *[his] father would surely invent a problem or he would write down a whole bunch of answers because [his] father is really good at mathematics.*

These results show that exchanges between parents and children regarding emotions toward mathematics – whether those of the youngsters or their parents – could influence the development of pupils' emotional competency in mathematics. To further these results, it would be interesting for the pupils to ask their parents to draw mathematics and discuss their thoughts on the subject with them. This would be akin to the IRA implementation project to be done at home with the parents.

7. Interpretation, discussion and conclusion

From the results presented in this text, it can be surmised that parents have a role to play in youngsters' attitudes toward mathematics. Their influence may be due to their own emotional reactions concerning this discipline, to the manner in which they help their child, or to their understanding of the source of their child's trouble. As such, it seems important to develop emotional competency in mathematics, in parents just as in pupils. We believe that a number of parents find it difficult to help their children because they transfer their feelings regarding mathematics to their child, either by exaggerating the difficulty of participating in the mathematical activity, or by avoiding helping their child, or by giving away the entire problem-solving process in an attempt to be helpful. According to us, the development of emotional competency in mathematics, for both parents and pupils, leads to more judicious exchanges, to attentive listening, and to a mutual understanding of difficulties encountered and emotions experienced.

According to the results presented in this chapter, parents' comments drive youngsters away and keep many of them from asking for help. Lehrer and Shumow (1997) show that, more than teachers, parents tend to help their child by controlling the problem-solving process he or she suggests while the children prefer to be given clues. As school years go by, lack of parent comprehension regarding their children's needs causes a decrease in exchanges, and parents end up no longer knowing what their children do in school — which they deplore. Youngsters eventually develop ready-made sentences that close the door to any help from their parents. Yet, youngsters could benefit from this help and would like to take advantage of it, but they prefer to manage on their own, or with their schoolmates, so as not to be subjected to undue tension and the stifling attention of their parents.

We also note that it is difficult for teachers to adopt a parental perspective when teaching. This parental perspective presupposes a concern for the possibility of pursuing certain classroom activities at home. Spontaneously, the teachers consider suggested activities according to what can be done in the classroom. We believe heightening teacher awareness would be relevant in helping parents participate in their children's learning of mathematics. As such, using IRA is a relevant means to stimulate exchanges at home, without limiting homework to practicing repetitive exercises that complete what was learnt in class.

We would like to emphasize the fact that the teachers we met were open to using innovative activities to teach mathematics. We know that we cannot compel teachers to innovate in this sense. However, meeting with them could help heighten their awareness of the relevance of using IRA. A single parent (out of 9 classrooms; approximately 200 pupils) refused to sign the protocol allowing his child to participate in this experience. This leads us to suppose that parents are open to collaboration and to the exploration of new avenues.

Furthermore, youngsters that predict their parents' drawings seem to bestow rather negative reactions upon their mother, in comparison to those bestowed upon their father. When learning mathematics, these differences in reactions according to gender can have a negative influence on girls who, although they enjoy as much success as boys do, do not choose fields with high concentrations of mathematics, science and technology as often as boys do. Girls perpetuate stereotypes regarding their ability to use technology (Lafortune and Solar, 2003). Heightening parent awareness in relation to this situation could help girls reduce their anxiety toward mathematics and increase their self-confidence. Such an action could also help boys who express indifference, by giving them the opportunity to express what is hidden behind this lack of motivation.

In this text, we wished to present results of a process of validation and implementation of Interactive-Reflexive Activities for an at-home follow-up of classroom mathematics. Following an explanation of emotional competency, we attempted to explain the contribution of the implementation of IRA to the development of such a competency. To these results, we added those of an exploratory process where youngsters present their perception of their parents' attitudes toward mathematics.

Results show that teachers are open to using innovative activities to ensure an at-home follow-up of classroom mathematics and that they made some discoveries regarding the knowledge parents have of their children. They realized that youngsters do not speak much with their parents about the stress they experience in mathematics. However, teachers do not seem to realize that several youngsters keep silent because of parental pressure and that they would like to have better communication with their parents. As to the parents, they deplore the fact that they lose track of what youngsters do in class as they progress in school, but they do not realize that they try too hard to help their youngsters. The latter would prefer a nudge or a clue rather than an answer or a complete process. Youngsters prefer to exchange with their parents without feeling judged or without giving their father or mother a cause for concern.

To pursue this work, we would have to take a closer look at the effect(s) of using IRA on the emotional competency of youngsters and parents. To this end, we could meet youngsters and their parents to foster awareness of the parental relationship in mathematics, before carrying on with the experimentation stage. We believe the implementation of IRA would be more profitable and would give rise to an increase in parent awareness. It would then be easier to communicate with them, to discover and to understand how they evolve when using this approach.

We could also take a closer look at the role of parents according to gender (mother or father) with regard to the attitudes youngsters adopt toward mathematics. How do influences differ according to gender? How could we elicit parental awareness of these influences?

In addition to studying the role of emotional competency, we could add that of social competency. Webster-Stratton (1999) relates these two competencies in the parental relationship; this seems important to do from a child's earliest years. With regard to learning mathematics, this could equally influence emotions concerning this discipline and beliefs that hinder the learning process.

Moreover, it would be interesting to help teachers in developing a parental perspective; which is to say a concern with parental follow-up at home in mathematics. The development of such a perspective could orient the manner in which several activities are accomplished in school, so that they may be pursued at home. This would be a way of showing that the educational reform provides means to communicate with one's child, furthering its implementation.

References

Anthony, G. (1996). Active learning in a constructivist framework. *Educational Studies in Mathematics, 31*, 349-369.

Baruk, S. (1973). *Échec et maths.* Paris: Éditions du Seuil.

Baruk, S. (1977). *Fabrice ou l'école des mathématiques.* Paris: Éditions du Seuil.

Baruk, S. (1985). *L'âge du capitaine: de l'erreur en mathématiques.* Paris: Éditions du Seuil.

Bouffard, T., & Bordeleau, L. (2002). Le rôle des parents dans l'ontogénèse des ressources motivationnelles du jeune élève. In L. Lafortune, & P. Mongeau (Eds.), *L'affectivité dans l'apprentissage* (pp. 185-207). Sainte-Foy: Presses de l'Université du Québec.

Dauber, S.L., & Epstein, J.L. (1993). Parents' attitudes and practices of involvement in inner-city elementary and middle schools. In N. Chavkin (Ed.), *Families and Schools in a Pluralistic Society* (pp. 53-71). Albany, NY: Suny Press.

De Serres, M., & Groleau, J.D. (1997). *Mathématiques et langages.* Montréal: Collège Jean-de-Brébeuf.

De Serrec, M. (Ed.) (2003). *Intervenirsur les langages en mathématiques et en sciences.* Montréal: Modulo.

Dehaene, S. (1997). *La bosse des maths.* Paris: Odile Jacob.

Dodd, A.W., & Konzal, J.L. (1999). *Making our High Schools Better.* New-York: St. Martin's Press.

Fennema, E., & Sherman, J.A. (1976). Fennema-Sherman mathematics attitude scales: Instruments designed to measure attitudes toward the learning of mathematics by females and males. *JSAS Catalog of Selected Documents in Psychology* (Wisconsin Center for Education Research, University of Wisconsin-Madison), *1225*(6), 31.

Goos, M., & Galbraith, P. (1996). Do it this way! Metacognitive strategies in collaborative mathematical problem solving. *Educational Studies in Mathematics,*

30, 229-260.

Harris, P.L. (1985). What children know about the situations that provoke emotion. In M. Lewis, & C. Saarni (Eds.), *The socialization of emotions* (pp. 161-185). New York: Plenum.

Harris, P.L. (1989). *Children and emotion: The development of psychological understanding.* Oxford: Basil Blackwell.

Harris, P.L. (1995). Children's awareness and lack of awareness of mind and emotion. In D. Cicchetti, & S. Thoth (Eds.), *Rochester Symposium on Developmental Psychopathology: Emotion, Cognition and Representation*, Volume 6 (pp. 35-57). Rochester, NY: University of Rochester Press.

Hatchuel, F. (2000). *Apprendre à aimer les mathématiques.* Paris: Presses Universitaires de France.

Hoover-Dempsey, K.V., & Sandler, H.M. (1997). Why do parents become involved in their children's education? *Review of Educational Research,* 67(1), 3-42.

Jitendra, A., & Xin, Y.P. (1997). Mathematical word-problem-solving instruction for students with mild disabilities and students at risk for math failure: A research synthesis. *Journal of Special Education,* 30, 412-438.

Jonnaert, P., & Masciotra, D. (Eds.) (2004). *Constructivisme. Choix contemporains. Hommage à Ernst von Glaserfeld.* Sainte-Foy: Presses de l'Université du Québec.

Jonnaert, P., & van der Borght, C. (1999). *Créer des conditions d'apprentissage: Un cadre de référence socioconstructiviste pour une formation didactique des enseignants.* Brussels: De Boeck University Press.

Kogelman, S., & Warren, J. (1978). *Mind over Math.* New York: McGraw-Hill.

Lafortune, L. (1992a). *Élaboration, implantation et évaluation d'implantation à l'ordre collégial d'un plan d'intervention andragogique en mathématiques portant sur la dimension affective en mathématiques.* Doctoral thesis, Montréal: Université du Québec à Montréal.

Lafortune, L. (1992b). *Dimension affective en mathématiques, Recherche-action et matériel didactique.* Mont-Royal: Modulo Éditeur.

Lafortune, L. (1994). *Des maths au-delà des mythes.* Montréal: CECM.

Lafortune, L. (2002). *Suivi scolaire en mathématiques à la maison. Activités interactives-réflexives.* Unpublished manuscript used for the implementation of intervention programs.

Lafortune, L. (2003). Le suivi parental en mathématiques: intervenir sur les croyances. In L. Lafortune, C. Deaudelin, P-A. Doudin, & D. Martin (Eds.), *Conceptions, croyances et représentations en maths, sciences et technos* (pp. 121-145). Sainte-Foy: Presses de l'Université du Québec.

Lafortune, L. (2004a). Des intuitions constructivists. In P. Jonnaert, & D.

Masciotra (Eds.), *Des réflexions constructivists* (pp. 187-196). Sainte-Foy: Presses de l'Université du Québec.

Lafortune, L. (2004b). Des activités interactives-réflexives pour favoriser le lien école-famille: une démarche de validation, In *Actes du GDM*.

Lafortune, L., & Deaudelin, C. (2001). *Accompagnement socioconstructiviste. Pour s'approprier une réforme en education.* Sainte-Foy: Presses de l'Université du Québec.

Lafortune, L., & Fennema, E. (2002). Situations des filles à l'égard des mathématiques: anxiété et stratégies utilisées. *Recherches féministes, 15(1)*, 7-24.

Lafortune, L., & Fennema, E. (2003). Anxiété exprimée et stratégies utilisées en mathématiques: une comparaison entre les filles et les garcons. In L. Lafortune, & C. Solar (Eds.), *Femmes et maths, sciences et technos* (pp. 205-224). Sainte-Foy: Presses de l'Université du Québec.

Lafortune, L., & Lafortune, S. (2002). *Chères mathématiques. Susciter l'expression des émotions en mathématique: Huit capsules video.* Sainte-Foy: Presses de l'Université du Québec.

Lafortune, L., & Martin, D. (2004). L'accompagnement: processus de coconstruction et culture pédagogique. In M. D'Hostie, & L.-P. Boucher (Eds.), *L'accompagnement en education* (pp. 47-62). Sainte-Foy: Presses de l'Université du Québec.

Lafortune, L., & Massé, B. with the collaboration of Lafortune, S. (2002). *Chères mathématiques. Des stratégies pour favoriser l'expression des émotions en mathématiques.* Sainte-Foy: Presses de l'Université du Québec.

Lafortune, L., & Mongeau, P. (2003a). Les dessins des élèves: des révélateurs des croyances à l'égard des mathématiques et des sciences. In L. Lafortune, C. Deaudelin, P-A. Doudin, & D. Martin (Eds.), *Conceptions, croyances et représentations et maths, sciences et technologies* (pp. 59-90). Sainte-Foy: Presses de l'Université du Québec.

Lafortune, L., & Mongeau, P. (2003b). Approche des mathématiques par le dessin: une analyse qualitative et quantitative de dessins. In L. Lafortune, C. Deaudelin, P.-A. Doudin, & D. Martin (Eds.), *Conceptions, croyances et représentation en maths, sciences et technologies* (pp. 91-120). Sainte-Foy: Presses de l'Université du Québec.

Lafortune, L., Mongeau, P., Daniel, M.F., & Pallascio, R. (2000). Approche philosophique des mathématiques et affectivité: premières measures. In R. Pallascio, & L. Lafortune (Eds.), *Pensée réflexive et education.* Sainte-Foy: Presses de l'Université du Québec.

Lafortune, L., Mongeau, P., & Pallascio, R. (2000). Une mesure des croyances et préjugés à l'égard des mathématiques. In R. Pallascio, & L. Lafortune (Eds.),

Pour une pensée réflexive et education (pp. 209-232). Sainte-Foy: Presses de l'Université du Québec.

Lafortune, L., Mongeau, P., Daniel, M.L., & Pallascio, R. (2002a). Anxiété à l'égard des mathématiques: applications et mise à l'essai d'une approche philosophique. In L. Lafortune, & P. Mongeau (Eds.), *L'affectivité dans l'apprentissage* (pp. 49-79). Sainte-Foy: Presses de l'Université du Québec.

Lafortune, L., Mongeau, P., Daniel, M.F., & Pallascio, R. (2002b). Philosopher sur les mathématiques: Évolution du concept de soi et des croyances attributionnelles de contrôle. In L. Lafortune, & P. Mongeau (Eds.), *L'affectivité dans l'apprentissage* (pp. 27-48). Sainte-Foy: Presses de l'Université du Québec.

Lafortune, L., & Pons, F. (2004). Rôle de l'anxiété dans la métacognition: une réflexion vers des actions. In L. Lafortune, P.-A. Doudin, F. Pons, & D. Hanckock (Eds.), *Intervenir sur les émotions à l'école* (pp. 145-169). Sainte-Foy: Presses de l'Université du Québec.

Lafortune, L., & Solar, C. (2003). L'utilisation des technologies en mathématiques et en sciences: réactions des filles et des garçons au cégep. In L. Lafortune, & C. Solar (Eds.), *Femmes et maths, sciences et technos* (pp. 43-76). Sainte-Foy: Presses de l'Université du Québec.

Legendre, R. (1993). *Dictionnaire actuel de l'éducation.* Montréal-Paris: Guérin-Eska.

Lehrer R., & Shumow, L. (1997). Aligning the construction zones of parents and teachers for mathematics reform. *Cognition and Instruction, 15*(1), 41-83.

Ma, X., & Kishor, N. (1997). Assessing the relationship between attitude toward mathematics and achievement in mathematics: A meta-analysis. *Journal for Research in Mathematics Education, 28(1)*, 26-47.

Martin, B.L., & Briggs, J.L. (1986). *The affective and cognitive domains: integration for instruction and research.* New Jersey: Educational Technology Publications.

Martinez, J.G.R., & Martinez, N.C. (1996). *Math without fear.* Boston: Allyn and Bacon.

McLeod, D.B. (1994). Research on affect and mathematics learning in the JRME: 1970 to the present. *Journal for Research in Mathematics Education, 25*(6), 637-647.

Meravech Z.R., & Kramarski, B. (1997). A multidimensional method for teaching mathematics in heterogeneous classrooms. *American Educational Research Journal, 34,* 365-394.

Ministère de l'Éducation (2001). *Programme de formation de l'école québécoise. Éducation préscolaire. Enseignement primaire.* Quebec: Gouvernement du Québec.

Ministère de l'Éducation (2004). *Programme de formation de l'école québécoise: Enseignement secondaire*. Quebec: Gouvernement du Québec, Ministère de l'Éducation.

Mongeau, P., & Tremblay, J. (2002). *Survivre. La dynamique de l'inconfort*. Sainte-Foy: Presses de l'Université du Québec.

Nimier, J. (1976). *Mathématiques et affectivité*. Paris: Stock.

Nimier, J. (1985). *Les Maths, le français, les langues, à quoi ça me sert ?* Paris: Cedic-Nathan.

Petit, M., & Zawojwoski, J.S. (1997). Teachers and students learning together about assessing problem solving. *Mathematics Teacher, 90,* 472-477.

Pons, F., Doudin, P.-A., Harris, P.L., & de Rosnay, M. (2002). Métaémotion et intégration scolaire. In L. Lafortune, & P. Mongeau (Eds.), *L'affectivité dans l'apprentissage* (pp. 7-28). Sainte-Foy: Presses de l'Université du Québec.

Saarni, C. (1999). *The Development of Emotional Competency*. New York: Guilford Press.

Sillamy, R. (1980). *Dictionnaire encyclopédique de psychologie*. Montréal: Borduas.

Thagard, P. (2000). *Coherence in Thought and Action*. Cambridge: MIT Press.

Tobias, S. (1978). *Over-coming Math Anxiety*. Boston: Houghton Mifflin.

Tobias, S. (1987). *Succeed with Math: Every Student's Guide to Conquering Math Anxiety*. New York: College Entrance Examination Board.

Tobias, S. (1990). *They're not Dumb, They're Different: Stalking the Second Tier*. Tucson: Research Corporation.

Webster-Stratton, C. (1999). *How to Promote Children's Social and Emotional Competency*. London: Paul Chapman Publishing Ltd.

Weyl-Kailey, L. (1985). *Victoire sur les maths*. Paris: Robert Laffont.

Zaslavsky, C. (1996). *Fear of Math*. New Jersey: Rutgers University Press.

CHAPTER 8

Emotional competency in accompaniment: Analysis of the manifestations of emotions in a context of change[1][2]

Louise Lafortune, Lise St-Pierre, and Daniel Martin

1. Introduction

Two elements of context in education stimulate interest regarding the affective dimension in accompaniment. Firstly, reforms have produced changes in educational practices, which place accompaniers (teachers, educational advisers, trainers) in sometimes difficult situations of uncertainty (Lafortune & Deaudelin, 2001; Lafortune & Mongeau, 2002; L'Hostie & Boucher, 2004). Based on observations and discussions, we believe that the emotions of those being accompanied greatly influence the accompanying process. Moreover, these

---

[1] We use the word "accompaniment" to translate the French word "accompagnement". We are using this word in a new sense in education. Its sense is different from "training" or "coaching". "Accompaniment" includes some training, but must be seen in a broader perspective; it is a "support given to persons in a learning situation so that they may progress in the construction of their knowledge" (Lafortune and Deaudelin, 2001, p. 199). The definition of "accompaniment" in a socio-constructivist theoretical context is: "A socio-constructivist accompaniment is a support centered around the construction of the accompanied persons' knowledge while in interaction with peers. Such an accompaniment aims to activate prior experiences in order to favor the construction of knowledge, give rise to socio-cognitive conflicts while making the most of those that appear in discussions, co-construct in action, track down erroneous conceptions and profit from self-awareness arising from certain constructions. This accompaniment supposes an interaction between the accompanier and the accompanied person" (Lafortune and Deaudelin, 2001, p. 200). This accompaniment supposes frequent meetings where the changes in the professional lives of the participants are discussed and studied.
[2] We thank Nathalie Girardin and Bernard Massé, respectively for the translation and the revisions of the translation of this text.

changes influence the way continuing education is used (Lafortune, Deaudelin, Doudin & Martin, 2001). More or less adapted university educations or specific training with minimal reinvestments should evolve towards a form of accompaniment (associating theory and practice) that presupposes the involvement of both accompanier and accompanied. This implies emotional interactions between them, based on a relatively long-term and sustained approach.

With this text, we wish to stimulate a reflection on the influence of the affective dimension in an accompaniment process and thus contribute to establishing new ways of approaching continuing education. We suggest a theoretical reflection on the affective dimension's influence during accompaniment and on the development of emotional competency in accompaniers. The description of a self-analysis approach, which takes into consideration emotions in preparation for accompaniment, and includes a training-intervention research from which an analysis grid is drawn (Lafortune 2004a-b) sustains this theoretical reflection. Subsequently, we add the results of some exploratory research focused on knowledge and analysis of situations of accompaniment influenced by emotions.

2. Reflection resulting in theoretical choices

Our observations regarding the accompaniment approaches of different groups of accompaniers (teachers, educational advisers, and heads of schools) show they stress the importance of the affective dimension in their interventions, on a relatively constant basis. Nevertheless, developing this dimension in accompaniment, which is directly focused at emotions, is not a priority for them.

There is a perception according to which emotions hold a transversal place in accompaniment and that it is difficult to define which aspects of accompaniment elicit emotions. Could it be the context, the task, or the attitudes of the accompaniers or of the accompanied … ? There seems to be a lack of models, of training, or of means to act on the affective dimension of accompaniment. Our reflection makes us cautious of searching for simple means of intervention insofar as considering emotions in accompaniment is a complex process that presupposes self-examination, examination of others, of occurrences, and of the perceptions of group members' interactions.

We therefore ask ourselves how to provide the persons becoming an accompanier a treatment that integrates both theoretical elements and elements linked to communication and interrelations. We favor a cognitive rather than emotional treatment of emotions. The latter, according to us, only leads to so-called "group therapies." We believe that an emotional treatment is not relevant in the current context of change in the educational system whereas favoring a cognitive treatment of emotions is conducive to awareness of one's own emotions and those of others in an accompaniment approach. This perspective stimulates the search for means that are easily adaptable to classroom situations for the development of competencies, or to a school-team or cycle-team situation intended at finding means of interventions to put into action — not to analyze the behaviors and attitudes of others but rather to understand them. We believe that to facilitate such an understanding, accompaniers should develop an emotional competency that aims at cognitively viewing the emotions involved in an accompaniment approach.

3. Emotional competency

Saarni (1999) is the author most referred to regarding comprehension of emotional competency in a perspective that can be transposed to accompaniment. She explains emotional competency based on eight components. In the following, we specify these components by first formulating and explaining each component (Lafortune, 2005). Then, we add information regarding the meaning of each component for socio-constructivist accompaniment in a metacognitive and reflective perspective (Lafortune & Deaudelin, 2001).

First component
The awareness of one's own emotional states refers to recognizing one's own emotions and to the relationships between emotions and the events that cause them. This awareness is connected to meta-emotion. Indeed, meta-emotion requires this awareness to comprehend emotions and to make adjustments that take this comprehension into account (Pons, Doudin, Harris & de Rosnay, 2002). Mongeau and Tremblay (2002) speak of conscious attention in relation to the awareness of one's own emotional states. According to them, conscious attention fosters the desire to act in order to dissipate any uneasiness, such as discomfort. Despite the fact that these authors refer to conscious attention, they consider that reactions towards discomfort are instantaneous, unconscious, and reflexive or stem from a reflected and differed analysis.

According to us, becoming aware of their own emotions when involved in an accompanying process would be to the accompaniers' advantage. This awareness not only enables them to choose interventions that favor the success of the process, but it also facilitates adjusting the intervention by taking into account their own emotional reactions. Furthermore, this awareness leads to a search for the means to control emotional reactions (rather than avoid them and act as if no emotion was involved).

Second component
The ability to recognize and understand the emotions of others is complementary to the comprehension of one's own emotions. Knowledge of other people's emotions helps one understand one's own emotional reactions. This component of emotional competency shows the importance of looking into the construction of emotions and to accepting the limits of constructing one's own emotions as well as those of others (Lafortune, 2004c).

This component of emotional competency is important for accompaniers who should recognize and understand the emotions of those being accompanied. This aspect is particularly useful in a context of imposed change (reform and new training programs); since some people maintain (rightly or wrongly) that what was done up till now was quite valid and did not warrant being changed. Recognizing that others experience emotions in this context of change favors communication and diminishes the negative influence of resistance that is manifested by fear of the unknown, feelings of incompetence, etc. Recognizing and understanding the emotions of others leads to interventions that help those being accompanied to feel less isolated in their experience. However, better awareness of one's own emotions (first component) is essential so that comparisons with the emotions of others will be relevant and not disparaging.

Third component
The ability to use the vocabulary associated with emotions, through words, images, symbols, or others makes it possible to communicate emotional experience to others and to access one's own representations of emotional experiences. This helps to contextualize these representations and compare them to those of others.

This component of emotional competency favors the description of experiences that implicate emotions (pleasant or unpleasant) in an accompaniment process. It also encourages the discussion and sharing of emotions by trying to explain emotions to favor understanding, without being limited to naming the emotion or presenting anecdotes. While favoring the expression of emotions in an appropriate vocabulary, we believe it is necessary to collectively explore the means to control these emotions in the act. In an accompaniment process, these means are directly associated to emotions experienced ("What emotions were experienced during such a situation?") or deduced from a conceptual treatment of emotions ("Which emotions might be experienced in such a type of situation?")

Fourth component
The capacity for empathy is necessary in establishing relationships with others. According to Saarni (1999), empathy refers to feeling *with* others whereas sympathy refers to feeling *for* others; these emotional states favor communication with others. According to Legendre (1993, p. 488), empathy is the "capacity to identify the emotions and representations of others"; since it is a capacity, it can be developed and learned.

For accompaniers to show empathy towards those they accompany, they should recognize the emotions of others (even though they may not be verbalized) to encourage their explanation or understanding through a questioning process, for example. This capacity favors communication and comprehension of emotions and avoids hasty judgments on the accompanier's part. This empathy can help to create a climate of respect, active listening, and openness. This climate can in turn foster mutual help and comprehension during those moments of interventions that prove difficult.

Fifth component
The ability to understand that the internal emotional state does not necessarily correspond to what is expressed refers to the fact that a person does not always outwardly express the emotions he/she feels. One anticipates the reactions of others which may have negative effects. Understanding this phenomenon greatly aids interpersonal relationships. Developing this aspect of emotional competency favors attributions that are relevant to the situation and results in increased coherence between thoughts and actions (Thagard, 2000).

In an accompaniment situation, paying attention to the difference between what people express and what they feel is important since there is generally a difference between the two. The same goes for the difference between beliefs and practices linked to teaching and learning (Lafortune, 2004d). This difference between thoughts and actions is not too serious as long as the person has some awareness of it. In this sense, the ability to understand the difference between the feeling and the expression of an emotional state is conducive to developing awareness through coherent and relevant means.

Sixth component
The capacity to manage emotions of aversion or distress through self-regulation strategies enables a person to endure high-intensity emotions over a relatively long period. This capacity presupposes the development of self-regulation strategies that produce adjustments while emotions are experienced. Perhaps self-observation during emotional experiences is necessary to understand what

is occurring. This observation makes it possible to observe what is happening in the course of an action and to act accordingly (Lafortune & Martin, 2004). This capacity can develop the ability to point out the positive aspects of supposedly negative emotions such as anxiety (Lafortune & Pons, 2004).

In accompaniment, instead of denying the presence of emotions (one's own or those of others), it is preferable to see the positive influence of these emotions or to search for means of adjusting one's intervention so as to willingly engage in a process of change by demonstrating one's own involvement in the process.

Seventh component
The awareness of the nature of relationships, or of communication, depends on emotions and particularly on the degree of reciprocity and of symmetry in the relationship. This component integrates the previously described components and encourages the person to become aware that not everyone communicates emotions in the same way, which influences relationships with others. This presupposes that taking into account the emotional factors that facilitate or hinder communication helps a person adjust according to the reactions of those being addressed.

In accompaniment, this awareness fosters active listening of the accompanied, and the development of the means to observe the influence of emotions in relationships or interactions. It is true that this awareness necessitates an accompaniment approach that presupposes various observations of the situation (what is occurring, the emotions involved, their influence in the interaction, an explanation of their emergence, a search for means to control them, and the transition to action that implies adjustments), while keeping in mind the accompaniment intentions.

Eighth component
The capacity to accept one's emotional experiences and develop a feeling of self-efficiency is linked to personal beliefs as to what is socially acceptable as emotional stability. This means that we construct our own theory of emotions to develop our feeling of emotional self-efficiency which is already more or less solid.

In accompaniment, observing one's own emotional experience improves a person's feelings of competency in supporting others. For example, accepting the fact that changing educational practices can bring out emotions such as anxiety or pleasure, can contribute to increasing feelings of competency in living with the instabilities that necessarily accompany change.

This being a new subject, our perspective is exploratory. Therefore, we present two research projects: one that resulted in the creation of a self-analysis grid regarding consideration of the affective dimension during accompaniment, and another that consisted in collecting data. This data came from accompaniers that described experiences concerning emotions and explained the means used to manage these more or less difficult situations. After presenting the results of each in relation to the affective dimension, we will look into the relationship with emotional competency during accompaniment.

4. Self-analysis of taking into account the affective dimension in a context of an accompaniment project

The idea of self-analysis of taking into account the affective dimension came to us from comments made during interventions in schools. In response to the question "What did you learn during this intervention?" a number of respondents said that they became aware of the importance of the affective dimension. Nevertheless, in the experiments in which this observation was made, the need to consider the affective dimension was not part of the principal conceptual aspects of the intervention. It is therefore possible that although awareness of the need to develop emotional competency may be present, the emotions involved, their source, their influence, and their solutions could not be specified. This fostered our interest in analyzing some of the four levels of interventions made during preparation for accompaniment to extract an auto-analysis grid that could be used as an instrument of reflection or for research in other contexts. This accompaniment training came within the scope of a training-intervention research (Lafortune, 2004a-b).[3] All the sessions were taped and the transcripts of these interventions allowed us to create a grid.

Construction of the self-analysis grid of taking into account of the affective dimension

To create a self-analysis grid taking into account of the affective dimension, we proceeded to an emergent analysis of the types of interventions that took place. After studying the transcripts of a few sessions, three types of interventions emerged regarding the affective dimension; these are shown in Table 1.

---

[3] This research-training-intervention, subsidized by the *Direction régionale des régions de la Capitale-Nationale et de la Chaudière-Appalaches* of the *Ministère de l'Éducation*, concerns the socio-constructivist approach as well as cycle-team work in elementary schools (SCA-CTW). The group of people trained in accompanying was comprised of school administrators, pedagogical counselors and teachers (2 or 3 participants from each of 9 schools and 6 school boards).

We then elaborated on them with principles and strategies. The grid was used to analyze all the transcripts (approximately 400 pages). The complete analysis will be published later.

In what follows there are three types of interventions that take into consideration the affective dimension that emerged from the analysis. They provide a self-analysis grid of personal interventions to identify types of interventions and the means that were used.

Table 1
Types of interventions that consider the affective dimension

Affective dimension consideration levels	Explanations
(1) Considering the affective dimension with accompaniers or persons formed to accompany	This first level refers to interventions made during accompaniment so that the affective dimension (emotions) of accompaniers-in-training is directly taken into account.
(2) Showing that we take into account the affective dimension in interventions with accompaniers	This second level refers to the outlook on the interventions made with accompaniers (those formed to accompany) so that they become aware that the affective dimension is taken into consideration and can give it more weight when accompanying others.
(3) Provide ideas to take into account the affective dimension with reference to those being accompanied.	This third level refers to ideas that were provided for interventions. The suggested interventions consider the affective dimension of those being accompanied (generally teachers) in an accompaniment process.

These three types of interventions are linked to emotional competency, because they require awareness of one's own emotional states (1st component), recognition of those of others (2nd component), a certain degree of empathy (4th component), and the capacity to manage more or less pleasant, more or less difficult (6th component) emotions so as to consider the influence of the affective dimension (1st type). Furthermore, to use interventions according to the 2nd type, it is important to use the vocabulary associated with emotions (3rd component) and to understand that what is expressed is not necessarily what is felt (5th component). Finally, the third type presupposes comprehension of the importance of the affective dimension in accompaniment (7th component) and having strategies at hand to manage emotional experiences (8th component) to suggest ways to consider the affective dimension, according to the situation.

Explanations of Types of Interventions

Below, we provide explanations for the three types of interventions leading to awareness of the affective dimension and also provide the intervention principles or strategies that are linked to each type.

Type 1: What is done
This type is split into two parts. The first part proposes general intervention principles or ideas that are valid for any intervention that presupposes a follow-up. The second part suggests other intervention principles or ideas that come within the scope of a socio-constructivist perspective.

First Part
Getting accompaniers to talk of the people they accompany before speaking of themselves (from impersonal to personal) reassures the person with whom one interacts. Even though providing elements of observation regarding those being accompanied can give the impression of not being involved, these observations provide a great deal of information regarding the person with whom the accompanier interacts. The choice of observations is not objective and points to what is bothering the accompanier. (Development of a vocabulary associated with emotions, 3rd component)

By first listening to descriptions of in-class attempts without judging prematurely (without prejudging), the accompanier can then ask questions or ask for the advice of those who made these attempts or of other people participating in the meeting. It is important not to undermine the value of what is already being accomplished, unless it is timely and contributes something to the accompanier. (Capacity for empathy, 4th component)

Avoiding saying that a method or a strategy is easy to use, to achieve, or to implement prevents the accompanier from feeling incompetent if things do not turn out well. It can even be said that a first attempt can cause difficulties and that this is completely normal. Too often, in a perspective of motivation, one is tempted to say that what is coming up will be easy; however, nothing is easy the first time it is done. (Comprehension of the emotions of others, 2nd component)

Including oneself as part of the group means generous use of "we" and not just "you". For example, the accompanier can speak of "the priorities of our group". This creates a group climate, which has a better chance of resembling a community of learning. (Recognition and comprehension of the emotions of others, 2nd component)

Establishing relationships by referring to ideas generated by people in the group – by naming these people by their name, if possible is another means. By referring to the ideas of others, the accompanier gives them importance. However, if he or she can also name those who came up with the idea, a climate of thoughtfulness is created. This shows active listening and the importance one gives not only to ideas but also to individuals. This is a form of recognition of the person. It can even encourage others to speak. Without prejudging the intentions or the representations behind the ideas, they should not all be treated on the same level. They can be compared, interrelated confronted, questioned. (Recognition of the need for people to be considered as emotional beings, 2nd component)

Diversifying intentions is essential. It is important to diversify the forms of intervention and interaction. The accompanier's goal might be to reach each person in different ways of learning based on 4 to 6 interventions or given situations. (Development of a feeling of self-efficiency, 8th component)

"Coming to terms with" or accepting the fact that the accompanier will not accomplish all the tasks or situations planned is helpful. In order to accomplish the tasks or situations while respecting the individuals with whom there is an interaction and to favor the reflective process while respecting schedules, the accompanier should accept that it is not necessary to accomplish all that was planned and to try to satisfy all the cognitive needs of the participants. This acceptation leads to respecting schedules. This principle may seem unimportant, but respecting the schedule places those being accompanied in a more positive listening position. Too often, meetings do not proceed according to the announced schedule and participants become inattentive to the last part. Furthermore, to respect the schedule, and satisfy those being accompanied, it is sometimes necessary to break off interventions that drift and that don't go in the anticipated direction. This could mean not making the most of an activity, or, at other times, being strict about the time allotted for interventions. For example, when participants or teams present the result of their work or of their reflections, it may be important to limit the time allocated and to respect this allocation. Sometimes it is necessary to stop the two first people or teams in their presentations, which could last up to 30, 40 or 50 minutes. This is usually appreciated, since a number of people do not find it appropriate to listen to others "talk about themselves" during a session. After two teams, the pace is established and everyone conforms to the time allotted. Each person or team ends up making choices regarding their presentation. They choose what is essential. What is presented becomes more interesting and anecdotal forms are avoided. This mode of operation is

more stimulating for the group. (Recognition of the emotions of others and capacity for empathy, 2nd and 4th components)

Avoiding anecdotes will help the group focus on what is important. The accompanier should find ways to prevent participants from confining their accounts to anecdotes; these do not help the reflection process. This type of account does not contribute to the construction process needed for the accompaniment. Participants are generally truly interested in learning, and details regarding what goes on in school or in a classroom are of little interest. If the accompanier gets participants to recognize the structure of what they do, their intervention will be more to the point. It is the sharing of this aspect that is interesting and provides food for thought. (Comprehension that communication depends on emotions and importance of developing a feeling of self-efficiency, 5th and 8th components.)

Second Part

The following aspects are more directly related to socio-constructivism.

Showing that the accompanier is also in a research process and progressing, helps participants experience the accompaniment approach as an evolutionary process. This also helps the accompanied persons come to terms with the fact that they won't find all the answers and that answers may be slow in coming. Knowing everything in advance takes pleasure away from creation. (Capacity to accept emotional experiences, 8th component)

Showing how the construction process is prepared will ease the work. Training routines create expectations. For example, customarily, theoretical elements are provided at the beginning, and examples and practice are given afterwards. To encourage active listening, it is necessary to specify that the approach will be different this time and that the synthesis that establishes links with the theory will come later. This method is different from the usual and requires knowledge of the approach to engage in the process: "I haven't given you a presentation, but you can feel that it will come. In my mind, establishment of the theory of what we are now preparing could take place four sessions from now; to me, it is part of the construction (or co-construction) process." (Development of a feeling of self-efficiency, 8th component)

In the context of a collective syntheses or brainstorming, for example, not taking for granted that everything is valid. In a brainstorming session, it is important to take note of all the ideas and not to criticize them during compilation. However, if brainstorming leads to a presentation of team definitions, it is necessary to give one's opinion and even to be critical. Too often, socio-constructivism is perceived as a theory that presupposes everyone is constructing their knowledge and that one should not influence these constructions. We do not feel the latter statement is justified. Socio-cognitive conflicts can change constructions, concepts and representations. Participants in a process of continuing education want to progress and they know that what they do and think is not perfect. They are looking for ideas and want the accompanier to intervene, correctly and respectfully, regarding what they express and accomplish. One could even say that accepting everything does not mean considering the affective dimension because this gives the impression that the participants cannot tolerate any criticism. This could be taken as extreme protection; it could even undermine the efforts made. (Knowledge of self-regulation strategies and acceptance of emotional experiences, 6th and 8th components)

Accepting that the goal is not to transform others, since in a constructivist perspective, even if one can help someone construct knowledge and skills, these belong to the person who constructed them. This is even truer in an accompaniment approach of adults, experienced teachers, who will use what they have been presented as they please. (Recognition and comprehension of the emotions of others, 2nd component)

Intervening by questions rather than statements helps establish a co-construction relationship between the accompanier and the participants. This makes it possible to perceive that the process is an evolution, that there is room for ideas, and that all is not decided beforehand. (Knowledge of self-regulation strategies and development of a feeling of self-efficiency, 6th and 8th components)

Regulating the intervention according to the course of events shows the accompanied persons that whatever occurs in the session is taken into consideration. Nevertheless, we believe that this regulation should be done while respecting the main orientation or the intentions that were decided upon at the start. (Feeling of self-efficiency, 8th component)

Highlighting the positive aspects of the interventions or the presentations encourage the accompanied persons to be open-minded towards what is said, the questions, and even the criticism. When the accompanier underlines positive aspects of an intervention, he or she should provide reasons that show why the intervention is interesting. In a description of tasks or situations, the accompanier should present the suggestions as complementary to what is already being done, not as a replacement or a true addition. They should be presented as a continuity and represent adjustments rather than radical changes. This way of thinking requires that one progresses with the person and attempts to understand the person's mental processes (his or her metacognition). It is preferable to help him or her construct ideas, thoughts or means of intervention based on his or her beliefs (conceptions and convictions) while at the same time confronting some ways of thinking or doing. Imposing one's vision is not possible even if one can ask questions to sway the other person's vision. (Comprehension of one's emotions and those of others and capacity for empathy, 1st, 2nd and 4th components)

Type 2: Examining what is done
In type 2, the interventions of the first type can be repeated in a perspective where accompaniers are made aware of what is being done. This process is called "double observation" of the interventions. These two observations represent "experiencing the formation", being able to "observe one's own experience" and extracting intervention means for one's own accompaniment process. (Relations can be established with the eight components of emotional competency.)

Lafortune and Martin (2004) consider that the development of accompaniment skills requires the practice of what they call the "meta perspective", which is a way of looking at what is occurring during action to be able to reflect it to those being accompanied. This "meta perspective" contributes to the process of co-construction. If it is to be effective, it should be done respectfully. It requires: 1) observing the situation, while avoiding hasty judgments (attitude); 2) sharing and analyzing actions; and 3) making adjustments based on the observations. Using such a perspective, in relation to the affective dimension, requires the development of emotional competency for the recognition and understanding of one's own emotions and those of others but also requires the use of the appropriate vocabulary and actions.

A way of encouraging accompaniers to become aware of these two observations consists in doing some intervention in that sense and then, to show the process, generating a list of the strategies used. With regard to the affective dimension, this method helps developing accompaniers play a part. It provides a means based on experiences rather than on a list with no practical reference. Such a method favors the self-confidence required for interventions in a process of accompaniment and the development of a feeling of self-efficiency (8th component). It is true that achieving these two observations is deemed difficult, but practice of this method and mostly getting those present to participate increases self-confidence regarding the ability to do so. The person leading the session could serve as a model in regards to awareness of the affective dimension rather than telling others what must be done; as such, the accompanier should show the development of emotional competency.

Specifying that what is accomplished while constructing one's accompaniment capacities can and must be adapted to all circumstances. Sharing this preoccupation helps future accompaniers to increase their feeling of competency and self-efficiency (8th component), because they perceive the possibility of transforming what has been presented, as they please. Even if one wants them to adopt what they are shown as a method that should be followed, in a socio-constructivist perspective, it will not be used as planned. Various transformations are carried out either because of different personalities, or through an interpretation of what was suggested, which may even go against the grain of the accompanier's intention. Such a perspective presupposes comprehension of the emotions of others and an outlook that enables one to discern what emerges beyond what is expressed (2nd and 5th components).

Allowing time for learning and informing the participants of this allows the accompaniers to accept experiences which were more or less successful. It also allows them to realize they are not required to implement experiences that they consider complex in an immediate future. For example, one can stress that "it takes time [...], it takes energy, [...] it's not that easy". Developing a capacity for empathy and awareness of the emotions involved are essential for the belief that short or long-term actions can produce results (4th and 7th components).

Sharing one's own realizations helps people understand what can or cannot be done within the context of their interventions as accompaniers. Once a climate of confidence has been established, one can share what choices were made in the action and the reasons for these choices. Sometimes, it is necessary to say why an intervention was not pursued, because of the consideration for the emotions of those participating. To do so, it is important to recognize one's own emotional states, and accept one's emotional experiences so they can be shared (1st and 8th components).

Type 3: How to transpose an experience to other situations of accompaniment
The third type of intervention is made up of ways of taking into consideration the people being accompanied. In this type of intervention, one can speak of the insecurities of those with whom one intervenes, of the resistance to change they will manifest... It is a starting point to suggest means of intervention in an accompaniment process.

Insisting on differences means making accompaniers aware of the differences that may emerge in those they accompany. Some people want to understand why a concept is being used or need to search for definitions before participating in the task, whereas others prefer to participate in the task and understand the meaning of this task as it emerges from the action. To help understand these differences, one can also insist on the range of educational approaches a person will use, according to situations and contexts. Inability to comprehend these differences can lead to managing intense emotions (6th component) which can make the accompaniment approach difficult.

Insisting on what one believes to be reality is of a perceptive or interpretative nature. In a constructivist viewpoint, it is important to pay attention to one's convictions or judgments in relation to others (link with the 5th component). These are perceptions or interpretations based on observations, which are restricted in time and filtered by the accompanier's previous conceptions. In this sense, if one believes that a person is "traditional in their teaching, one cannot tell them to change to become 'something else'". It is preferable to ask questions to find out whether "the person feels like trying a given strategy". The answer provided gives clues to the judgment that was previously made and places the accompanied person in a state of open-mindedness towards these attempts because she or he feels understood (2nd and 4th components).

With these three types, these principles and these strategies, we note that by keeping in mind the components of emotional competency, it is possible to refine interventions to favor the development of such a competency in those being accompanied. An analysis of one's own interventions can enable a person to recognize the influence of her or his interventions on others. Assessment of data gathered in Switzerland and Quebec allows us to refine comprehension of the development of emotional competency.

5. Analysis of data from accompaniers: Quebec and Switzerland

Exploratory research was conducted in Switzerland and in Quebec during the spring of 2003 to explore the nature and place of emotions in situations of accompaniment. A questionnaire (annex 1) served to collect data with teacher trainers at the *Haute École Pédagogique du canton de Vaud* (16 out of 20 answered the questionnaire) and with educational accompaniers in Quebec CEGEPs[*] (13 out of 53 answered the questionnaire). The respondents, as a whole, mentioned 57 accompaniment situations that elicited emotions (35 in Switzerland and 22 in Quebec) and produced changes in practice.

Below are some results concerning the nature of the situations of accompaniment that were reported in relation to the emotions involved and their

---

[*] In Quebec, CEGEPs are pre-university (12th and 13th years of study) and vocational (12th to 14th years of study) colleges that have been involved, in the last few years, in an important reform of all their educational programs. Educational accompaniers accompany teachers in the elaboration, implementation, and evaluation of educational programs.

manifestations, the interventions mentioned by the accompaniers, and the means used to prepare themselves for the intervention (questions 1a, 3 and 4 in the questionnaire, annex 1). These results are not presented as a comparison between Switzerland and Quebec; they are studied in relation to emotions and emotional competency to help understand how various interveners identify situations that, according to them, elicit emotions.

Situations of Accompaniment: Emotions and Manifestations of Emotions

Two contexts of accompaniment situations are identified in Switzerland and in Quebec: the first occurred in a context of change chosen by those being accompanied and the second occurred in a context of change prescribed by the authorities. In Switzerland, the situations in which a team's continuing education projects were done corresponded to chosen changes, whereas those that provided for a concerted project to improve the evaluation of learning practices came within the scope of a prescribed change. In Quebec, situations of professional insertion of teachers and the accompaniment requiring individual follow-up by an educational accompanier, in the wake of student complaints or evaluation of teaching, were chosen by the accompanied persons. Other situations were prescribed or imposed by the school, such as the development or the revision of an educational program, or in some cases, those relative to a mandatory follow-up in the wake of student complaints or of an administrative evaluation of teaching.

Emotions expressed by the respondents in situations of accompaniment were diverse; it may in fact be necessary to examine whether it is a question of emotions or feelings, of attitudes, or even of elements hardly linked to the affective dimension. Several basic emotions have been recognized in written works; for example: *fear, sadness, anger, happiness, surprise, disgust,* and *distress* (Martin & Briggs, 1986). The vocabulary that refers to emotional aspects is much more diversified in the data collected. In Switzerland and in Quebec, both pleasant and unpleasant, favorable and unfavorable emotions were mentioned. They can be the same whether the situation is chosen or prescribed (tables 2 and 3). To interpret tables 2 and 3 correctly, it is important to note that manifestations were coded according to the type of emotions by the Swiss researcher, and according the type of situations, by the Quebec researcher.

Table 2
Emotions according to the nature of the situation of change and manifestations of these emotions according to their type (Switzerland)

Type of emotion	Chosen change: Training	Prescribed change: Reform of evaluation	Manifestations according to type of emotions
Pleasant or neutral emotions	Happiness, pleasure, enthusiasm, jubilation, positive feeling, relaxation, restraint, reserve.	Happiness, pleasure, positive stimulation, calm, serenity, relaxation.	Tone of voice, degree of involvement, sharing, and solidarity with colleagues.
Unpleasant emotions	Anger, fear, anxiety, deception, worry, timidity, depression, apprehension, frustration, embarrassment, insecurity, guilt, sadness, despondency.	Anger, fear, anxiety, deception, worry, injustice, exasperation.	Criticism from others, tone of voice, annoyance, lack of respect, lack of motivation, disinterest, regret, loss of self-worth, loss of confidence, discouragement, aggressiveness, tears, degree of involvement, shouting, stuttering, hesitation, comments, non-verbal behavior, tense speech, shaky voice, reading the newspaper, resistance, doubt, perplexity, unrestrained activism, closed expression, evasive looks, justifications of what has been done up to now, request for confirmation, leaving the room.

Table 3
Emotions according to the nature of the situation of change and manifestations of these emotions according to their type (Quebec)

Quebec	Chosen change: professional integration	Chosen or prescribed change: student complaints and follow-up, imposed or chosen	Prescribed change: Elaboration or revision of an educational program
Pleasant or neutral emotions	Open-mindedness, confusion: worry and satisfaction.		Enthusiasm, competition, open-mindedness, fascination, respect, admiration.
Unpleasant emotions	Fear, insecurity, uneasiness, confusion: worry and satisfaction.	Shame, concern, feelings of loneliness, anger, injustice, distress, anxiety, destabilization, feelings of incompetence, of being overcome, or loss of control.	Fear, stress, anger, frustration, powerlessness, bitterness, fear of losing face, destabilization, fear of losing control, curiosity.
Manifestations according to the type of situations	Loss of control, alternation of tears and smiles, if uneasiness is present: evasive looks, mistrust, resistance to change, motivation, if achievements are at play: smiles, straightforward looks.	Discouragement, tears, silences, abstruseness, body movements of discomfort, lack of interest, wanting to give up, in a group: collective anger or, if sadness, respect and support, lack of motivation, minimal actions, no openness to change, no confidence, apparent openness, loss of self-esteem, evasive looks, defensive position.	Resignation or refusal to collaborate, lack of active listening, aggressiveness, alternating between open-mindedness and closed-mindedness, questions, digressions, sudden change of mood, depreciative remarks regarding the process, value judgments, refusal of new ideas, negation.

We note the great variety of emotional aspects evoked; we also note that the people who were questioned sometimes confuse emotions with other emotional aspects. For example, confusion between two emotions is not an emotion, no more than the feeling of injustice, even if it generates a feeling of sadness in one person and a feeling of anger in another. These observations show the need to develop emotional competency not only to recognize emotions but to name them (2nd and 3rd components) and also to control potentially intense emotions and to develop a feeling of self-efficiency (6th and 8th components).

Accompanier's interventions

The interventions used in Switzerland and in Quebec were of the same nature. This is why we present them together. The vocabulary used in this section and in the following is comprised of the very words of the people questioned, without reformulation. Our aim was to categorize the types of interventions and means of preparation and give the narrative a flowing style. Accompaniers mentioned interventions regarding management of their own attitudes and emotions, management of the accompaniment process, and use of facilitation techniques.

Management of attitudes and emotions[5]

Interventions of this type consist in *adopting an attitude of partnership, of encouragement, in showing empathy, in recognizing one's own emotions and accepting them, in sharing one's emotions, in speaking about oneself, in not being overwhelmed by one's emotions, in avoiding contaminants that are despondent, in calling upon and trusting the group* and even, *in not doing anything particular*. Also mentioned are *adopting a neutral look, keeping distance, stepping back* whereas others, in contrast, are involved in the situation and speak of *our problem*. These strategies of management of attitudes and emotions have ties to several components of emotional competency such as recognition of one's emotions and those of others, but also the capacity for empathy, as well as the realization that communication depends on emotions (1st, 2nd, 4th and 7th components). However, it is unclear whether the respondents were aware of the need to develop this competency in order to carry out the process of accompanying changes of practice. Answers to the questionnaire do not confirm such awareness.

Management of the accompaniment process

The rich and varied interventions of this category are without a doubt the result of field experience. Accompaniers say they *establish and maintain a climate of trust, provide a place to speak of emotions during the process, approach change gradually, suggest a realistic plan of action, co-animate, work on the sense of*

---

[5] Statements in italics come from the transcripts.

change, analyze the sense of change, sustain the accompaniment for a sufficient period, analyze situations experienced, start off with the participants' experience, shift from the emotional level to the intellectual level. After an accompaniment experience, *some attempt to understand the emotions in context, to analyze the dynamics, their emergence and their evolution, the reactions of people . . . or to verify or validate their perception with a colleague that is not involved in the situation.* These suggested interventions show the development of emotion management strategies; in a subsequent phase, it would be interesting to explore what accompaniers think of the influence of these actions on those being accompanied. It would be an opportunity to better assess the level of development of emotional competency and to foster awareness.

Facilitation techniques
Several facilitation techniques are exploited to intervene on emotional aspects. Thus, accompaniers note that it is possible *to listen, encourage verbalization, let people express themselves, reflect, validate, value, reframe, generalize, inform, help identify facts, objectivize, use questions to bring out solutions, encourage, meta-communicate, recognize the legitimacy of an emotion, identify an emotion without judging, adjust, pave the way, negotiate, explain the objectives, the process, the steps and the timeframe of the change process, identify the zones of imbalance and elicit exchanges in relation to these, establish relationships between current practices and requested changes, recognize what is already being done, reframe – using constructive aspects.* It is also important, according to the persons questioned, *to emphasize progress and improvements, both orally and in written form.*

Such a variety of means of interaction may give the impression that accompaniers are skilled in the situations mentioned and have developed in-depth emotional competency. However, it should be noted that these ways of intervening were compiled from a total of 29 people, and no individual uses all of them. Moreover, people probably do not always react the same way, and their reactions are probably not based on explicit foundations when studying emotional aspects during situations of accompaniment; likewise when preparing accompaniment situations.

Preparation of situations of accompaniment

With regard to preparation of situations of accompaniment and training interventions, we have activities related to training, anticipation of accompaniment, and attitude control. They are similar in both samples (Switzerland and Quebec).

Training
When referring to training, accompaniers first mention the importance of *up keeping one's abilities in helping relationships, of training, of getting information about the subject discussed prior to the session, of participating in groups of professional practice analysis, of working on listening skills.* For some, it is a matter of enriching *theoretical and practical instruments.* A technique consists in *analyzing each session a posteriori and discussing it during the next session.* The *metacognitive and critical perspective on an experience* becomes a preparation activity for a subsequent accompaniment session. The vocabulary of emotional competency is not really used but is implicitly referred to when speaking of abilities in helping relationships. Nevertheless, it would be important to understand what these abilities encompass to find ways to improve them and thus become better accompaniers during a process of change.

Anticipation of Accompaniment
Some persons accompanying or training others to accompany try to *anticipate the emotions likely to surface and condition themselves to adopt a neutral outlook* and *to stand back somewhat.* They say they *use visualization and are aware of what can occur,* including consequences and obstacles. They *think of intense situations that were not catastrophic* and *try to anticipate zones of imbalance.* They *prepare themselves to encourage verbalization, to listen, to open up, to validate, to question, to testify, to objectivize, to rationalize, to confront.* Some say they *meticulously prepare content and interventions.* Thus, they *attempt to introduce one new thing at a time and without haste.* They say they *construct a learning environment that is compatible with the public's culture* or *analyze a priori what could happen.* They *question one or several people about the work context.* One mentions *the importance of recognizing and understanding how the team or the department usually operates and to conform to it.* Others *review all the subjects, the adopted strategy, the planned roles, and discuss all of this with one or two persons.* Proposing an anticipation approach in the preparation of an accompaniment process shows concern for knowing and acknowledging the persons being accompanied. This anticipation helps to: recognize and understand the emotions that can emerge, control more or less intense emotions, show empathy, and develop a feeling of self-efficiency (2nd, 4th, 6th and 8th components).

Attitude Management
Some accompaniers try to *adopt a position of accompanier rather than trainer, remain stable over quicksand, distance themselves from the missionary role, participate while keeping a distance* and *avoid defensive positions.* Others speak of *distancing*

themselves from the problem and *focusing on the search for solutions.* They try to think that *teachers will show them a lot, to put themselves in the other person's shoes, to stay humble.* They say that *progressing in managing their own emotions* is a way to prepare for them. They *search for a balance between empathy and efficiency* by being both helpful and showing solidarity. Some do *breathing exercises,* take up a *welcoming position,* and take *for granted that some events will affect the session's progress.* One mentioned that she *trusts facts and her own intuitions;* when they both coincide, she is *confident in her decision.*

Finally, some admit that they *do not prepare in any special way and became aware of what they did or could do when they answered the questionnaire.* This instrument enabled them to *look at the things they do during action in a metacognitive way.*

Apparently, although several actions show some development of emotional competency, awareness of the degree of development of this competency is not always explicit. Naming some attitudes, or ways of organizing these attitudes, does not directly presuppose being able to provide explanations or justifications for the actions undertaken. However, it can be surmised that those who accepted to answer the questionnaire already had a certain awareness of the emotions involved in accompaniment, or that they became aware of them in answering the questionnaire. In such a context, and to take advantage of the data collection situation, the results could be sent back to the accompaniers to discuss possible interpretations in relationship with emotional competency.

6. Discussion and conclusion

Certain links can be made with the previous self-analysis of accompaniment sessions. The two studies differ in certain respects and any interpretation must be made with care. During the self-analysis experience, the researcher helped accompaniers to better accompany; data was collected with accompaniers that intervened in different contexts, without focusing on accompaniment process of the people with whom they intervene. Those who answered the questionnaire on emotions in accompaniment are situated at another level of intervention; a level that refers to accompaniers, whether or not they were trained to accompany.

With regard to the types of interventions, related to awareness of the affective dimension (table 1), we find examples of each type, but with less variety than in the self-analysis situation for types 1 and 2 and more variety regarding type 3. Among the fifteen strategies noted in the self-analysis of the accompanier responsible for accompaniers, those that refer to awareness of the affective dimension, type 1, which could be referred to as "emotional presence", only two correspond to actions mentioned by the persons questioned. These were

(i) creating a place for the expression of emotions and (ii) including themselves in the group. With regard to the second type, which consists in showing that the affective dimension is considered in the intervention, which we refer to as "emotional modeling", *speaking of one's awareness*, and *giving time to learn* are two strategies mentioned by those questioned. Recall that, for some people, filling out the questionnaire was their chance to take a "meta"-viewpoint at their interventions, which is what this type of intervention is about. Type 3 interventions regarding awareness of the affective dimension deal with "emotional instrumentation" — in other words providing intervention ideas to consider the affective dimension. It is about this type of intervention that people provided the most data. Indeed, intervention and intervention preparation strategies are rich in teachings. They show an idea of the interest in analyzing accompaniment practices in a perspective of dealing with emotional aspects within the framework of training activities. They also allow us to probe the possibility of elaborating and validating a varied and rich base of practical knowledge in this field. However, in a socio-constructivist perspective, we may question the contribution of the presentation of strategies that can be used in comparison to the richness of modeling strategies used in action and awareness that there is indeed modeling in the action.

In several countries, significant educational reforms now being implemented require profound changes in concepts and practices on the part of educators. For these reforms to succeed, it is necessary to count on the accompaniment of persons and groups of persons whose traditional ways are called into question and submitted to a critical review. This elicits sometimes intense emotions that may perturb the accompaniment process. Accompaniers should consider these emotions and treat them so they will not negatively affect undertaking the proposed changes. But this is a complex and delicate task that cannot be improvised. The accompaniers we accompanied often expressed the feeling that they did not have a sufficient grasp of these situations and would have appreciated being better prepared to be efficient in their interventions. They did not use the expression "emotional competency", but their remarks could easily be related to this competency. Few researchers have looked into this question with regard to the work of adults with other adults in education. Theoretical reflections, and the experiences presented, contribute to a better understanding of the phenomena involved and suggest possible avenues of interventions for accompaniers and reflections concerning emotional competency.

These people experience imbalances themselves, perhaps even "paradigmatic changes", concerning the conceptual foundations and the organizational reference frameworks at the root of educational reforms. They do not always feel they have full control in relation to these foundations. Treating emotional aspects, which should be done in concert with cognitive treatment of ideas, within the scope of the goals pursued by the accompaniment situation, adds an additional difficulty to the accompaniment process. Some of the data collected highlighted the fact that they were sometimes influenced by the negative views of those being accompanied, by an excess of "empathy". According to us, this underscores the importance of preparing accompaniers with regard to emotional competency. To do this, it is necessary to construct a basis of scientific knowledge in this field and then to develop activities and training instruments for accompaniers.

With regard to pursuing research in this field, first, it is important to specify, on the conceptual plane, the definitions of the terms and expressions used to describe the phenomena involved: for example, concepts of emotions, feelings, attitudes, manifestations, but also of meta-emotion and emotional competency. We also recommend describing and explaining the dynamics of the emotions experienced in the context of accompaniment: for example, their emergence, treatment, effects, evolution cycles, etc. Second, it would appear justified to better recognize the perceptions and representations of accompaniers regarding the emotions of those they accompany, their manifestation, their meaning, and their role in the accompaniment process. Indeed, a better knowledge of the role of the accompanier's emotions in treating the emotions of others is an avenue that could be explored. Third, it seems necessary to develop and validate research approaches and instruments: data collection instruments that would allow a more in-depth analysis and instruments for a better comprehension of the emergence of emotions and comprehension of emotions and relationships. Finally, research including training and intervention would favor increased scientific knowledge while refining concepts and increase the skills of accompaniers. Within the context of such activities, models of intervention could be developed and perfected. For example, the following is a possible three-step model of intervention: 1) affective presence; 2) affective modeling, and 3) affective instrumentation while establishing relationships with the three types of interventions defined in the self-analysis approach and with the eight components of emotional competency.

Based on our experience and the data collected, it would seem that accompaniers react to and treat manifestations of emotions rather intuitively and often feel dissatisfied or worried about their performance. They would like to feel better prepared. For the professional development of accompaniers, we note the need for preparation concerning theoretical and practical knowledge about emotions in situations of accompaniment. Theoretical knowledge is that which we previously mentioned, whereas practical knowledge concerns the development of emotional competency in accompaniment. To develop this competency, a wide range of approaches and instruments for formation is needed, including among others approaches and instruments to sustain analysis of practices. In addition to theoretical and practical knowledge, the accompaniers should be given support of the development of a critical perspective regarding emotional manifestations and the effects of different interventions (Lafortune & Robertson, 2005). In this regard, some people mentioned that answering the questionnaire was in itself a learning instrument because it fostered a metacognitive reflection on their practice. This exercise is a first step in the development of this critical perspective. Developing this instrument to amplify the movement would prove interesting.

Dealing effectively with the emotional aspects that emerge in a situation of accompaniment requires a prerequisite relation to pedagogical culture (Lafortune & Martin, 2004): experience in the field pertaining to the accompaniment process, such as evaluation of learning, cooperative education, professional integration, elaboration of programs, etc. According to our concept of accompaniment (which includes elements of preparation relative to both content and process), this prerequisite is crucial for the accompanier to have the mental freedom needed to perceive what is going on and also act, bearing in mind the intentions of change. Therefore, a person's pedagogical culture should be strengthened, either prior to or concomitantly with the development of accompaniment skills, including its emotional component. Paradoxically, one of the avenues worth exploring in the development of emotional competency in accompaniment would be interventions intended at developing the "pedagogical culture" of accompaniers.

References

Doudin, P.-A., Martin, D., & Albanese, O. (2001). *Métacogntion et éducation: aspects transversaux et disciplinaires.* Berne: Peter Lang.

Jonnaert, P. (2002). *Compétences et constructivisme: un cadre théorique.* Brussels: De Boeck.

Jonnaert, P., & van der Borght, C. (1999). *Créer des conditions d'apprentissage: Un cadre de référence socioconstructiviste pour une formation didactique des enseignants.* Brussels: De Boeck University Press.

Lafortune, L. (1992a). *Élaboration, implantation et évaluation d'implantation à l'ordre collégial d'un plan d'intervention andragogique en mathématiques portant sur la dimension affective en mathématiques.* Doctoral thesis, Montreal: Université du Québec à Montréal.

Lafortune, L. (1992b). *Dimension affective en mathématiques, recherche-action et matériel didactique.* Mont-Royal: Modulo Éditeur.

Lafortune, L. (2004). Des intuitions constructivists. In P. Jonnaert, & D. Masciotra (Eds.), *Constructivismes. Choix contemporains. Hommage à Ernst von Glasersfeld* (pp. 187-196). Sainte-Foy: Presses de l'Université du Québec.

Lafortune, L. in collaboration with Cyr, S., & Massé, B. and the participation of Milot, G., & Benoît, K. (2004a). *Travailler en équipe-cycle. Entre collègues d'une école.* Quebec: Presses de l'Université du Québec.

Lafortune, L. (Ed.) (2004b). *Le questionnement en équipe-cycle. Questionnaires, entretiens et journaux de réflexion.* Quebec: Presses de l'Université du Québec.

Lafortune, L. (2004c). Des intuitions constructivists. In Ph. Jonnaert, & D. Masciotra (Eds.), *Constructivismes. Choix contemporains. Hommage à Ernest von Glasersfeld* (pp. 187-196). Sainte-Foy: Presses de l'Université du Québec.

Lafortune, L. (2004d). Croyances et pratiques: deux questionnaires de recherche, de formation et d'autoréflexion. In L. Lafortune (Ed.), *Le questionnement en équipe-cycle. Questionnaires, entretiens et journaux de réflexion* (pp. 97-143). Sainte-Foy: Presses de l'Université du Québec.

Lafortune, L. (2005). Le développement de la compétence émotionnelle par l'utilisation d'activités interactives-réflexives pour assurer le suivi parental en mathématiques. In L. Lafortune, M.-F. Daniel, P.-A. Doudin, F. Pons, & O. Albanese (Eds.), *Pédagogie et psycohologi des émotions: vers la compétence émotionnelle* (pp. 35-60). Sainte-Foy: Presses de l'Université du Québec.

Lafortune, L., & Deaudelin, C. (2001). *Accompagnement socioconstructiviste. Pour s'approprier une réforme en education.* Sainte-Foy: Presses de l'Université du Québec.

Lafortune, L., Deaudelin, C., Doudin, P.-A., & Martin, D. (Eds.) (2001). *La formation condinue: de la réflexion à l'action.* Sainte-Foy: Presses de l'Université du Québec.

Lafortune L., & Martin, D. (2004). L'accompagnement: processus de co-construction et culture pédagogique. In M. L'Hostie, & L.-Ph. Boucher (Eds.), *L'accompagnement en éducation. Un soutien ou renouvellement des pratiques* (pp. 47-62). Sainte-Foy: Presses de l'Université du Québec.

Lafortune, L., & Mongeau, P. (Eds.) (2002). *L'affectivité dans l'apprentissage.* Sainte-Foy: Presses de l'Université du Québec.

Lafortune, L., & Pons, F. (2004). Le rôle de l'anxiété dans la métacognition: une réflexion vers des actions. In L. Lafortune, P.-A. Doudin, F. Pons, & D. Hancock (Eds.), *Les émotions à l'école* (pp. 145-169). Sainte-Foy: Presses de l'Université du Québec.

Lafortune, L., & Robertson, A. (2005). Une réflexion portant sur les liens entre émotions et pensée critique. In L. Lafortune, M.-F. Daniel, P.-A. Doudin, F. Pons, & O. Albanese (Eds.), *Pédagogie et psycohologi des émotions: vers la compétence émotionnelle* (pp.61-84). Sainte-Foy: Presses de l'Université du Québec.

Lafortune, L., Deaudelin, C., Doudin, P.-A., & Martin, D. (Eds.) (2001). *La formation continue: De la réflexion à l'action.* Sainte-Foy: Presses de l'Université du Québec.

L'Hostie, M., & Boucher, L.-Ph. (Eds.) (2004). *L'accompagnement en éducation. Un soutien au renouvellement des pratiques.* Sainte-Foy: Presses de l'Université du Québec.

Martin, B.L., & Briggs, L.J. (1986). *The Affective and Cognitive Domains: Integration for Instruction and Research.* New Jersey: Educational Technology Publications.

Ministère de l'Éducation (2001). *Programme de formation de l'école québécoise. Éducation préscolaire. Enseignement primaire.* Quebec: Government of Quebec, Ministère de l'Éducation.

Ministère de l'Éducation (2003). *Programme de formation de l'école québécoise. Enseignement secondaire.* Quebec: Government of Quebec, Ministère de l'Éducation.

Mongeau, P., & Tremblay, J. (2002). *Survivre. La dynamique de l'inconfort.* Quebec: Presses de l'Université du Québec.

Pallascio, R., Daniel, M.-F., & Lafortune, L. (Eds.) (2004). *Pensée et réflexivité.* Quebec: Presses de l'Université du Québec.

Pons, F., Doudin, P.-A., Harris, P.L., & de Rosnay, M. (2002). Métaémotion et intégration scolaire. In L. Lafortune, & P. Mongeau (Eds.), *L'affectivité dans l'apprentissage* (pp. 7-28). Québec: Presses de l'Université du Québec.

Saarni, C. (1999). *The Development of Emotional Competency.* New York: The Guilford Press.

Thagard, P. (2000). *Coherence in Thought and Action.* Cambridge, MA: MIT Press.

Tobias, S. (1978). *Over-coming Math Anxiety.* Boston: Houghton Mifflin.

Appendix

Questionnaire – Exploratory Research – February - March 2003

The place of emotions in accompaniment

1a Identify and briefly describe two or three situations of accompaniment (during which the objective is to support a change in practices). What do you note about the emotions that emerge from the individuals affected by the change you wish to elicit or support? What type of emotions are they? How are they manifested?

1b What are the potential impacts of these emotions on others that are being accompanied and on the accompaniment process? How do you experience the emergence of these emotions?

2. Why do you think people experience this?

3. How do you help the people you accompany turn "insecure" experiences into secure imbalances? How do you manage this?

4. How do you prepare yourself to face these situations?

5. How do your own emotions interact with what is occurring?

CHAPTER 9

A study of children's representations of four basic emotions

Marie-France Daniel, Emmanuelle Auriac, Catherine Garnier, Martine Quesnel, and Michael Schleifer

1. Introduction

Within the framework of a research project subsidized by the Social Sciences and Humanities Research Council (SSHRC) of Canada from 2001 to 2005, focused on primary prevention of violence, one of our objectives consisted in studying the modification process of preschool-aged children's Social Representations (SR) of four basic emotions. We related violence prevention to a refinement of SR based on studies in which the internal source of violence was associated with the biased representations a person had of a situation.

The three questions we attempt to answer in this chapter are the following: (a) What are 5- and 6-year-old children's social representations of four basic emotions, specifically: happiness, anger, fear and sadness?[1] (b) Without specific stimulation, are the social representations of children in this age group stable? (c) With cognitive stimulation, how is the process of modifying representations manifested by these children? To answer the third question, our methodological postulate is that, with regular classroom practice during a school year, the Philosophy for Children approach could serve as a useful instrument to cognitively stimulate children and thus contribute to modifying their representations of emotions.

In the following pages, after defining the problem of violence prevention, we introduce a theoretical framework comprised of three interrelated components:

---

[1] Some researchers, such as Wallon (1925) name four basic emotions: happiness, fear, anger, and sadness. Other researchers (see Frijda, 1993; 2003) add four more basic emotions: pride, guilt, disgust, and surprise. Within the scope of our research project, we focus on the four basic emotions noted by Wallon.

social representations, emotions, and the Philosophy for Children approach. Subsequently, we present and discuss the preliminary results of a current experiment with preschool children.

2. Primary prevention of violence

Violence is an increasingly decried phenomenon in our societies. For Bergeret (1999), violence exists in each person; it is innate, natural, and fundamental. Under positive conditions, it is desirable, in that it represents a motor to love, energy and creativity; it is an instrument to ensure a person's survival. It is only when violence is not integrated that it can generate aggression and abuse.

This research project focuses on non-integrated violence, that which generates abuse and disorders. According to the *Ministère de l'Éducation* (1990), it is a question of "using power (physical, hierarchical, psychological, moral or social), in a manner that is open or concealed, spontaneous or deliberate, motivated or not, through the behavior or structures of an individual or a group and which has as its effect to compel or destroy, partially or completely, by physical, psychological, moral or social means, an object (material goods, persons, symbols) to ensure a response to a legitimate need or to react to this unfulfilled need." This type of violence can and must be fought and indeed prevented. However, to accomplish this, its source must first be known.

Researchers disagree as to the internal source of violence. Some establish a link between acts of violence and rupture of thought (Damasio, 1994; Malherbe, 2000; Wallon, 1925). Others link violence to the quality of an individual's SR of a situation or, more specifically, to the limits of these representations, inasmuch as when they are distorted, these representations may bias judgment concerning the situation and generate an act of violence (Libersan, 2003; Jodelet, 1993). Yet to others, emotions influence perceptions (Dantzer, 1988); moreover, violence is often linked to mismanaged emotions (Doudin & Erkohen-Markùs, 2000). We consider that it is relevant to study whether children's "SR of emotions" have an impact on their behaviors.

Our research project is situated within a perspective of prevention. There are three levels to violence prevention: primary, secondary, and tertiary. Our research project focuses on "primary" prevention; in other words it is intended for a healthy population, and its objective is to anticipate acts of violence. Schools can play a fundamental role in primary prevention of violence. In fact, a number of preventive approaches can be found within schools. However, most of these approaches emphasize the acquisition of pro-social skills in school-aged children (from ages 6-7), whereas our work is intended for preschool-aged children (ages 5-6) and focuses on their global development through cognitive development.

Some believe that investing in cognitive work with young children is inappropriate. Nevertheless, actions conducted in accordance with the *Convention on the Rights of the Child* ratified in 1989 by the United Nations Organization (UNO), which recommends that children's right to free speech and to autonomous and critical thought (see articles 5, 13, 14, 15 and 16) should be taken into account. We would further point out that studies have shown that young children are able to reflect upon their emotions so as to understand their causes and consequences (Pons, Harris, & de Rosnay, 2003; Pons, Lawson, Harris, & de Rosnay, 2003), and that this reflection can have an incidence on the quality of their social interactions (Villanueva, Clemente, & Garcia, 2000). Finally, we would mention works that show that SR serve to regulate behaviors in relation to the social norms within which an individual acts, and that the modification of a person's social representations influences that person's judgment and behavior (Duveen, 1999; Garnier, 1999.)

In sum, our research project is situated within a perspective of primary prevention of violence. As a complement to what is already being accomplished in schools, we have decided to work with preschool children. On one hand, studies have shown that violent behaviors appear very early in children (Dodson, 1972; Dumas, 2000), and, on the other hand, a review of the literature indicates that children are capable of understanding their emotions and of thinking of them in terms of causal relations. One of the objectives of this research project was to describe five- and six-year-old children's social representations of emotions and to understand how their SR evolve during the course of a school year. To this end, we recall the questions entertained in this chapter: (1) What are 5- and 6-year-old children's social representations of four basic emotions (happiness, anger, fear and sadness)? (2) Without specific stimulation, are the social representations of children in this age group stable? (3) With cognitive stimulation, how is the process of modifying representations manifested by the children?

3. Social representations of emotions

In the following pages, to ensure a better understanding of the meaning of "social representations of emotions," we will first address the "social representations" aspect, then the "emotions" aspect before focusing on the philosophical approach.

Social representations (SR)

At the end of the nineteenth century, Durkheim introduced the notion of *collective representations* as legitimate scientific subjects. Following his lead, mentality historians surfaced: Aries studied child and family; Vovelle looked into death; Foucault into insanity and sexuality; Elias into morals and hygiene; Vigarello into cleanliness and filthiness, etc. Piaget too, in his epistemological studies, was led to pose the problem of representations, in particular that of moral judgment in children, when he looked into the modification of their ideas regarding notions of discipline, rules, respect, cooperation, etc. (see Mannoni, 1998). In social psychology, the notion of *social representation* was introduced by Moscovici (1961). Moscovici provided a scientific definition of the concept and described a method of analysis that can be used to interpret it.

The theoretical foundation of Social Representation (SR) is constructivist and postulates the absence of a rupture between the world and the individual and between the interior and the exterior of an individual or a group. In other words, it presupposes that objective reality does not exist, but that it is always represented. That is, it is appropriated by an individual or group, reconstructed within that person's or group's symbolical universe, and integrated into the person's or group's value system (Doise, 1992). The SR is then both the "product and the process of a mental activity through which a person, or group, reconstitutes the reality to which he is confronted, and gives it a specific meaning" (Abric, 1994, p. 13).

Some theoreticians specify that the basis of SR is necessarily socio-constructivist, since SR is determined by the social system in which the person moves, and by the nature of the relations the person maintains with the system. From this perspective, representation is a form of socially-elaborated and shared knowledge that contributes to the construction of a common reality (Jodelet, 1989). It corresponds to opinions, beliefs, and attitudes linked to an object or a situation.

As a world vision developed by social players, SR work as an organized and hierarchical system of interpretation of social data. They enable individuals to decode the expectations and anticipations of other members, and they are interdependent in relation to the actions of each and all (Abric, 1994). SR and social practice are correlative and co-constituent. Indeed, representations guide and determine practice, and practice creates or transforms representations. In other words, SR serve to interpret situations and to justify behaviors with regard to the social norms that influence individuals (e.g. Doise, 1969). Hence, SR have two functions: identification and orientation.

In short, representations are the individual and spontaneous construction of reality as it evolves within a social context. The functions of representations are (i) identification of an individual with his reference group and (ii) orientation with regard to expectations and conduct. As for the study of representations, it allows one to understand, comprehend and explain (knowledge function) this reality (Abric, 1994.)

In the particular context of our study, we first ensured theoretically that emotions constitute an object of representation. Unlike Doise, Moliner (1993) maintains that not all objects stem from SR since, if this were the case, SR would be our only means of interpretation of the world. According to Moliner "there will be a representational elaboration when, for structural or conjectural reasons, a group of individuals is confronted with a polymorphic subject whose command constitutes an issue in terms of social cohesion or identity. Moreover, when command of this subject constitutes an issue for other social players that interact with the group. Finally, when the group is not subjected to a regulation or control authority that defines an orthodox system." (p. 13). Thus, the Molinerian criteria concern, on the one hand, the polymorphic character of an object (varying forms and meanings) and, on the other hand, the value of the issue (impact on the individual and on social issues).

In the case of our study, emotions are a human product (in opposition, for example, to social practices or physical objects), that presuppose a twofold issue: individual and social. Individual issues are notably situated on cognitive and emotional levels insofar as refining children's SR of emotions provides them with a better comprehension of the ins and outs of actions (theirs and those of their peers) and, consequently, a better comprehension of the world that surrounds them and better control over their lives. The issues are also social, since refining children's SR of emotions may have an impact on their cooperative or aggressive pro-social behaviors and on classroom climate. From this perspective, Jodelet (1989) maintains that representations "fit into pre-existing thought frames while involving social ethics" (p. 34).

As for the polymorphic nature of SR, we note the complexity of emotions concerning their underlying manifestations and meanings. For example, happiness can be represented by laughter, jumping, blushing, tears, etc.; fear can be considered a sign of femininity in women (positive) or a sign of weakness in leaders (negative). But what about emotions themselves?

Emotions

A brief historical overview reminds us of the theorists' lack of consensus in defining emotion. At first, there were the peripheral theories of James, of Lange and of Cannon (end of the nineteenth century), which essentially linked emotional states to bodily perceptions. Then, Schachter and Singer (mid twentieth century) put forward a physio-cognitive theory of emotions. This theory is situated at the intersection of physiological and cognitive theories of emotion in that it includes physiological manifestations and their cognitive interpretations. Subsequently, cognitive theories appear with Arnold (mid twentieth century), who upholds that the brain is not the site of simple reflexes, but that it is active in decoding emotional stimuli. It calls upon the concept of recalling anterior emotional experiences and appraising possible consequences. Later, the relational theory of emotions appears in the 1970s with Lazarus, who introduced the interaction of the individual with his environment as a determinant of emotion. The latter would be influenced by the norms, rules and social characteristics of the environment, although the fundamental process at the root of the determination of an emotion would be an internal cognitive treatment. Likewise, Averill (1980) conceives of emotions as social constructions controlled by social rules and behavioral expectations, which, in turn, influence an individual's emotional experience.

Some psychologists concur in upholding that, no matter what type of situation is experienced by an individual, there is generally a desire and a belief (Harris & Pons, 2003) or a concern of a personal, relational or social nature at the root of emotion. Personal concern is linked to physical and psychological integrity. It includes issues such as protecting the body, satisfying basic needs and safeguarding self-esteem. Relational concern conveys fundamental links (family, etc.) which are the basis of cohesion in social groups. Social concern is linked to respect for norms, principles and values that perpetuate social order. The satisfaction or non-satisfaction of the latter would be at the root of emotional induction. With the exception of fear, which can assume a personal character, the other three emotions are generally triggered in a relational or social context. It would appear that protecting one's body and self-esteem is generally at the root of happiness and fear; that satisfying relational needs is generally linked to happiness and sadness; and that anger is often linked to respect of social norms (Cosnier, 1994.).

Studies that show the contribution of cognition to the emotional function of individuals maintain that pupils who have learning difficulties in school show more difficulty understanding emotions, even when compared to youngsters that have been abused (see Pons, Doudin, Harris & de Rosnay, 2005). Other studies (e.g. Harris & Pons, 2003) reveal that reflecting on emotions tends to regulate their intensity or, in other words, that reflecting on emotions is a process that is likely to alter an individual's emotional function, with a repercussion on social components. Furthermore, other studies specify that exchanges with parents can significantly contribute to a child's increased understanding of emotions. In this constructivist perspective, we postulate that exchanges among peers regarding philosophical (open) concepts are likely to contribute to the refinement of children's social representations of emotions. We now broach the third and last section of the theoretical framework: the philosophical approach.

The philosophical approach

As previously mentioned, the research objective pursued in this chapter concerns the description of children's SR of emotions, as well as the comprehension of the evolution process of these SR. Thus there is relevance in cognitively stimulating these children in order to ascertain that their SR evolve during the school year. To do this, the "methodological postulate" (see Van der Maren, 1996) we proposed was to the effect that the Philosophy for Children (P4C) approach, if practiced regularly in the classroom during a school year, can be a relevant instrument in the cognitive stimulation of children and can thus contribute to modifying their SR of emotions. Indeed, several studies have shown that P4C helps develop cognitive, social and communication skills in youngsters (e.g.: Camhy & Iberer, 1988; Cannon, 1987; Cannon & Weinstein, 1985; Gazzard, 1988; Lane & Lane, 1986; Schleifer, Daniel, Lafortune & Pallascio, 1999). Within the framework of our research project, P4C was thus considered a pedagogical tool that contributed to achieving the pursued goal.

P4C was conceived in the 1970s by American philosopher Matthew Lipman and his team from Montclair State University in New Jersey. It is now used in nearly 50 countries throughout the world, and its material has been translated into 20 languages (see Lipman, Sharp & Oscanyan, 1980). The philosophical support material written by Lipman includes seven philosophical novels intended for youngsters aged 6 to 15. It draws its inspiration from the fields of philosophy: logic, ethics, esthetics, etc.

The philosophical support material used within the framework of our research project is titled *The Tales of Audrey-Anne* (Daniel 2002, 2003). It is new material that falls within Lipman's perspective but is specifically intended for primary prevention of violence with five-year-old children. This support material has been previously validated. Experiments in Quebec and France have shown that, insofar as the *Tales* and the ensuing exchanges among peers are situated in the children's "proximal development zone" (Vygotsky, 1985), the children quickly learn to become involved in dialogical reflection focused on concepts such as violence, emotions, rights, etc. (see Daniel, 2004; Daniel & Michel, 2001; Schleifer, Daniel, Auriac & Lecompte, 2003.). The *Tales* are of a philosophical nature, because they favor the questioning of open concepts for which there is no single answer and upon which the children are invited to reflect as a group. The specific objectives of the *Tales* aim to develop cognitive (understanding and identifying causes, anticipating consequences, establishing relations, judging, etc.) and social (autonomy, empathy, dialogue, etc.) skills within the context of awareness of various manifestations of violence.

A three-step educational method is suggested to help the children "philosophize": (1) The adult reads a tale to the children. (2) The children are invited to ask philosophical questions (Why ___? What does ___ mean?) inspired by the reading, and which they would like to discuss as a group. (3) Together, the children attempt to answer the question(s) they have chosen and are led to hold a dialogue. A dialogue is said to be philosophical when the children, instead of lingering over personal anecdotes, search for the meaning of concepts, question, share their opinions, justify these opinions with valid reasons, find similarities and differences, give counter-examples, draw relationships between concepts, show criticism toward the statements of peers, self-correct, etc. The objective of dialogue is not to bring the children to recount personal situations in relation to manifestations of violence, but rather to encourage them to reflect as a "community of inquiry" upon concepts. It should be understood that the classroom is transformed into a community of inquiry only when the dialogue is marked with respect, open-mindedness and tolerance. Thus, it is not a question of getting the children to argue in a spirit of competition but rather to hold a dialogue with a focus on cooperation. Each child's intervention thus contributes to the enrichment of the group's perspective.

4. Method of analysis

This research is exploratory and includes: (a) an approach with experimental and control groups that enables us to study children's SR when they are stimulated cognitively, and when they are not stimulated on this level; (b) a grounded theory approach that allows analysis of the modification process of SR.

Our method of analysis draws its inspiration from the Grounded Theory (Glaser & Strauss, 1967; Huberman & Miles, 1991), which is characterized by among other things the need for a diversity of participants. In this perspective, we chose eight preschool classes (experimental and control), of which six were in Quebec and two in France. In Quebec, the classes were composed of 12 to 18 children, whereas in France they numbered 27. The socioeconomic backgrounds represented ranged from privileged to underprivileged. In this chapter we use only the data collected on the six groups (experimental and control) from Quebec.

All the children in the experimental groups received the benefit of a weekly philosophical intervention. The philosophical sessions, which varied between 30 and 45 minutes per week according to the children's ability to concentrate, took place between October and May. The control group children were from the same schools, but they were not subjected to philosophical interventions.

Variables associated with age and gender factors, as well as cultural, social, and socioeconomic factors were taken into account. The experimental and control groups were paired according to the following points: children's minimum age was 5 and maximum age was 6; proportion of girls and boys was close to 50%; children were French-speaking; and children were city-dwellers.

For the study of SR, we met 54 children in individual interviews, that is, nine per classroom, selected by the teachers in each experimental and control group, according to the children's level in school (three that were academically strong, three that showed weakness, and three that were average). A twenty-minute interview took place at the beginning of the experiment (end of September pre-test) and another at the end of the experiment (end of May post-test). At the beginning of the interview, to put the child at ease, the interviewer asked the child to draw a picture of herself or himself with friends at school. This drawing (pretext) served as a starting point for the interviewer's questions (see Galli & Nigro, 1990, 1992.)

The interview questions were based on word associations, which, in our study, focused on four basic emotions (happiness, anger, fear and sadness). For example, "In your drawing, I see a person that looks sad. What does feeling sad mean to you? Give me three words." The word-association technique is relevant, because it allows a concept's diversity of meaning to emerge (for example, children might represent "happiness" as eating cake, not crying, playing with friends, etc.) (Rouquette & Rateau, 1998). When studying SR while resorting to word-associations, salience (or the concepts' frequency of appearance) is used as an indicator. Thus, the fact that certain concepts are frequently stated indicates that they play an organizing role in the field of this particular group's SR (Abric, 1994). All the interviewers respected the same protocol. Individual interviews were videotaped.

To answer our research objective with regard to the description of children's SR as well as the comprehension of the evolution process of these representations (with and without cognitive stimulation), we followed the Grounded Theory's analytical process (Glaser & Strauss, 1967; Laperrière, 1998; Paillé, 1994), which took place in two phases.

Phase 1

We first transcribed the 53 children's answers in the pre-tests and post-tests, in relation to the four emotions, yielding a total of 424 elements to be analyzed.[2] The head of research coded each element with specific memos. To bring forth the more important aspects of this data, she grouped the codes into 10 preliminary conceptual categories. Furthermore, to specify or consolidate these categories, she assigned particular properties or characteristics to each one. To consider the data as a whole, and to further comprehend the modification process of SR, she related these categories to each other in order to reveal as many links as possible between them. This in turn led to the emergence of three main categories that enable the integration of the entire data set: non-representation or representation without naming the emotion, concrete or self-centered representation of emotion, and socializing representation of emotion. It should be mentioned that codification and categorization remained preliminary during the entire analysis process.

After four weeks, the head of research completed another analysis of the 424 elements. Subsequently, she submitted this analysis to two of the team's co-researchers (one from France and the other from Quebec) with the intention of confronting differences and consolidating interpretations. In case of divergence, exchanges took place until a consensus was reached.

Phase 2

The result from the first phase analysis, that is, the categorization that emerged from the word-association analysis, became the instrument of analysis for the second phase. In other words, during the second phase of the analysis, the head of research applied the categorization of the emotions' SR, as it had emerged from the first phase, to the analysis of the children's 424 answers. The intent was to understand the character (stable or dynamic) of five- and six-year-old children's SR both without the benefit of any particular cognitive stimulation and when cognitively stimulated by the philosophical approach.

For this second phase of the analysis, the researcher once again proceeded with a second analysis four weeks later and subsequently to a confrontation of results with team co-researchers.

---

[2] We asked the children to give three words; however, the majority gave only one. Consequently, we chose to deal only with the first word provided by each child.

5. Results

In the following pages, we present the categorization of children's SR of the basic emotions and then the dynamic of the representations when the children do or do not experiment with cognitive stimulation.

Children's SR of four basic emotions – A categorization

In this section, in table form, we illustrate the categorization of five- and six-year-old children's SR of emotions, as it emerged in the first phase of analysis. The example provided evolves from the word "happiness."

Ten sub-categories were grouped into three main categories which were organized into hierarchical stages: non-representation or representation without naming the emotion (1-2-3), concrete or self-centered representation (4-5-6-7), and socializing representation (8-9-10). However, it is important to note that within these three stages the order, from 1 to 3, from 4 to 7 or from 8 to 10, does not infer a hierarchy (for example that 1 is inferior to 3 or that 7 is superior to 5.)

Table 1
SR of emotions: Three categories (sub-categories, description and example)

Category 1: Representation without naming	
1	Indicates that the child does not know the inductor word (e.g.: I don't know).
2	Applies when the child states a definition that is unrelated to the inductor word (e.g.: spend the day, bandage).
3	Means that the child simply repeats the inductor word (e.g.: happiness).
Category 2: Concrete or self-centered representation of emotion	
4	Differs from the former in that it indicates a certain vision of what happiness is. It can be identified with a more or less lasting way of being. Thus, stage 4 indicates that children represent happiness by the well-being they experience (e.g.: being happy, feeling calm). This state is elaborated from self in a self-centered form.
5	Refers to the child's true feelings. The emotional state is expressed as a concept (e.g.: happiness) rather than with a substantive. Representation of emotion does not refer to others as participating in one's happiness.
6	Indicates that the child represents happiness through sensorial experiences (e.g.: eating a piece of chocolate cake) or through its concrete or observable manifestations (e.g.: smiling).
7	Refers to a cause rather than to a manifestation of happiness, as in 6. It should be noted that this cause can be either concrete (e.g.: when it's your birthday, when I'm in the garden), or self-centered, in other words included in a relation of exclusivity rather than reciprocity (e.g.: being alone with Mom).
Category 3: Socializing representation of emotion	
8	When taking the other into account plays a part. It differs from the former in that it introduces a social perspective. But it does not emphasize a mutual relationship with peers where "You" and "I" are equally active; it infers that happiness depends on others (e.g.: when someone plays with me, when someone likes us).
9	Indicates that the children represent happiness through the expression of a moral duty or a learned and integrated obligation (e.g.: you must share with your friend).
10	Indicates that the children's SR do not presuppose an exclusive relationship with others, but illustrate a relationship with peers in which "I" plays an active role. They refer to an interpersonal relationship that is constructed and based on reciprocity (e.g.: love, playing with my friends, having good friends, having fun with others).

Dynamic of children's SR of four basic emotions – With and without cognitive stimulation

In this section, we present the results of the second phase of the analysis, meaning that the second analysis we performed of the 424 elements was based on the categories and the characteristics of the SR that emerged from the first phase of the analysis and that are presented in the previous section (descriptive table). The objective consists in understanding the modification process of the children's SR of each of the basic emotions when cognitively stimulated (experimental groups) and not stimulated (control groups) with P4C during a school year. The results are examined sequentially, one emotion at a time: happiness, anger, fear and sadness.

Happiness
In the experimental groups, analyses of transcripts from the beginning of the school year bring to light a perspective of emotion "without denomination" by half the group (16/27). However, there is an emergence of a "concrete or self-centered" representation (8 children), and of a "socializing" representation (3 children) in the group. At the end of the school year, the group of children is increasingly characterized by representation shared among all three levels: 10 of 27 children show a representation of happiness "without denomination" (10/27 children), 9 children have a concrete representation, whereas 8 children have a socializing representation.

Hence, between the pre-test and the post-test, the experimental groups' SR evolved by tending increasingly toward a more socialized perspective: representation without denomination went from 16 children to 10; concrete representation went from 8 children to 9; socializing representation went from 3 children to 8. The developmental process observed in the groups of children's modifications can be invoked here, emotions fitting into dynamics that are more complex, but also resulting from a social effect in which representations develop in the midst of social interactions.

In the control groups at the beginning of the school year, as in the experimental groups, half the children (13/26 children) conceive of happiness "without denomination," whereas 8 children have a concrete representation, and 5 a socializing representation. At the end of the school year, the children show an evolution toward "concrete" representation, since 7 children manifest a conception of happiness without denomination and half (15) have a concrete conception, while the remaining 4 manifest a socializing representation.

Between the pre-test and the post-test, the control groups' SR also evolved, shifting toward concrete representation (representation without denomination went from 13 to 7 children, concrete representation increased from 8 to 15 children, and socializing representation diminished slightly from 5 to 4 children). These results confirm the interpretation regarding the evolution of the representation of happiness in the experimental groups; however, this transformation is less marked in the control groups. Indeed, it mostly affects the concrete representation, whereas the experimental groups seem to pursue a progressive tendency toward socializing representation.

In short, we note that the children's SR of happiness change during the school year, with or without cognitive stimulation. But the children that experienced cognitive stimulation achieved greater transformation in their representation of happiness.

Table 2
Number of answers concerning SR of happiness by group, phase and category

Group	Pre-test			Post-test		
	Category 1	Category 2	Category 3	Category 1	Category 2	Category 3
Experimental	16	8	3	10	9	8
Control	13	8	5	7	15	4

Anger
At the beginning of the school year, the representation of anger, for half of the children (14/27) in the experimental groups, is mostly marked by its concrete aspects, whereas 9 children have a "representation without denomination" of anger and the remaining 4 children have a socializing representation. At the end of the school year, modifications tend toward a socializing representation, since 9 children are situated in this third category whereas 14 have a concrete representation of anger, and 4 still conceive of anger "without denomination."

Thus, between the pre-test and the post-test, the transformation of the groups' representations of anger tends toward a greater integration of the social aspects of this emotion. The number of children "without denomination" decreases, and the number with a "socializing representation" increases. We can therefore hypothesize that, as is the case with happiness, this is due to a developmental process. This interpretation is even more plausible in this case if we consider the fact that, from the start, the emotion of anger (9/27) is more integrated than that of happiness (16/27).

In the control groups, at the beginning of the school year, 6 children out of 26 have a representation of anger "without denomination", 13 of them have a concrete or self-centered representation and, finally, 7 have a socializing representation. For these children, at the end of the school year, the tendency remains quite similar and modifications are slight: 5 children have a representation of anger "without denomination" (slight decrease,) and 15 have a concrete representation (slight increase). Finally, six have a socializing representation (slight decrease).

In short, regarding the SR of anger, the margin of transformation in the groups without cognitive stimulation remains limited, whereas that of the experimental groups is more significant.

Table 3
Number of answers concerning SR of anger by group, phase and category

Group	Pre-test			Post-test		
	Category 1	Category 2	Category 3	Category 1	Category 2	Category 3
Experimental	9	14	4	4	14	9
Control	6	13	7	5	15	6

Fear

From the outset, the representational development concerning fear is again proposed. From the beginning of the school year, the experimental groups include 7 children whose representation is "without denomination," whereas the majority (19/27) have a concrete or self-centered representation, particularly in relation to an imaginary cause linked to sub-category 5 (e.g.: fear of a monster,) and a single child expresses a socializing representation. At the end of the school year, we note a slight modification with respect to an evolution toward socializing representation (6 children have a representation of fear "without denomination", 17 have a concrete representation, this time in relation to a real cause linked to sub-category 7 (darkness, a loud noise, etc.), and 4 children express a socializing representation. Thus, between the pre-test and the post-test, we see a slight transformation in the group, but the tendency remains highly concrete because it is grounded in reality.

With regard to the control groups' representations of this emotion, the portrait at the beginning of the school year clearly differs from that of the experimental groups, with a similar distribution in the first two categories. Thus, 12 children out of 26 are situated in the "without denomination" category, 11 children have a concrete representation of fear (5 associate it with an imaginary cause and 6 with a real cause), and 3 children are situated in a socializing representation. At the end of the school year, modifications are few, with 9 children having a representation of fear "without denomination," 13 having a concrete representation (the majority [8/13] being situated in the imaginary dimension linked to sub-category 5), and 4 children having a socializing representation. Hence, between the pre-test and post-test, the modifications are modest, and can be attributed to developmental fluctuations, since the groups achieve a certain level of awareness of their emotions by the end of the school year.

In a certain sense, the children's SR of fear form a picture that resembles that of the SR of anger, but the evolution is more marked on the intermediary level; from the outset, at the beginning of the year, the control groups differ from the experimental groups.

In short, in the experimental group children's SR of fear were mostly refined in the transition from an imaginary cause of fear (10 children in the pre-test *versus* 4 in the post-test) to a real cause (5 in the pre-test *versus* 8 in the post-test). In the control group children, however, it is rather a transition from "without denomination" (from 12 children in the pre-test to 9 in the post-test) to a concrete or self-centered representation linked to an imaginary cause.

Table 4
Number of answers concerning SR of fear by group, phase and category

Group	Pre-test			Post-test		
	Category 1	Category 2	Category 3	Category 1	Category 2	Category 3
Experimental	7	19	1	6	17	4
Control	12	11	3	9	13	4

Sadness
At the beginning of the school year, the experimental groups show a pattern that is rather similar to that of their representations of anger (10 children out of 27 have a representation of sadness "without denomination," 13 have a concrete or self-centered representation, and 4 have a socializing representation). At the end of the school year, the modifications are significant and tend toward

a developmental process, as we previously observed with anger, but also with happiness (3 children have a representation of sadness "without denomination," 12 have a concrete representation, and 12 have a socializing representation).

As for the control groups, at the beginning of the school year, they show a more nuanced profile (11 children out of 26 express a representation of sadness "without denomination," 8 express a concrete or self-centered representation, and 7 a socializing representation). However, their evolution is less marked than the experimental groups, since at the end of the school year, 9 children express a representation of sadness "without denomination," 11 have a concrete or self-centered representation, and 6 have a socializing representation. Thus, between the pre-test and post-test, the evolution is developmental but tends mostly toward the concrete representation level.

In sum, if we compare both groups, clear progressions are noted in the SR of sadness. Indeed, the refinement of the experimental group children's SR of sadness are manifest between the beginning and the end of the school year. The evolution took place in the transition from "without denomination" to "socializing representation." On the other hand, the control group children have SR of sadness that are more concrete or self-centered. Refinement between the pre-test and the post-test took place in the transition from "without denomination" to "concrete representation."

Table 5
Number of answers concerning SR of sadness by group, phase and category

Group	Pre-test			Post-test		
	Category 1	Category 2	Category 3	Category 1	Category 2	Category 3
Experimental	10	13	4	3	12	12
Control	11	8	7	9	11	6

To conclude on these results, we must note the emergent general tendencies. The experimental groups systematically make greater progress in their evolution and reach socializing representation in higher numbers, whereas the control groups seem to persist at the concrete representation level. More specifically, in the pre-test, the majority of experimental group children have a representation of happiness "without denomination" and a mostly concrete or self-centered representation of the other emotions (anger, sadness and fear). In the post-test, refinement of the experimental group children's SR of the four emotions was manifest on the levels of both concrete and socializing representations, in other words, representations without denomination clearly decreased, in particular concerning happiness, anger and sadness, and socializing representations increased with regard to all four emotions, and in particular with regard to sadness.

Moreover, in the control groups, representations "without denomination" decreased for all four emotions, giving way to an essentially concrete representation for the four emotions, whereas socializing representations decreased slightly between the pre-test and post-test with regard to three emotions: happiness, anger and sadness.

Although the developmental process is perceptible in each group, the role of cognitive stimulation in the experimental groups is of interest. Without asserting that the profiles of the experimental groups result from this intervention alone, the fact that they differ so clearly from those of the control groups allows us to attribute this effect in part to cognitive stimulation.

6. Discussion and conclusion

As a result of the analyses, we are able to maintain that emotions are objects of representations in the same way as other objects (Moliner, 1993); that five- and six-year-old children's SR of emotions are a dynamic construction that evolve within a social context (Abric, 1994) and because of this context (Vygotsky, 1985).

In response to the second research question, concerning the stable or dynamic character of children's SR, the results of our analysis indicate that five- and six-year-old children's SR are dynamic, whether or not they receive cognitive stimulation. Modification of SR seems to take place with peer contact, and both formal and informal everyday learning situations, despite the fact that we often characterize children with a self-centered, or closed and not easily influenced, epistemology.

Furthermore, the experimental group children, instead of associating their emotions only with observable manifestations, begin to understand their social significance and recognize the role of others in the emergence of their own emotions (see Cosnier, 1994; Harris & Pons, 2003). Maturation, associated with the transition from age 5 to 6, is fundamental in modifying representations of emotions. However, it goes without saying that, in conformity with Vygotsky's thesis (1985), without cognitive stimulation of a socio-constructivist nature, in other words a stimulation based on social interactions (in this case, weekly philosophical dialogue among peers), the "socializing" nature of the modification of SR is not ensured.

To answer concomitantly the first and third research questions, which concern the description of preschool children's SR of four basic emotions when cognitively stimulated according to a philosophical approach, the following points emerged from the analysis. With regard to the SR of happiness, although non-representation dominates slightly, it can be said that the children's answers in the post-test are almost equally distributed among all three levels. What seems to be the central core of their representation of happiness comes down to two sub-categories: namely the way they feel (sub-category 4: "feeling happy," "feeling calm") and the social relationship of reciprocity (sub-category 10: "having fun with others," "love", etc.). Thus, a number of children acquired a certain degree of awareness that happiness occurs in the presence of others, that it necessitates a personal commitment or an active rather than a passive construction of the social relationship.

With regard to the SR of anger, at the end of the school year, two sub-categories emerged: the way they feel (sub-category 4: "feeling angry", etc.) and the contribution of others (sub-category 8: "when you say things that aren't nice," "when someone hits me", etc.). Thus, for several children, anger is henceforth linked to a cause, which places interpersonal relationships at the forefront.

With regard to fear, at the end of the school year, the experimental group children represented it with real causes (sub-category 7: "darkness," "nightmares," "noises I don't recognize", etc.), instead of the imaginary causes displayed at the beginning of the school year ("ghosts," "monsters," "vampires", etc.). Thus, a number of them seem not only to better comprehend the meaning of fear, but also to exert a better control over this fear, which leads us to suppose that they have probably acquired greater confidence in themselves and in the world surrounding them.

Finally, what predominates in these same groups of children regarding sadness are both its concrete manifestations (sub-category 6: "crying," "pouting", etc.) and the contribution of others as causes of sadness (sub-category 8: "when you're all alone," "when I'm being yelled at," "when my father died," "when my sisters hit me", etc.). Thus, not only do these children explicitly represent sadness, but also its representations indicate that they are most often subjected to it and, by corollary, that social relations are bearers of happiness, anger and sadness.

The fulfillment of the research objective treated in this chapter enables us to outline theoretical avenues linked to the process of internalization, appropriation and modification of the experimental group children's emotions: during exchanges among peers, words associated with new representations are created in the children's minds and are modified. It therefore becomes possible for the children to form "spontaneous" concepts with words that designate emotions. Shared definitions that tend toward a consensual tangent of social reality are then developed by the group (Abric, 1994; Doise, 1992; Jodelet, 1989; Moliner, 1993).

As previously mentioned, this study is exploratory in nature, and the results we share in this chapter are preliminary; therefore, we do not intend to generalize them. Nonetheless, we maintain that they represent an interesting starting point, and that they are worth looking into systematically. From this perspective, a larger team of researchers has received another subsidy from the Social Sciences and Humanities Research Council (SSHRC) of Canada to achieve the objectives with a larger sampling of children and more diversified data collection instruments. The preliminary results reached and discussed in this paper will become more relevant since we will then be able: to verify, with a larger number of subjects, the validity of the categories that emerged from this study; to theorize based on the emergent categories in order to better understand the evolution process of children's representations of emotions; to compare various educational approaches that strive toward the cognitive development of five- and six-year-old children to determine which components of these approaches most adequately stimulate the intellectual skills linked to the modification of children's SR; and primarily to study a possible correlation between children's cognitive development and their pro-social behaviors. Indeed, if we maintain that one of the internal sources of violence is situated in a person's biased SR of situations (Libersan, 2003), and that adequate stimulation is likely to positively influence children's SR of emotions toward a more "socializing" dimension, we should verify to what extent work on SR is likely to affect the primary prevention of violence, that is, to orient five- and six-year-old children's behavior with respect to more integrated and more cooperative social practice.

References

Abric, J.-C. (1994). *Pratiques sociales et Représentations*. Paris: PUF.

Averill, J. R. (1980). A constructivist view of emotion. In R. Plutchik, & H. Kellerman (Eds.), *Emotion. Theory, Research and Experience*, Tome 1, *Theories of Emotion*. New York: Academic Press.

Bergeret, J. (1999). La violence fondamentale. In P. Mazet, & S. Lebovici (Eds.), *Violences*, Cahier n°. 49 (pp. 1–18). Bobigny: UFR de médecine de Bobigny.

Camhy, D., & Iberer, G. (1988). Philosophy for children: A research project for further mental and personality development of primary and secondary school pupils. *Thinking, 7*(4), 18-26.

Cannon, D. (1987). Good reasoning: A reconsideration drawn from experience with Philosophy for children. *Analytic Teaching, 8* (1), 30-35.

Cannon, D., & Weinstein, M. (1985). Reasoning skills: An overview. *Thinking, 6*(1), 29-33.

Cosnier, J. (1994). *Psychologie des émotions et des sentiments.* Paris: Éditions Retz.

Damasio, A.R. (1994). *Descartes' Error: Emotion, Reason and the Human Brain.* New York: Putnam.

Daniel, M.-F. (2002). *Les contes d'Audrey-Anne.* Quebec City: Le Loup de Gouttière.

Daniel, M.-F. (2003). *Dialoguer sur le corps et la violence: un pas vers la prevention.* Quebec City: Loup de Gouttière.

Daniel, M.-F. (2004). Philosopher sur le corps et la violence. Récit d'une expérimentation auprès d'enfants de 5 ans. *International Journal of Early Childhood, 36*(1), 23-35.

Daniel, M.-F., & Michel, A.-M. (2001). Learning to think and to speak: Account of an experiment involving children aged 3 to 5 in France and Quebec. *Thinking, 15* (3), 17-26.

Dantzer, R. (1988). *Les emotions.* Paris: PUF.

Dodson, F. (1972). *Tout se joue avant 6 ans.* Paris: Robert Laffont.

Doise, W. (1969). Stratégie de jeu à l'intérieur et entre groupes de nationalités différentes. *Bulletin du CERP, 18*, 13-26.

Doise, W. (1992). L'ancrage dans les études sur les représentations sociales. *Bulletin de psychologie.* Numéro special, *Nouvelles voies en psychologie sociale*, XLV, 405, 189–195.

Doudin, P.-A., & Erkohen-Markus, M. (Eds.) (2000). *Violences à l'école. Fatalité ou défi ?* Brussels: De Boeck-Larcier.

Dumas, J. (2000). *L'enfant violent – le connaître, l'aider, l'aimer.* Paris: Bayard.

Duveen, G. (1999). Le développement des représentations sociales chez les jeunes enfants: un exemple, le genre. In M.-L. Rouquette, & C. Garnier (Eds.), *La genèse des représentations socials* (pp. 114-136). Montreal: Éditions Nouvelles.

Frijda, N.H. (1993). Les théories des émotions: un bilan. In B. Rimé, & K.R. Scherer (Eds.), *Les émotions* (pp. 21-72). Neuchâtel: Delachaux and Niestlé.

Frijda, N.H. (2003). Passions: l'émotion comme motivation. In J.–M. Colletta, & A. Tcherkassof (Eds.), *Les émotions. Cognition, langage et développement* (pp. 15–33). Sprimont (Belgium): Mardaga.

Galli, I., & Nigro, G. (1990). Les représentations sociales: la question de la genèse. *Revue internationale de psychologie sociale, 3*(3), 429-450.

Galli, I., & Nigro, G. (1992). La représentation sociale du pouvoir chez les enfants. *Bulletin de psychologie*. Numéro special, *Nouvelles voies en psychologie sociale, XLV,* 405, p. 4-7.

Garnier, C. (1999). La genèse des représentations sociales dans une perspective développementale. In M.-L. Rouquette, & C. Garnier (Eds.), *La genèse des représentations socials* (pp. 87–113). Montreal: Éditions Nouvelles.

Gazzard, A. (1988). Thinking skills in science and Philosophy for children. *Thinking, 7*(3), 32-41.

Glaser, B.G., & Strauss, A.L. (1967). *The Discovery of Grounded Theory. Strategies for Qualitative Research*. Chicago: Aldine.

Harris, P.L., & Pons, F. (2003). Perspectives actuelles sur le développement de la compréhension des émotions chez l'enfant. In J.–M. Colletta, & A. Tcherkassof (Eds.), *Les émotions. Cognition, langage et développement* (pp. 209–229). Sprimont (Belgium): Mardaga.

Huberman, A.M., & Miles, M.B. (1991). *Analyse des données qualitatives: recueil de nouvelles méthodes*. Brussels: De Boeck.

Jodelet, D. (1989). Représentations sociales: un domaine en expansion. D. Jodelet (Ed.), *Les représentations socials* (pp. 31–61). Paris: PUF.

Jodelet, D. (1993). Indigenous psychologies and social representations of the body and self. In U. Kim, & J. Berry (Eds.), *Indigenous psychologies. Research and Experience in Cultural Context* (pp. 177-192). London: Sage Publications.

Lane, N.R., & Lane, S.A. (1986). Rationality, self-esteem and autonomy through collaborative enquiry. *Oxford Review of Education, 12,* 263-275.

Laperrière, A. (1998). La théorisation ancrée: Démarche analytique et comparaison avec d'autres approches apparentées. In. J. Poupart, J.–P. Deslauriers, L.H. Groulx, A. Laperrière, R. Mayer, & A. Pires (Eds.), *La recherche qualitative: Enjeux épistémologiques et méthodologiques* (pp. 309–346). Boucherville: Gaëtan Morin Éditeur.

Lazarus, R.S., Averill, J.R., & Opton, O.M. (1970). Toward a cognitive theory of emotions. In M.B. Arnold (Ed.), *Feelings and emotions* (pp. 207-232). New York: Academic Press.

Libersan, C. (2003). *Cette peur qui rend violent*. Montreal: Liber.

Lipman, M., Sharp, A.M., & Oscanyan, F.S. (1980). *Philosophy in the Classroom,* 2nd ed. Philadelphia, PA: Temple University Press.

Malherbe, J.-F. (2000). *Petite philosophie de la violence*. Sherbrooke: Université de Sherbrooke.

Mannoni, P. (1998). *Les représentations socials*. Paris: PUF.

Ministère de l'Éducation du Québec (1990). *Prévenir et contrer la violence à l'école*. Quebec City: Bibliothèque nationale du Québec.

Moliner, P. (1993). Cinq questions à propos des représentations socials. *Les Cahiers internationaux de psychologie sociale, 20,* 5-14.

Moscovici, S. (1961). *La psychanalyse, son image et son public*. Paris: PUF.

Paillé, P. (1994). L'analyse par théorisation ancrée. *Cahiers de recherche sociologique, 23,* 147-181.

Pons, F., Doudin, P.-A., Harris, P.L., & de Rosnay, M. (2005). La compréhension des émotions. Entre affect et intellect. In L. Lafortune, M.-F. Daniel, P.-A. Doudin, F. Pons, & O. Albanese (Eds.), *Pédagogie et psychologie des emotions* (pp. 179-202). Quebec City: PUQ.

Pons, F., Harris, P.L., & de Rosnay, M. (2003). Emotion comprehension between 3 and 11 years: Developmental periods and hierarchical organizations. *European Journal of Developmental Psychology, 9* (2), 127-152.

Pons, F., Lawson, J., Harris, P.L., & de Rosnay, M. (2003). Individual differences in children's emotion understanding: Effects of age and language. *Scandinavian Journal of Psychology, 44*(4), 345-351.

Rouquette, M.-L., & Rateau, P. (1998). *Introduction à l'étude des représentations socials*. Grenoble: PUG.

Schleifer, M., Daniel, M.-F., Lafortune, L., & Pallascio, R. (1999). Concepts of cooperation in the classroom. *Païdeusis, 12*(2), 45-56.

Schleifer, M., Daniel, M.-F., Auriac, E., & Lecompte, S. (2003). The impact of philosophical discussions on moral autonomy, judgment, empathy and the recognition of emotion in 5 year olds. *Thinking, 16*(4), 4-13.

Van der Maren, J-M. (1996). *Méthodes de recherche pour l'éducation*, 2e éd. Montreal: PUM.

Villanueva, L., Clemente, R., & Garcia, F. (2000). Theory of mind and peer rejection at school. *Social Development, 9,* 271-283.

Vygotsky, L. (1985). *Pensée et langage*. Trad. Fr. Sève, Paris: Éditions sociales.

Wallon, H. (1925). *L'enfant turbulent: étude sur les retards et les anomalies du développement moteur et mental*. Paris: F. Alcan.

CHAPTER 10

Training social workers in intercultural realities: A teaching model to counter unreasoned affectivity and contribute to the development of reflective judgment

Jo Ann Lévesque

1. Introduction

In this chapter, we present the results of doctoral research based on the study of 80 Bachelor of Social Work students at the Université du Québec en Outaouais. The purpose of the study was to evaluate how the course's strategies had contributed to the development of the students' reflective judgment, so we described the context of the emergence of the study, the main analytical grid, the methodology, and the research results of the qualitative and quantitative analyses. The results show that a teaching model combining the transmission of information, educational conversation, and writing can counter the continuing of cultural preconceptions manifested in unreasoned affectivity and can promote awareness, leading to an openness to differences, as well as developing the students' capacity for reflective judgment on intercultural realities. A set of conditions are however attached to this teaching model so that it can contribute to reflective development. In particular, we should mention the quality of the completeness and amplitude of the information, the quality of the balance and the clarity of the transmission of information, as well as the coherence of the structure between pedagogical activities. In this chapter, we describe the conditions for the application of a teaching model in the reflective universe of social workers who will have to intervene with newcomers in this new millennium.

2. Social workers and intercultural realities

Immigration is part of the reality of every province in Canada. It is even a strategy for contributing to the country's future demographic, economic, and cultural growth. For example, between 1993 and 2002[1], the Province of Quebec welcomed 321,070 immigrants from every continent.[2] In 2002, most immigrants admitted to Quebec came from the following countries: France, China, Algeria, Morocco, Romania, Haiti, India, Pakistan, Lebanon, Sri Lanka, South Korea, the Democratic Republic of Congo, Colombia, Russia and the Philippines.[3] These people left their countries of origin for different reasons, but all hoped to create a better future for themselves by coming to Quebec. Although several mechanisms have been put in place to help the newcomers adapt to their new reality, they nonetheless will be confronted by a new culture with its different customs, behavior and ways of doing things, and a different social structure than the one in their country of origin. They will all experience culture shock, to varying degrees, which will translate for example into grieving for the past and disillusionment over the gaps between the country of their dreams and their actual situation. They will have to become familiar with new social practices, standards, and values. A series of adjustments will lead some to ask for help, which quite often will be provided by social workers, working in community organizations or public services.

At the same time, social workers are also confronted with the original culture of the newcomers who turn to them for help. They discover that their method of intervention no longer produces the same results. In their professional exchanges, they encounter a new tension called *intercultural incomprehension*. According to Cohen-Emerique (1985), this is manifested in the form of incidents related to a differentiated perception of space and time, differences in the structure of the family group, roles and statuses of its members, codes of interpersonal exchanges and codes of decorum, and finally, helper-helped tensions in the professional context of social services. The evolution of contemporary Quebec society imposes transformations in social relations, which inevitably lead to the aim of training social workers in intercultural intervention, to help them think differently about their relations with someone who comes from another country.

---

[1] Gouvernement du Québec, Direction générale de la population et de la recherche (2003, p. 22).
[2] Gouvernement du Quebec, Direction générale de la population et de la recherche (2003, p. 9).
[3] The list of countries presented is in descending order by number of arrivals.

3. The course on interethnic realities and social intervention

In the fall of 1995, doctoral research in education (Lévesque, 1999) was conducted among two third-year graduating groups of students in social work at the Université du Québec en Outaouais.[*] Approximately, 80 students participated in this anthropo-pedagogical study, with the general purpose of discovering and evaluating how all of the pedagogical strategies of the "Interethnic Realities and Social Intervention" course contributed to the development of the students' reflective judgment in intercultural matters.

The "Interethnic Realities and Social Intervention" course was designed to meet the new needs of social work practice with people of various cultural origins. Its general purpose was to sensitize social work students to the realities related to immigration and the coexistence of different cultural groups, as well as their rapid growth and transformation. It also sought to foster the development of abilities to reflect on the complexity of intercultural relations, the acquisition of appropriate attitudes, and the transfer of knowledge and general intervention skills in the intercultural field.

The course was divided into two parts. The first eight sessions, were of a more theoretical nature and were devoted to the study of key concepts and underlying realities related to intercultural understanding: immigration, culture, culture shock, tradition, modernity, post-modernity and intercultural intervention. Three kinds of teaching strategies were favored in the theory section of the course: theoretical presentations, idea sharing in small groups and full group discussion, as well as audiovisual presentations and invited specialists. The last five sessions were more practical, as the team of students presented the results of their field studies regarding specific problems experienced by immigrants. In addition to participating in this research, as learning activities, the students also (i) wrote an autobiography of ten experiences in intercultural situations and (ii) kept a reflective learning notebook in which they were to summarize the content presented in each of the first eight sessions and to formulate a critical reflection on a topic related to each of the eight sessions.

All of the teaching strategies and learning activities for the theoretical part of the course were inspired by the following teaching models: for the transmission of information, Ausubel's advance organizers (cited in Joyce, Weil & Showers, 1992), for educational conversation, Oliver and Shaver's conflict resolution

---

[*] The first group was composed of 39 students (30 women and 9 men). The second group also included 39 students (37 women and 2 men). Only the first group was the focus of qualitative research, while the second group was invited to participate in the quantitative component of the research.

or jurisprudential inquiry (cited in Joyce, Weil & Showers, 1992) and Paul's Socratic questioning (1993) and for writing, the reflective work of Nikerson (1984) and McSweeney (1994). These strategies were and still are recognized as facilitating the integration of subject matter and the development of students' reflective judgment.

4. An analytical tool and a methodology

An analytical tool: The reflective judgment development model

To determine whether all the teaching and learning strategies of the *Interethnic Realities and Social Intervention* course contributed to the development of students' reflective capacity, we used the latest model of the current of critical thinking perceived as intellectual development, the reflective judgment development model developed by King and Kitchener (1994). The reflective judgment model serves as a frame of reference for describing development from childhood to adulthood, the apprehension of the knowledge process and the justification for each stage and thus reveals beliefs on vague or unstructured problems. The development of epistemological cognition is described in the model. As individuals grow up, they acquire a capability to evaluate the postulates of knowledge and become capable of explaining and defending their point of view. This frame of reference determines how a person perceives and seeks to resolve poorly defined problems and puts emphasis on the perception of knowledge and the concepts of justification.

This cognitive process is divided into three levels (pre-reflective, quasi-reflective, and reflective) and seven stages, each with its postulates of access to knowledge and its own concept of justification. Each stage represents a way of accessing knowledge. The further one advances in the stages, the more complex and effective the form of justification becomes, enabling individuals to evaluate and defend their point of view. Each stage has its own problem-solving strategies. At the advanced stages, the individual can distinguish between problems that are clearly and poorly defined and integrate a whole set of data pertaining to a complex situation.

People who reason according to the first three stages think that knowledge can be acquired by observation or by expert discourse. They assume that knowledge is concrete and absolute and make no distinction between problems that are clearly or poorly defined. They believe that a solution exists to every problem. This type of reasoning is characteristic of the pre-reflective level of the King and Kitchener model (1994). Secondary school students generally think this way.

People who reason according to Stages 4 and 5 are capable of making a distinction between the two types of problems. They recognize that a certain degree of uncertainty exists in problem situations, but they do not know how to formulate a judgment in such situations. While they claim that judgment is based on evidence, they believe the evaluation of a situation is a matter of personal opinion. This type of reasoning belongs to the quasi-reflective level of the King and Kitchener model (1994). College and university students generally think this way.

Finally, people who reason according to Stages 6 and 7 are aware that an understanding of the world is constructed from a specific context and that certain interpretations or constructions are more plausible than others. In this case, judgment is based on solid validated data. The coherence, depth and relevance of the concepts are part of the evaluation criteria. This type of reasoning belongs to the reflective level of the King and Kitchener model (1994). University professors and doctoral students generally think this way.

A methodology: The anthropo-pedagogical approach

In addition to the reflective judgment development model, we were greatly inspired by the characteristics of Morin's anthropo-pedagogical approach (1992b), which is defined as follows:

> A pedagogical research method which uses the essential of the anthropological approach to the benefit of pedagogy to foster an understanding and active evaluation of educational phenomena. (Morin, 1984, cited in Legendre, 1993, p. 1074, and Morin & Vautour, 1994, p. 29.).

As this definition implies, anthropo-pedagogy attaches great value to cultural and social considerations and to anthropological tools to study pedagogy or, in other words, the teaching-learning relationship. Its ultimate goal is to understand the meaning of events as they are interpreted by the stakeholders in the field of education environment. With this approach, the main instrument becomes the researcher, who uses a variety of tools, such as a notebook, participatory observation and formal and informal meetings, in order to better probe the educational phenomenon.

In this research, all the stakeholders contributed through their reflections on the purpose of the study. First, two people acted as participating observers by recording and analyzing, according to a predetermined scoring model (Morin, 1992a), all the interactions that took place in each course session. They were recorded and transcribed so that no comments made in the classroom escaped analysis. We also kept our own notebook according to the scoring method favored by Morin (1992a). The students also kept a reflective learning notebook with a summary and reflection on one of the topics of each theoretical session. They also participated in the formal and informal meetings, focusing both on the progress of the course and on their perception of the changes in their own ability to judge in the area of intercultural relations. In addition to these anthropological tools, a pretest and post-tests on cognitive reflection (Wood, King, Kitchener & Lynch, 1994) served to measure the changes in the levels and stages of the students' reflective judgment.

All of the data and their relationships were examined in three analyses. The first, a vertical analysis,[5] combined the interactions of each course session[6], collected by means of the following data gathering tools: tape recordings, notes of the participating observers and the professor/researcher in the notebooks. It also presented a qualitative analysis of the reflective judgment of the students' critical reflections[7]. All of these data combined constituted the first data triangulation for this study. The second, a horizontal analysis[8], tracked the changes in the students' reflective judgments in accordance with the course sessions, a reflective process which was linked to their pretest and post-test results on cognitive reflection. This second analysis also combined all the observations from the first analysis, allowing the emergence of conditions conducive to the development of the students' critical judgment. It constituted the second research data triangulation. The third, a statistical analysis[9], allowed quantitative validation of the changes in the students' reflective judgment. The originality of this research lies in the in-depth study of the changes in the students' oral and written reflective judgment, the analytical framework of the changes in this reflective judgment, and the approach used to understand the meaning given by the different stakeholders. Thanks to all the tools and the two triangulations,

---

[5] The vertical analysis corresponds to the first part of the fourth chapter of Lévesque's thesis (1999).

[6] All course sessions were treated in the same manner, according to each teaching strategies: teaching strategy, objectives of the strategy, proposed activity, student participation, and observations.

[7] It should be noted that the study includes analysis of the reflective learning notebook (8 critical reflections per notebook) of 10 students from the first group who were selected according to their representation of the levels and stages of the development of reflective judgment, based on their results in the pretest on cognitive reflection.

[8] The horizontal analysis corresponds to the second part of the fourth chapter of Lévesque's thesis (1999).

[9] The cognitive reflection test was given to the 39 students in the first group and to 15 students in the second group.

380 observations were identified, allowing the formal recognition of eighteen pedagogical conditions which resulted in the emergence of a teaching model for the development of reflective judgment in social workers in an intercultural education context.

5. The teaching model based on the development of reflective judgment

The results of the study led to a teaching model combining the three pedagogical axes of the *Interethnic Realities and Social Intervention* course: the transmission of information, educational conversation, and writing. While they were implicit at the beginning of the research, these three pedagogical axes were transformed by their close interrelations and interdependencies into essential components of an integrative teaching model focused on the development of reflective judgment in intercultural education.

The model includes other attributes which qualify each of the pedagogical axes. For example, the transmission of information raises the necessity of providing pedagogical documents and calls for clear and well-balanced course presentation. Educational conversation is the key pedagogical orientation that allows for a direct connection with the student's experiences and fosters a deeper exploration of the subject matter through democratic, even Socratic, exchanges in small work groups or full group sessions. Writing raises the necessity of training in the rudiments of critical thinking, requiring the diligent practice of writing and rigorous correction to develop reflective abilities.

The model also includes other components related to the quality of the information during the pedagogical activities which belong to each axis. As a result, in order to contribute to the development of reflective judgment, the content in the information transmission activity benefits most when it is ample, complete, rich and coherent. The same principle applies to the educational conversation axis and the writing axis.

To increase the quality of reflection, the model's three axes should connect with the students' experiences through illustrations during the pedagogical activities of the transmission of information, educational conversation, and writing. The illustrations can take several forms – case studies, videos and other types of activities which facilitate the integration and reflection on content in each strategy or pedagogical axis.

Figure 1

Teaching model for the development of reflective judgment

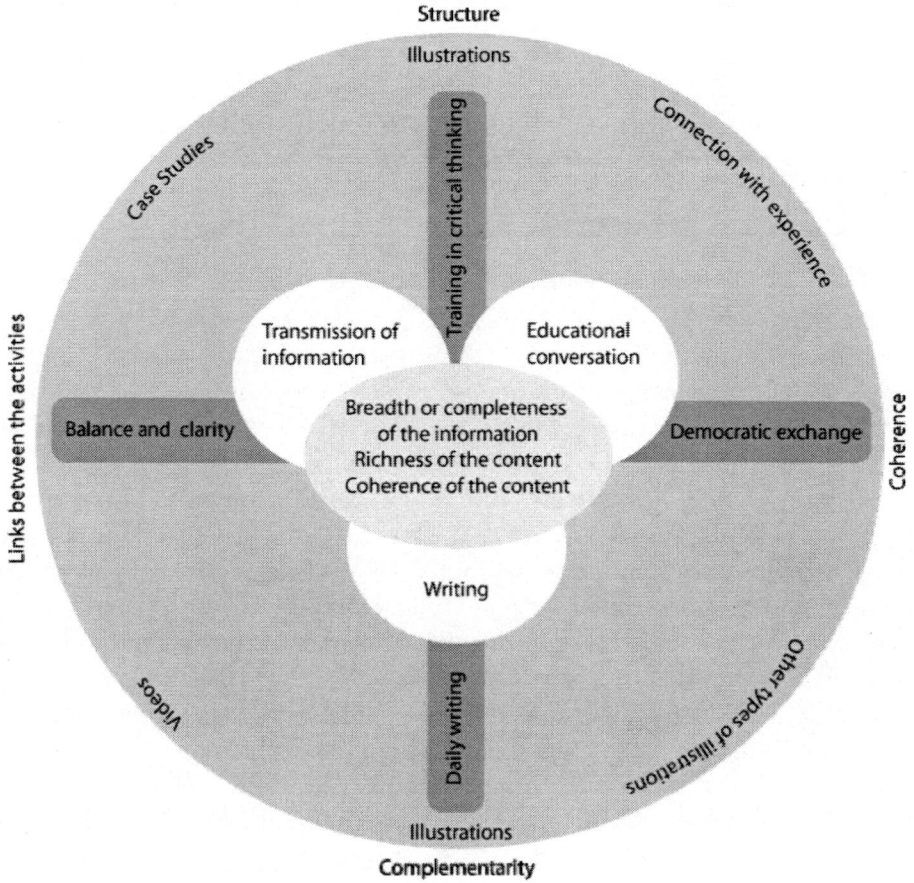

The model's structure, complementarity, links between activities and coherence are other qualities that provide a context for the three axes and their attributes. These superior qualities tie the model's components together, enrich the performance of each of the axes and their attributes, and are essential to the interactivity between all components of the model.

The dynamics of all the components of the reflective judgment development model make it a system (Lévesque, 2004) with multiple interactions which are modeled on the actions or behavior of the model's stakeholders as they evolve. Seen in this way, this system leads to the necessity of creating conditions to guide the stakeholders' behavior in order to contribute to the development of the students' reflective judgment.

6. Conditions derived from the data on each axis of the model

With the help of contextual situations, it is possible to show how we have qualified the three axes on which the teaching model of reflective judgment development is based, in an intercultural relations context. The only pedagogical situations chosen will be those that best illustrate the observations generated both by classroom interactions and by the content of the students' critical reflections in their reflective learning notebooks.

Transmission of information

The first eight sessions of the *Interethnic Realities and Social Intervention* course all include a lecture segment. For example, one of the pedagogical activities of the second session deals with the immigration profile in Quebec in the form of charts. Approximately 30 charts were presented for an hour and ten minutes. In reaction to this teaching strategy, one student wrote the following comments in his reflective learning notebook:

> I must say that, at first, none of the figures given in class really surprised me. What astounded me is that you used them to describe the immigration profile in Quebec without giving more details which, in my opinion, could have helped us form an accurate idea on the subject. Take for instance the example of learning French. In response to the question "what language do they speak?", you answered "English" and then you gave the percentages – that's all. My initial reaction was the same as that of my classmates: they don't want to learn French! Then I started to look for reasons […] (Lévesque, 1999, p. 120).

The analyses of all the writings and interactions indicated that a partial transmission of information, awakening curiosity through questioning, followed by a presentation of charts and their conclusions, can incite reflection. However, if the information transmitted, along with other pedagogical activities, cannot respond correctly to the students' questions, it becomes a counter-strategy for the development of reflective judgment, since the students seem to be left to their own devices in reflective relativism and they display a pre-reflective or quasi-reflective, Stage 4, tendency. The following condition arises from this observation:

> Partial information can awaken intellectual curiosity however, to foster the development of reflective judgment, complete and full-breath information must be presented (Lévesque, 1999, p. 322).

In the session on culture, we recognized the different meanings attached to the concept of culture: culture perceived in its primary sense, *agri-culture*; culture perceived as all human knowledge, cultures perceived in an ethnographic sense, culture perceived in a spiritual sense, and culture perceived in a technical sense. We then moved on to the ethnographic classification of culture as defined by ethnologists. A note from a participating observer reveals the following regarding this treatment of information:

> In the first part of this module segment, the students' questions or comments show a desire to know more about the subject, but their protests due to an insufficient explanation of the Age of Enlightenment seem to have affected the seriousness of the responses towards the end of the course [...] (Lévesque, 1999, p. 191).

The transmission of information in light of the classroom interactions and the reading of the students' reflections showed that information overflow, too rapid a delivery, or confusion in the transmission of information influences the comprehension of realities, affects students' ability to judge them, and limits or hinders the development of reflective judgment on the subject matter. The following condition can be deduced:

> Balance and clarity in the transmission of well-structured information are necessary for understanding the subject matter studied and having the ability to judge it (Lévesque, 1999, p. 322).

In the session dealing with culture shock, we discussed the different facets of culture shock experienced by newcomers. The content of this topic was presented through appealing clever titles, followed by examples taken from everyday life. Following the course, one student wrote the following in her reflective learning notebook:

> The content of this course covers several points with focus on important dimensions to consider in psychosocial intervention. Even though the course's subject matter concerns the special conditions of intercultural reality, it still presents differences that cause us to experience culture shock without having to go any further.
>
> I choose to explore the limits of intervention with culture shock because this aspect of social work is often ignored to the detriment of the person

seeking help. Social workers remain trapped in their fear and ignorance without reconsidering their approach.

In reflecting on the problem of intervention in an unfamiliar context (culture shock), I became aware that every day that I encountered opportunities to confront my value system, my habits, the way I understand and decode life's events [...] (Lévesque, 1999, p. 243).

This short excerpt shows a transmission of information that is meant to be conceptually rich with its content seen as linked to learning: it logically explores a topic while emphasizing that which is essential. It also contributes to the understanding of the topic, stimulates reflection, fosters remaining at higher stages of the reflective judgment development model or increasing reflective judgment on the topic discussed. This observation gives rise to the following condition:

A structure of pedagogical activities that coherently enhances the richness of the content based on experienced facts, linked to personal experience, stimulates and contributes to keeping reflective judgment at the higher stages or moving it to higher stages (Lévesque, 1999, p. 323).

In the session on intercultural intervention, we discussed attitudes, perspectives, and irritants in a context of intercultural assistance. The session concluded with situations experienced by social workers in their daily lives. In conducting this teaching activity, we noted:

The students' questions in the situational exercises reflect the characteristics of the quasi-reflective level, Stage 5 and the reflective level, Stage 6. The teaching structure (theory – application) plays a role here, because it seems to correspond to the style of teaching the students like and that immediately allows them to show the integration of their knowledge or make the necessary adjustments (Lévesque, 1999, p. 296).

One student recorded the following reflection in his notebook:

When the video was shown in the classroom, we became aware of the problems that many newcomers may face as showed by Francesco and his family. The family values adhered to in their country of origin are no longer appropriate in Canada. This family thus experienced upheavals, upsets and confrontations, often followed by tears and frustrations, all in an attempt to integrate the new values of our postmodern society. Integration was however was simpler for some of his family as I mentioned by Francesco's daughter and his wife. Francesco obstinately refused to integrate, and rightly so [...] To understand Francesco's family situation better, it is important to compare the sociological traits or values of this immigrant family with those of North American citizens [...] (Lévesque, 1999, p. 303).

The notebooks reveal that the transmission of information by appealing titles, clear and coherent explanations of the content, illustrated by facts or accompanied by audiovisual or written situational exercises close to the reality of the individuals, contributes more to understanding, integration of subject matter, and the development of reflective judgment for all the students than the conceptual transmission of information without immediate illustration of the content. This observation gives rise to the following condition:

> Pedagogical activity that structures the transmission of information, followed by other activities for the integration of the subject matter with links to the students' personal experiences, contributes to the development of their ability to judge this information (Lévesque, 1999, p. 323).

Educational conversation[10]

All the sessions of the *Interethnic Realities and Social Intervention* course include an educational conversation in which there is formal or informal interaction among the students or between the students and the professor/researcher. For example, the session on immigration included two types of educational conversations: one in which the students were invited to answer a question formulated from graphs and another in which the students formed groups to answer the following question: Why do immigrants leave their homeland? The comparison revealed that an educational conversation, after sharing ideas in small groups, gains more depth in the ideas expressed than a conversation based on individual reflection. This leads to the following condition:

> Sharing ideas in small groups fosters a more exhaustive exploration of ideas required to formulate an informed and reflective judgment (Lévesque, 1999, p. 324).

---

[10] For Potvin (1994), educational conversation is a major pole of educational teaching activity. He sees it as a deliberate and conscious educational action in which the teacher interacts and "communicacts" with the student in the spontaneity of the situation and overall dynamics of everyday life.

In the activity on the reasons favoring immigration, the comments made by one team inspired intense debate which was difficult to control. We heard the following reasons:

> It's easy to get into Canada. It's less expensive than other industrialized countries. Immigrants are drawn by our democracy, the neutrality of our country which is not involved in conflicts. There are a lot of free services, such as health insurance, and social welfare. In fact, they have a guaranteed income when they arrive. They have freedom of speech here. It's more permissive. For example, they can wear their veils when we can't wear a "Heavy Metal" cap or sweatshirt in public places (Lévesque, 1999, p. 139).

In response to these words, one student wrote the following reflection in her notebook: [...] When we conducted this activity in class, there was one important detail that really offended me. There was one team which instead of talking about reasons jokingly cited prejudices that Quebecers have against them [immigrants]. As a person from an ethnic minority, these statements and the way they were made upset me because these prejudices really exist and aren't easy to forget. However, I would have accepted their message better if the team had presented in a serious manner. In my opinion, they hadn't thought much about this exercise [...] (Lévesque, 1999, p. 151).

There was also a group discussion following a short presentation on First Nations in the session dealing with the situation of aboriginals in Quebec. One student said:

> There is a trap in the way we perceive aboriginals. We can't trust what we hear on Channel 10 or what we read in the Journal de Montréal (Lévesque, 1999, p. 255).

If we compare the level of reflection emerging from both discussion activities, we find that most of the comments made by the students in an educational conversation, as in the first activity, reflect popular prejudices or the characteristics of the quasi-reflective level, Stage 4. More often than not, the comments aroused controversy. This can foster an exchange of ideas, tending to raise the level of opinions to the higher stages of the reflective judgment development model (5+) if they were facilitated in a manner inspired by Socratic questioning. As a result the following condition thus appears:

> Democratic, even Socratic discussion erases preconceptions based on popular prejudices and encourages opinions that tend to reach the highest stages of the reflective judgment development model (Lévesque, 1999, p. 324).

In the educational conversation, activities that focused on the realities of immigration and on culture compared to the activities on intercultural intervention, the researcher discovered that the arguments provoked during the educational conversation stimulate reflection with a diversity of opinions on a given topic. In response to the comments made in class, one student wrote:

> To help you understand, Mario, I'm going to paint you a picture. It's still the turn of last week's small group to be the centre of attention. This group questions the professor on the concept of culture. They challenge her comments by confirming that, for them, culture means partying hard, listening to Paul Piché and eating tourtière. The professor then tries to explain that there are different forms of culture and that tourtière (popular culture) was one of these forms. However, she also tried to get them to recognize a second form of culture, a global culture, the culture of the soul and of evolution.
>
> All this to tell you, my dear Mario, that I was astounded, once again, to hear the words coming from such closed minds. For these individuals, culture gravitates around their immediate surroundings environment. Yet it's constantly repeated that social workers must learn not to impose their Quebec, Canadians and North Americans values on others. How can they understand the poor Islamic mother who suffers isolation with a closed and self-centered "Habitant pea soup" mentality? In my opinion, it's not going to be easy for this small group of individuals when they begin their careers [...] (Lévesque, 1999, p. 449).

An educational conversation can give rise to writing themes that contribute to maintaining or increasing reflective judgment. Maintaining or increasing judgment is achieved if there had previously been a transmission of rich conceptual information that sheds light on a specific topic and if it is followed by audiovisual presentations with content related to the students' questions. Thus, the following condition is created:

> Arguments in educational conversation stimulate reflection and contribute to maintaining high reflective capacity or increasing reflective judgment, if the downstream transmission of information is conceptually rich and if the upstream integration activities shed light on certain aspects of the

transmission of information, while at the same time connecting with the students' questions. (Lévesque, 1999, p. 325).

The last two conditions clearly imply that educational conversation contributes to the development of reflective judgment, but also that it can benefit from being guided by a special teaching syntax[11]. If it is not guided, the result is that educational conversation can develop or contribute to reflective judgment, but it does not channel it sufficiently because the students are left to their own devices in reflective relativism. It can even turn out to be a counter-strategy by playing on unreasoned affectivity[12] and prevent an analysis of the propositions. The student who expressed shock at the students' comments on the reasons for immigration continued with the following reflection on racism in Quebec.

[…] This classroom activity allowed me to think about the attitude of Quebecers to immigrants. In fact, I felt that if this team could voice all these ideas that they claim are held by most people in Quebec, how far does their tolerance of immigrants go? For example, a long time ago, I watched a program on Radio-Quebec, dealing with Quebecers' opinion on the massive arrival of immigrants of color. There were some racist statements that struck me. Among other things, they claimed that they steal jobs, they smell bad, and their taxis are dirty. After this program, I was left wondering: "Why do Quebecers have all these reservations about accepting us in their country?" I asked to my parents and friends, as well and I looked into immigration at the Library and came to the conclusion that this is because most immigrants come to Quebec to succeed at all costs, which means that they take on the hardest jobs, and they go to school to get an education. Quebecers (at least most of them) don't do either. On the contrary, they watch what they're doing and then fear, above all, that these newcomers will become stronger than them. So I believe that racism comes from a fear of differences. (Lévesque, 1999, p. 152).

Indeed, unreasoned affectivity clouds the ability to form reasonable judgments, due to the tenor of the comments, and thus confines judgment to the lower

---

[11] The research has revealed the following teaching syntax: putting in context, presentation of content, oral or audiovisual illustration, summarizing comments made in light of the presentation of the content, and writing (Lévesque, 1999, p. 343).
[12] Unreasoned affectivity is defined as an emotion that clouds any ability to reason on one or more propositions at a given time. Channouf and Rouan (2002) show how emotion alters the processing of information.

stages of the reflective judgment development model. The following two conditions thus emerge:

> Educational conversation can turn out to be negative if it fosters a reflective relativism influenced by unreasoned affectivity, thus limiting the analysis of propositions and confining judgment to the lower stages of the reflective judgment development model (Lévesque, 1999, p. 325).

> The more students are able to establish a relationship between the statements of the educational conversation and the activities that precede or succeed it, the more their reflective judgment tends to rise on the scale of stages. Conversely, the less they are able to establish this relationship, the more their judgment tends to reflect the characteristics of the lower stages of the reflective judgment development model (Lévesque, 1999, p. 325).

In short, the conditions emerging from educational conversation make it possible to understand that it certainly stimulates reflection, but that it has serious limitations because it doesn't exercise sufficiently the capacity for judgment of the students, most of whom are at the quasi-reflective level, Stages 4 and 5. The weakest students have difficulty judging the value of the propositions expressed in the educational conversation. They let themselves be influenced by ideas or beliefs which, in their eyes, seem to reflect what they think or believe they have understood about the situation discussed. They base their arguments on popular beliefs or clichés, which is a characteristic of Stage 4. Stage 5 retains only those beliefs that can be supported by evidence, but this does not lead students to think further about the topic. In Stages 6 and 7, students are able to evaluate the depth and accuracy of the assertions. Setting aside quasi-reflective interpretations of reality or using them to justify their point of view on the topic discussed. At this level, reflection is not dictated by beliefs, but by an integrating theme which allows incorporation into the writing of the most significant beliefs and evidence discussed in the educational conversation, the audiovisual documents, and the transmission of information.

Writing

Writing is a basic skill in education, recognized for its high cognitive virtues. As mentioned previously, the students wrote eight critical reflections on a theme of their choice, related to the content of each of the course's theoretical sessions. The following figure illustrates the evolution of one student's reflective judgment:

Figure 2
Marc's reflective judgment by stage and session

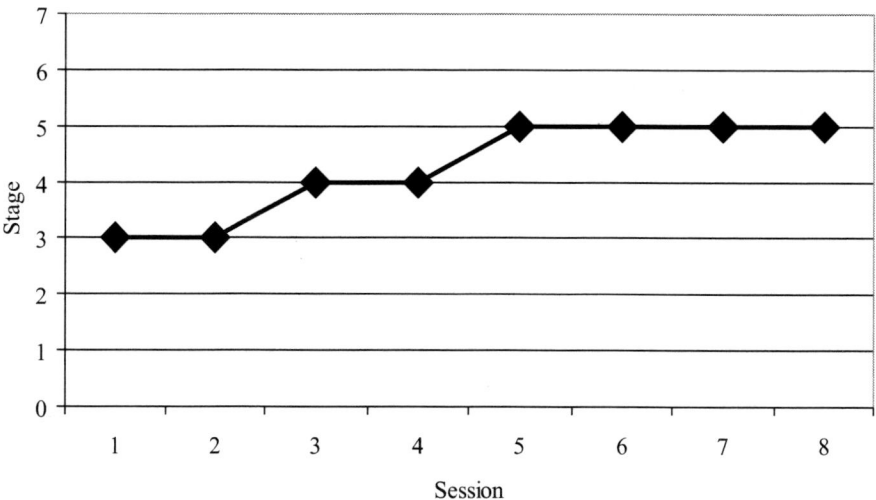

The given name used here is fictitious. The figure shows that Marc's reflective judgment evolves gradually, in the form of reflective plateaus, progressing from the pre-reflective level, Stage 3 to the quasi-reflective level, Stage 5, between the first and eighth session, in overlapping stages (Lévesque, 1999, p. 319).

Analysis of the evolution of reflective judgment through all of the students' writings allowed us to arrive at the following conditions:
> The weekly or even daily exercise of writing contributes to the development of the students' reflective judgment by the effort of integrating the subject matter it covers (Lévesque, 1999, p. 327).

However, writing skills are more deeply honed if the teaching activities provide serious arguments that confront individual preconceptions, a reality which ultimately maintains high reflective capacity or contributes to an increase in reflective judgment. It would appear that the quality of the arguments certainly depends on the students' individual characteristics, but it is also due to the way the subject matter is organized. Thus, the following conditions are stated:
> The line of argument in the text is based on individual preconceptions that limit or hinder the development of reflective judgment if the or-

ganization of the content does not foster sufficient comprehension of the subject matter studied and if no personal research is done to make up for a lack of comprehension (Lévesque, 1999, p. 328).

The ability to make connections between teaching activities fosters a transfer of knowledge and contributes to an increase in reflective judgment or maintaining a high reflective capacity, but difficulty in making these connections affects reflective judgment, which is maintained at its current stage or regresses (Lévesque, 1999, p. 330).

Writing assignments inevitably involves the correction of the students' work during a course. As a final condition, the professor/researcher arrived at the following observation:
> Training in critical thinking and the rigorous correction of the written assignments also appear to be conditions related to the development of reflective judgment (Lévesque, 1999, p. 329).

All of the conditions we have presented and illustrated regarding the transmission of information, educational conversation, and writing made it possible to develop a teaching model which contributes to the development of reflective judgment in an intercultural education context.

7. The reflective judgment development model and pedagogy

The reflective judgment development model is a tool designed to improve pedagogy which contributes immensely to developing the reflective judgment of individuals – particularly those at the quasi-reflective level, Stage 4 or maintaining the reflective gains of individuals at the quasi-reflective level, Stage 5. This is what the pretest and the post-tests on cognitive reflection showed with the two groups of students. In fact, the score obtained on the post-test (4.71 + 0.78) was significantly higher than the one obtained on the pretest (4.54 + 0.75), $p = 0.014$ in the first group. In the second group, however, there was no significant difference between the post-test (5.02 + 0.090) and the pretest (4.90 + 0.087), $p = 0.134$. This difference could be explained by the fact that the second group's post-test results were not significantly better than those of the pretest. However, the score obtained on the pretest (4.90 + 0.087) by the second group was significantly higher than the first group's score (4.54 + 0.75). These differences between the groups thus led to the hypothesis that it may be more difficult to increase the reflective judgment of a group of students who closely reflect the characteristics of the quasi-reflective level, Stage 5, rather than those of Stage 4.

Conclusion

The reflective judgment development model, by its teaching and learning strategies, has contributed to the development of the first group's reflective judgment and maintained the reflective gains of the second group of students. Its results attest to the model's richness, because it accounts for all the human dimensions that are challenged by a structure of pedagogical activities, such as the structure of the *Interethnic Realities and Social Intervention* course, which seeks a better understanding of intercultural realities. While laying the foundation for learning intercultural realities, it can accommodate pre-reflective propositions, which very often are unreasoned, and lead the students to quasi-reflective and reflective levels, which are much more reasoned. It helps them grow intellectually and emotionally in understanding cultural universes other than their own.

It is important, however, to make certain that the application and observation of the conditions attached to the model's three pedagogical axes are a *sine qua non* for the development of reflective judgment. Indeed, the reflective judgment development model acquires its full scope and dynamism in the observance of the conditions which must be seriously taken into account for there to be a real difference in the capacity to judge intercultural realities of individuals, particularly social workers who will have to help people from other countries.

The reflective judgment development model is part of the family of models that contribute to the development of critical thinking. Because of its objectives, it mainly belongs to the family of development models based on reflective judgment (King & Kitchener, 2004). It illustrates the difficulty in training people to think in complex situations. It calls for a systematic look at realities – a look that is, and will be, particularly necessary in our contemporary societies.

References

Channouf, A., & Rouan, G. (2002). *Émotions et cognitions. Série Neurosciences et cognition*. Brussels: De Boeck Universite.

Cohen-Emerique, M. (1985). La formation des praticiens en situations interculturelles. Le choc culturel: méthode de formation et outil de recherché. *L'interculturel en éducation et en sciences humaines* (pp. 66-120). Toulouse: Université de Toulouse – Le Mirail.

Cohen-Emerique, M. (2000). L'approche interculturelle auprès des migrants.

In G. Legault (Ed.), *L'intervention interculturelle* (pp. 161-184). Boucherville: Gaëtan Morin Éditeur.

Gouvernement du Québec. (2003). *Caractéristiques de l'immigration au Québec. Statistiques.* Québec: Ministère des Relations avec les citoyens et de l'Immigration, Direction générale de la population et de la recherche.

Joyce, B., Weil, M., & Showers, B. (1992). *Models of Teaching*, 4th ed. Boston: Allyn and Bacon.

King, P., & Kitchener, K.S. (1994). *Developing Reflective Judgment.* San Francisco: Jossey-Bass Publishers.

King, P., & Kitchener, K.S. (2004). Reflective judgment: Theory and research on the development of epistemic assumptions through adulthood. *Educational Psychologist*, *39*(1), 5-18.

Legendre, R. (1993). *Dictionnaire actuel de l'éducation*, 2nd edition. Montréal: Guérin.

Lévesque, J. (2004). "L'anthropopédagogie: une méthodologie au service d'un modèle de développement du jugement réflexif", Recherche-action, recherche systémique? *Questions vives, État de la recherche en éducation*, *2*(3), 123-132.

Lévesque, J. (1999). Les conditions liées au processus de développement du jugement réflexif. Une anthropopédagogie d'un cours universitaire portant sur les réalités interculturelles. Unpublished doctoral thesis, Montréal, Université de Montréal.

McSweeney, A. (1994). Internationalité dans la formation. *UISG*, 41-56.

Morin, A. (1984). L'évaluation anthropopédagogique. In C. Paquette (Ed.), *Des pratiques évaluatives* (pp. 159-203). Victoriaville: Éditions HHP.

Morin, A. (1992a). *Recherche-action intégrale et participation coopérative. Vol. 1, Méthodologie et études de cas.* Laval: Éditions Agence d'Arc.

Morin, A. (1992b). *Recherche-action intégrale et participation coopérative. Vol. 11, Théorie et rédaction du rapport.* Laval: Éditions Agence d'Arc.

Morin, A., & Vautour, C. (1994). L'analyse des données en recherche qualitative anthropopédagogique. *Repères*, *16*, 29-71.

Nikerson, R.S. (1984). Kinds of thinking taught in current programs. *Educational Leadership*, *41*(1), 26-37.

Paul, R. (1993). *Critical Thinking: How to Prepare Students for a Rapidly Changing World.* Santa Rosa, CA: J. Wilsen & A.J.A. Binker Foundation for Critical Thinking.

Potvin, G. (1994). Les actions, les discours, les savoirs et la recherche en education. *Repères*, *16*, 185-195.

Wood, P.K., King, P., Kitchener, K.S., & Lynch, C. (1994). *Techniques Manual to Accompany Reflective Thinking (Version 1.0).* Reflective Thinking Associates.